PRAYING
the
NAMES
of
JESUS

A DAILY GUIDE

PRAYING
the
NAMES
of
JESUS

ANN
SPANGLER

ZONDERVAN®

ZONDERVAN.com/
AUTHORTRACKER
follow your favorite authors

ZONDERVAN

Praying the Names of Jesus
Copyright © 2006 by Ann Spangler

Requests for information should be addressed to:
Zondervan, *Grand Rapids, Michigan 49530*

Library of Congress Cataloging-in-Publication Data

Spangler, Ann.
    Praying the names of Jesus : a daily guide / Ann Spangler.
      p. cm.
    Includes bibliographical references.
    ISBN-13: 978-0-310-25345-7
    ISBN-10: 0-310-25345-4
    1. Jesus Christ — Name — Meditations. 2. Devotional calendars. I. Title.
BT590.N2S69 2006
  232 — dc22   2006009335

All Scripture quotations, unless otherwise indicated, are taken from The Holy Bible, *New International Version®, NIV®.* Copyright © 1973, 1978, 1984 by Biblica, Inc.™ Used by permission. All rights reserved worldwide. Also, Holy Bible, *Today's New International Version®, TNIV®.* Copyright © 2005 by Biblica, Inc.™ Used by permission. All rights reserved worldwide.

The author gratefully acknowledges material reprinted from *Exalting the Names of Jesus* by William D. Watley, copyright © 2002 by Judson Press. Used by permission of Judson Press, www.judsonpress.com.

Interior production: Beth Shagene

Printed in the United States of America

---

13 14 15 16 17 18 19 20 /DCI/ 24 23 22 21 20 19 18 17 16 15 14 13 12 11 10 9 8 7 6

To Katie and Luci Spangler
May you know Jesus so completely that neither death nor life,
neither the present nor the future, neither height nor depth,
nor anything else in all creation, will ever separate you from him.

CONTENTS

PRONUNCIATION GUIDE TO THE NAMES OF JESUS

Akrogoniaios Lithos	ah-kro-go-nee-EYE-os LI-thos
Alpha kai Omega	AL-fah kai oh-MAY-gah
Arnion, Amnos tou Theou	ar-NEE-on, am-NOS tou the-OU
Aryeh Lammatteh Yehudah, Leon ek tou Phyles Iouda	ar-YEH la-mat-TEH ye-hou-DAH, LE-own ek tou fu-LAYS YOU-dah
Artos Zoes	AR-tos zo-ASE
Aster Lampros Proinos	as-TAIR lam-PROS pro-i-NOS
Basileus Basileon	ba-si-LEUS ba-si-LE-own
Christos, Mashiach	KRIS-tos, ma-SHEE-ach
Ebed, Pais tou Theou, Ish Makoboth	E-bed, PAIS tou the-OU, ISH mak-uh-BOTH
Ego Eimi	e-GO ay-MEE
Ga'al, Lytron	ga-AL, LU-tron
Hiereus, Prophetes	hee-uh-REUS, pro-PHAY-tays
Huios Dauid	hui-OS da-WEED
Huios tou Theou, Huios tou Anthropou	hui-OS tou the-OU, hui-OS tou an-THROW-pou
Iatros	ee-a-TROS
Iesous Soter	yay-SOUS so-TAIR
Immanu-el, Emmanouel	im-ma-nu-AIL, em-man-ou-AIL
Kyrios	KU-ree-os
Logos	LO-gos

Lytron	lou-TRONE
Nymphios, Aner	Num-FEE-os, an-AIR
Philos	FEE-los
To Phos tou Kosmou	to FOHS tou KOS-mou
Poimen Kalos	poi-MAIN ka-LOS
Sar Shalom	SAR sha-LOME
Rhabbi, Rhabbouni	ra-BEE, ra-BOU-nee
Yeled, Pais	YEL-ed, PICE
Yeshua	ye-shu-AH

INTRODUCTION

I had little idea when I first began working on this book that the world would soon be in the throes of some of the worst natural disasters in living memory. In the midst of the chaos of hurricanes and earthquakes and the heartbreak of people across the earth so compellingly portrayed in the media, I hunkered down to the work, wondering what God might reveal about himself at such a time. It went well at first, until unexpectedly my own personal hurricane hit, a turbulent time in which I began to question God's love. It became difficult to focus on the writing. But as I kept seeking God, kept reading and praying about the various names and titles of Jesus, I discovered not a God who is far from my troubles or who disdains my questions but Immanuel, a God who lives in the same world I inhabit, a God who has entered my suffering, holding nothing of himself back. I found a God whose forgiveness, love, and determination to help and to save is utterly consistent. As I researched name after name, praying for insight, I began to realize more deeply that the face of God comes into clearest focus in the life and person of Jesus Christ.

That is the premise behind *Praying the Names of Jesus* — that we can experience God more deeply by focusing on the names and titles of the man who was known by his contemporaries as *Yeshua*. His many titles, including such rich descriptions as the "Good Shepherd," "Bread of Life," "Light of the World," "Prince of Peace," and "Bright Morning Star," reveal who Jesus is and why he came into this world. They also show us something about God's intentions and plans for our own lives.

Praying the Names of Jesus is the companion volume to *Praying the Names of God*. Unlike its predecessor, which focused primarily on the names and titles of God in the Hebrew Scriptures, this book focuses on the key names and titles of Jesus, particularly as they are found in the New Testament. Generally these names are recorded in Greek. As in the previous volume, many of what I call "names" are more properly called titles. Most often I refer to them as names for the sake of simplicity. Because the New Testament does not reveal any kind of logical sequence regarding the names of Jesus, I have not attempted to present them here in any particular order.

As in *Praying the Names of God*, this book is divided into twenty-six weeks. Each week is devoted to studying and praying a particular name of Jesus. Here's how each week unfolds:

- *Monday* is devoted to reading and study. It provides a key Scripture passage that reveals the name, background information, and a brief Bible study to help you understand the name.
- *Tuesday, Wednesday,* and *Thursday* contain devotional readings to help you pray specific Scripture passages that contain the name or relate closely to it. The devotional readings are meant as a springboard for your own prayer life. It will be helpful to keep your Bible handy while reflecting on the relevant Scripture passages.
- *Friday* helps you reflect on how the name connects to God's promises in Scripture. It offers key Bible passages that can be read, reflected on, or even memorized. A section entitled "Continued Prayer and Praise" lists additional passages related to the name that can be studied on the weekend.

Though not every title of Jesus is included in this volume, I have tried my best to include the most significant ones. At the end of twenty-six weeks, I hope you will have a much deeper understanding of who Jesus is and of the remarkable way in which he has loved you.

I have done my best to carefully research the material in this book, and I know that it is a much better book than it would have been because of the help and support of several people. Particular thanks are due to senior editor Verlyn Verbrugge, who did his best to make sure that this non-scholar, non-theologian presented the material in a way consistent with both solid scholarship and sound theology. To associate publisher and longtime editor and friend Sandy VanderZicht are due thanks for her enthusiastic support, careful review of the manuscript, seasoned wisdom, unflagging prayers, and steady patience as she listened to my ongoing complaints about how slowly the writing was progressing. Thanks to Sue Brower and Sherry Guzy and the other members of marketing and publicity as well as to the dedicated sales team at Zondervan for believing in this book and enthusiastically supporting it. Thanks to creative director Cindy Davis for lending her considerable talent to the book jacket and the interior design.

Thanks also go to my assistant, Lucinda Poel, for carefully making corrections to the manuscript, and to my agent, Linda Kenney, whose advice I greatly value. Her friendship, encouragement, and insight have buoyed me up more than once.

Finally, but importantly, I am grateful to those who have prayed for me and for the book, especially at times when I felt discouraged—Linda Bieze, Leslie Dennis, Joan Huyser-Honig, Nancy Sabbag, and Patti Swets. To say thank you doesn't do justice to your unflagging support. Your prayers have made an incalculable difference. And thank you, Kathy High, for supporting me and my family on the home front during the long months when I was working on the book. As always, you have been flexible, patient, faithful, and kind. You continue to be an answer to prayer.

Despite its many shortcomings, I hope that God will use this book to reveal the beauty, the power, and the grace of Jesus Christ in your life. As you learn about his names and titles, may your confidence in his love and your grasp of his mercy grow strong, enabling you to reproduce his character so that others may recognize his goodness and encounter his love.

I

IMMANUEL

עִמָּנוּ אֵל   Ἐμμανουήλ

IMMANU-EL, EMMANOUEL

The Name

The name "Immanuel" appears twice in the Hebrew Scriptures and once in the New Testament. One of the most comforting of all the names and titles of Jesus, it is literally translated "with us is God" or, as Matthew's Gospel puts it, "God with us." When our sins made it impossible for us to come to him, God took the outrageous step of coming to us, of making himself susceptible to sorrow, familiar with temptation, and vulnerable to sin's disruptive power, in order to cancel its claim. In Jesus we see how extreme God's love is. Remember this the next time you feel discouraged, abandoned, or too timid to undertake some new endeavor. For Jesus is still Immanuel—he is still "God with us."

Key Scripture

All this took place to fulfill what the Lord had said through the prophet: "The virgin will be with child and will give birth to a son, and they will call him Immanuel"—which means, "God with us."

MATTHEW 1:22–23

Monday

HIS NAME REVEALED

This is how the birth of Jesus Christ came about: His mother Mary was pledged to be married to Joseph, but before they came together, she was found to be with child through the Holy Spirit. Because Joseph her husband was a righteous man and did not want to expose her to public disgrace, he had in mind to divorce her quietly.

But after he had considered this, an angel of the Lord appeared to him in a dream and said, "Joseph son of David, do not be afraid to take Mary home as your wife, because what is conceived in her is from the Holy Spirit. She will give birth to a son, and you are to give him the name Jesus, because he will save his people from their sins."

All this took place to fulfill what the Lord had said through the prophet: "The virgin will be with child and will give birth to a son, and they will call him Immanuel"—which means, "God with us."

MATTHEW 1:18–23

Immanuel, I praise you for your faithful love—drawing near when I was far from you. Instead of casting me away from your presence, you came to call me home. Instead of punishing me for my sins, you came to free me from them. Immanuel, my God, you are here with me today. Live in me and glorify your name, I pray.

Understanding the Name

The name "Immanuel" (im-ma-nu-AIL) first appears in Isaiah 7:14 as part of a prophetic word that Isaiah spoke to King Ahaz of Judah (the southern kingdom) at a time when Syria and Israel (the northern kingdom) had formed a coalition against Assyria. The prophet Isaiah counseled Ahaz not to join in their uprising against Assyria, the region's greatest power, assuring him it would not succeed. He urged Ahaz to trust in the Lord rather than to appeal to Assyria for help against Syria and Israel, who were threatening to invade Judah for not joining their uprising. Then he invited Ahaz to ask the Lord for a sign to confirm the prophetic word, but the unfaithful king refused, having already decided to place his trust not in the Lord but in Assyria.

In response to Ahaz's refusal to trust God, Isaiah proclaimed: "Hear now, you house of David! Is it not enough to try the patience of human beings? Will you try the patience of my God also? Therefore the Lord himself will give you a sign: The virgin will be with child and give birth to a son, and will call him Immanuel."

Shortly after that Syria and Israel were soundly defeated, exactly as Isaiah had prophesied. Many years later the southern kingdom of Judah was destroyed by Babylon, its people taken captive.

Matthew's Gospel recalls Isaiah's prophecy, applying it to the child who would be born of Mary, the virgin betrothed to Joseph. The sign given hundreds of years earlier to an apostate king was meant for all God's people. In fact the Bible is nothing if not the story of God's persistent desire to dwell with his people. In Jesus, God would succeed in a unique way, becoming a man in order to save the world not from the outside, but from the inside. *Immanuel, God with us*, to rescue, redeem, and restore our relationship with him.

Studying the Name

1. How have you experienced "Immanuel"—God being with you, in your life thus far?

2. Matthew begins and ends his Gospel (see Matthew 28:20) with the promises that God is with us. How would your life be different if you began and ended each day with the firm belief that God is with you?

3. What does this title of Jesus reveal about his nature?

Tuesday

PRAYING THE NAME

"Go away, Lord; I am a sinful man!"

LUKE 5:8

Where can I go from your Spirit?
     Where can I flee from your presence?
If I go up to the heavens, you are there;
     if I make my bed in the depths, you are there.
If I rise on the wings of the dawn,
     if I settle on the far side of the sea,
even there your hand will guide me,
     your right hand will hold me fast.

PSALM 139:7–10

Reflect On: Psalm 139:7–10.
Praise God: For his promise to be with you.
Offer Thanks: For God's persistence in pursuing you.
Confess: Any pattern of sin in your life.
Ask God: To increase your confidence in his desire to be with you.

∽

One of the most encouraging of all the promises in the Bible is this: *I am with you.* Jesus said it to his disciples (and to us) at the end of Matthew's Gospel: "Surely I am with you always, to the very end of the age." If the Lord is with us, what do we have to fear? What do we lack? How can we lose? The same Lord who walked on water, healed the sick, and rose from the dead is saving us, watching over us, guiding our steps. Knowing this, why don't we dance in the streets and throw more parties? Why do we sometimes act as though God is not only *not* with us but that he is nowhere in the vicinity?

There may be many reasons why we feel God's absence in our lives. One of these is surely that our "spiritual sensors" often don't work very well. We are like malfunctioning radar that can't spot a supersonic jet flying straight overhead. But another common reason is that we are the ones who go AWOL, not God.

Consider Peter. One day Jesus climbed into Peter's boat, telling him to row out into the lake and cast his nets out despite the fact that Peter had been up all night fishing with nothing to show for it. But this time when Peter threw out the nets, he caught so many fish that his boat began to sink. Instead of jumping with joy, Peter fell down and implored Jesus to leave him, saying, "Go away from me, Lord; I am a sinful man!"

There's something right about Peter's response. Jesus is holy and sin is his implacable enemy. Still the Lord didn't leave Peter. Instead he stayed and transformed his life. And that's what Jesus wants to do with our lives. We make a mistake when we let our sin drag us down and away from the One who has promised to be with us. Instead of running to him, we let a cloud settle over us. Finding it hard to pray, we move farther away. In a thousand different ways, we say, "Depart from me, O Lord!"

At times like this we need to recall the words of Psalm 139:11–12:

> If I say, "Surely the darkness will hide me
>   and the light become night around me,"
> even the darkness will not be dark to you;
>   the night will shine like the day,
>   for darkness is as light to you.

If you are troubled by some persistent failing, by some entrenched sin, don't run away from Jesus. Instead express your sorrow and ask for his forgiveness—and then receive it. After that try praying this famous ancient prayer known as St. Patrick's Breastplate:

> Christ be beside me, Christ be before me,
> Christ be behind me, King of my heart;
> Christ be within me, Christ be below me,
> Christ be above me, never to part.

Christ on my right hand, Christ on my left hand,
Christ all around me, shield in the strife;
Christ in my sleeping, Christ in my sitting,
Christ in my rising, light of my life.

Christ be beside me, Christ be before me,
Christ be behind me, King of my heart;
Christ be within me, Christ be below me,
Christ be above me, never to part.

Wednesday

PRAYING THE NAME

"I am with you and will watch over you wherever you go, and I will bring you back to this land. I will not leave you until I have done what I have promised you."

GENESIS 28:15

> *You have been a refuge for the poor,*
> *a refuge for the needy in his distress,*
> *a shelter from the storm*
> *and a shade from the heat.*

ISAIAH 25:4

Reflect On: Genesis 28:15 and Isaiah 25:4.
Praise God: Because he is present, even in the midst of great
                suffering.
Offer Thanks: For all the ways the Lord has watched over you.
Confess: Your inability to reflect Christ's presence without his
                grace.
Ask God: To open your eyes to the ways he is at work in the
                world and in your own life.

What if God had jurisdiction only in your city, county, or state? Leaving the area would mean leaving behind his protection and care, putting yourself outside the circle of his influence. At such times you wouldn't even bother praying to him because he could neither hear nor help you. Odd as it sounds, that's precisely how many ancient people thought about their gods. They believed in gods whose power was limited to a particular region or locality.

But listen to what God said to Jacob when he was on the run from Esau, the brother whose birthright he had stolen: "I will watch over you wherever you go." Clearly, this God was not confined to a particular territory or region. His protection and power were available wherever his people went. Indeed, as they were to discover, his power extended over the whole earth.

Many of us are taught this truth as little children, barely able to mouth the bulky words—God is omnipresent and omnipotent, everywhere and all-powerful. Yet as we grow older, some of us find ourselves restricting him, shrinking him down, setting boundaries around his ability and his love. I caught myself doing this as I listened to media reports of a tropical storm that slammed into Haiti a few days ago. More than 1,500 people drowned, and another 1,300 were missing, many of them swept out to sea or buried beneath debris. Of those who survived, many of the 300,000 homeless were perching on rooftops or living on debris-strewn sidewalks where the water had subsided.

But it got worse. Unburied bodies, raw sewage, and animal carcasses were everywhere, and there was not enough food to feed the living. Without adequate roads and supplies, relief efforts seemed like Band-Aids pasted over gaping wounds. How could anyone, I wondered, solve Haiti's intractable problems? It seemed like such a God-forsaken place.

As I prayed, I began to realize that God isn't the one who is absent in Haiti or in any other part of the world. It may only seem that way because so many of us are absent, withholding our prayers because of our little faith, withholding our gifts because of our little love. True, we can't do everything, but we can do something. We can tackle the problem that is in front of us, helping to bring God's presence to those who suffer.

If we want to experience Immanuel, "God with us," we need to be where he is, to do what his love compels, to reflect his image to the rest of the world. Today, I pray that Christ will pierce my heart with the things that pierce his. I ask for the grace to look for him in the midst of the world's suffering, whether close to home or far away. I pray that he will give you and me the faith to join him there, transforming our prayers, our time, our talents, and our financial resources into evidence of his presence in the world—Immanuel, a God who is truly with us.

Thursday

PRAYING THE NAME

As the Father has loved me, so have I loved you. Now remain in my love. If you obey my commands, you will remain in my love, just as I have obeyed my Father's commands and remain in his love. I have told you this so that my joy may be in you and that your joy may be complete. My command is this: Love each other as I have loved you.

JOHN 15:9–12

Don't you know that you yourselves are God's temple and that God's Spirit lives in you?

1 CORINTHIANS 3:16

Reflect On: John 15:9–12 and 1 Corinthians 3:16.
Praise God: For calling you to be his image bearer.
Offer Thanks: That God lives in you.
Confess: Any failures that mar the image of God in you.
Ask God: To show you how to bear his image, to magnify him by expressing his love to others.

Randy Frame was part of a team of journalists and business leaders invited to Haiti in the mid-1990s to view its problems close up. Trained as a reporter to maintain his distance, Randy wasn't prepared for what happened on the last day of his trip.

That day the group visited *La Cay Espwa,* the "House of Hope," a refuge for starving children cared for by a small group of nuns. As soon as Randy entered the two-room structure, a nun by the name of Sister Conchita approached, offering him the child she cradled in her arms. Reluctant at first to take the child lest he violate his role as an objective observer, he finally gave in, deciding it would be rude to refuse.

"Her name Maria," the Sister said with broken English and a quiet smile.

Frame writes:

I took Maria into my arms, gingerly at first. She seemed so fragile: I could practically see the skeleton beneath her skin. Only her eyes seemed to have escaped the circumstances of her young life. Her eyes were deep brown and as shiny as any healthy child's ought to be. She focused them not on me, but on Sister Conchita. It was clear I was "second string." Perhaps my arms were not as soft or comfortable. Yet she didn't cry. Maybe she was too weak to protest being held by a stranger. Or perhaps she was glad to be in anyone's arms. How could I tell?

After they left, Randy's tour guide explained that on average one in four of the children in the House of Hope die because their internal organs are too damaged by the time they arrive. You can spot the ones who won't make it. Lethargic, with pale, rigid skin, their hair has a reddish hue. She could have been describing Maria.

Despite being warned about the danger of venturing out alone in Port-au-Prince, Randy left the security of his hotel that night to make the two-mile trek back to the House of Hope. When he found Sister Conchita, she was still sitting on her rocker with Maria in her arms.

As I approach Sister Conchita, she stands, sensing exactly why I have returned. She says nothing, but offers me the child. And also her chair.... I have arrived at the place where I want to be. And as I live out what I'd earlier in the day envisioned, I am suddenly and fully aware of my weaknesses, my limitations. And aware also of the limitations and shortcomings of humanity, which has somehow failed this child and many others like her....

I am utterly powerless to determine whether this child, who bears the image of God, will live or die this night. But I do have power—complete power—to make certain that if and when her frail body finally yields, she has felt the security, the comfort, of someone's loving arms. Tonight they are my arms. It's the least I can do for her, and also, perhaps, the most. Her weak but gracious eyes look up to mine. And hold their gaze. And in the sacred silence of this moment, there is no other power I crave, no other purpose I desire.

Randy's story made me sad—and happy. God's love is so evident. It is "God with us," "God with Randy," "God with Maria"—the Lord expressing himself to and through human beings. Like Randy, we are called to be Christ-bearers, to reflect God to others. Today let us ask for the grace to make Immanuel known, to allow his light and his life to shine through us.

Friday

PROMISES ASSOCIATED WITH HIS NAME

What does it mean to say that God is with us? Surely it doesn't mean our lives will be easy. It doesn't mean we will be insulated from failure or doubt or that God will take our side in every argument. But it does mean we will never face even a single struggle alone. It means the Lord will never withhold the help we need to do his will. It means that ultimately we will come out on top even if we feel we're living most of our life on the bottom.

What difficulties are you facing? Chronic illness? Troubled children? A broken marriage? Financial hardship? Take a moment today to stop imagining yourself surrounded by all your difficulties and instead begin to envision yourself as you really are—surrounded by the presence of your faithful God. Invoke his name—Immanuel. Decide today to do everything in your power to follow him. Then ask for his peace, pray for his protection, and open your life to his power.

Promises in Scripture

But Moses said to God, "Who am I, that I should go to Pharaoh and bring the Israelites out of Egypt?"

And God said, "I will be with you."

EXODUS 3:11–12

"I will never leave you nor forsake you. . . . Have I not commanded you? Be strong and courageous. Do not be terrified; do not be discouraged, for the LORD your God will be with you wherever you go."

JOSHUA 1:5, 9

When you pass through the waters,
I will be with you;
and when you pass through the rivers,
they will not sweep over you.

When you walk through the fire,
  you will not be burned;
  the flames will not set you ablaze.
For I am the LORD, your God,
  the Holy One of Israel, your Savior.

ISAIAH 43:2–3

Surely I am with you always, to the very end of the age.

MATTHEW 28:20

Keep your lives free from the love of money and be content with what you have, because God has said,

"Never will I leave you;
  never will I forsake you."

So we say with confidence,

"The Lord is my helper; I will not be afraid.
  What can human beings do to me?"

HEBREWS 13:5–6

Continued Prayer and Praise

Pray this verse when you are afraid. (Joshua 1:9)

Be encouraged because no one can prevail against you if God is with you. (Isaiah 8:10)

Remember that Jesus will not leave us orphans. He will show himself to those who love him. (John 14:15–21)

2

LIGHT OF THE WORLD

τὸ φῶς τοῦ κόσμου
To Phos tou Kosmou

The Name

According to Jewish tradition, one of the names for the Messiah is "Light." How fitting, then, that Jesus is called the "Light of the world." John's Gospel portrays Jesus as the light that vanquishes the darkness brought on by sin—a darkness that ends in death. Christ has opened the eyes of a sin-darkened world to the truth of the gospel. We who believe in him have moved from darkness to light, from death to life. When we pray to Jesus as the Light of the world, let us remember that we are calling on the One who was so determined to draw us into his light that he spent nine months in the darkness of his mother's womb in order to become one of us. Let us ask Jesus, our Light, to make us shine with his reflected glory.

Key Scripture

I am the light of the world. Whoever follows me will never walk in darkness, but will have the light of life.

John 8:12

HIS NAME REVEALED

Through him all things were made; without him nothing was made that has been made. In him was life, and that life was the light of all people. The light shines in the darkness, and the darkness has not overcome it.

There was a man sent from God whose name was John. He came as a witness to testify concerning that light, so that through him all might believe. He himself was not the light; he came only as a witness to the light.

The true light that gives light to everyone was coming into the world.

JOHN 1:3–9

When Jesus spoke again to the people, he said, "I am the light of the world. Whoever follows me will never walk in darkness, but will have the light of life."

JOHN 8:12

Lord, how strange it must have been to enter the world as the only sighted man and to encounter a world so enshrouded that people could not see your light. Forgive me for my self-imposed blindness. Help me to follow you faithfully so that I can see you more clearly, reflecting your light and glory now and forever. Amen.

Understanding the Name

The Hebrew Scriptures are full of images that link God with light — pillars of fire, burning lamps, consuming fire. Such images are often associated with God's nearness or his presence. John's Gospel portrays Jesus as the embodiment of the divine light, a light so powerful that it cannot be overcome by the darkness of sin and death. Though Satan tries to disguise himself as an angel of light, he is light's opposite — the prince of darkness.

The phrase "light of the world" — *to phos tou kosmou* (to FOHS tou KOS-mou) — appears three times in the New Testament (Matthew 5:14; John 8:12; 9:5). It is a distinctive phrase spoken only by Jesus, who uses it twice to refer to himself and once to refer to his disciples, who are to reflect his light through their good deeds.

Just as natural light is essential to life on earth, Christ's light is essential to unending life with God. Whoever believes in his light becomes like him, reflecting his brightness by walking in his light and obeying his commands.

Studying the Name

1. Why do you think John's Gospel uses images of light and darkness to describe Jesus and the world's response to him?

2. What do the terms "light" and "dark" mean to you?

3. Have you ever felt you were living through a time of darkness? Describe what it felt like.

4. Have you experienced Jesus as light? If so, how?

Tuesday

PRAYING THE NAME

> *The people walking in darkness*
> > *have seen a great light;*
> *on those living in the land of the shadow of death*
> > *a light has dawned. . . .*
> *See, darkness covers the earth*
> > *and thick darkness is over the peoples,*
> *but the* LORD *rises upon you*
> > *and his glory appears over you.*
>
> > ISAIAH 9:2; 60:2

When Jesus spoke again to the people, he said, "I am the light of the world. Whoever follows me will never walk in darkness, but will have the light of life."

> JOHN 8:12

Reflect On: John 8:12.
Praise God: For the brightness of his light.
Offer Thanks: That Christ has given you the light of life.
Confess: Any alliance with the darkness through sin.
Ask God: To help you walk in obedience and in the light.

Every night my seven-year-old looks under her bed, checking for monsters. Even though Luci has never encountered anything more frightening than an occasional dust ball or tennis shoe, it seems a required bedtime ritual. Recently I introduced her to a device I invented in my childhood. I call it the Magic Bubble. After prayers and a good-night kiss, I walk around her bed waving my arms while describing the big, impenetrable bubble I am constructing around her. If she's lucky, I even add a little dance to the mix. Most nights Luci lies down with a smile before issuing the same last-minute orders: "I want music ... door open ... light on." So I crank up her music box and step quietly out, leaving the door open a crack to let light slip through from the hallway. Just a sliver of light puts her mind at rest.

I understand how my daughter feels. In the darkness our fears have a tendency to multiply, failings become exaggerated, challenges seem insurmountable. We need daylight to restore our perspective.

But even the daylight holds its share of darkness. The prophet Isaiah speaks of a world covered in thick darkness. He is talking about the spiritual darkness brought on by sin. Sin, in fact, is pregnant with darkness. It gives birth to famine, war, genocide, drug addiction, child abuse, divorce, petty hatred, and even small-town gossip. Some of us have become so conditioned to the world's darkness that we've begun to call crooked things straight and good things bent. Because of sin and its attendant darkness, even the happiest life ends tragically, in a grave.

But Jesus came in order to recast our "unhappily ever after" endings, to put a stop to what had been a nonstop tragedy. He did this by confronting the darkest of our fears — by taking on death itself. Happily, as St. Paul says, death has been swallowed up in Christ's victory. Darkness has been extinguished by light. In his light we see light.

But still we fear. We tremble before life's substantial challenges — difficult marriages, problems with children, personal weaknesses, illness, financial instability. There are times when we find ourselves walking into the darkness and crying out for the light. When that happens, we need to affirm the words of the psalmist who said to our powerful God:

> If I say, "Surely the darkness will hide me
>   and the light become night around me,"
> even the darkness will not be dark to you;
>   the night will shine like the day,
>   for darkness is as light to you.
>
> PSALM 139:11 – 12

Wednesday

PRAYING THE NAME

After six days Jesus took with him Peter, James and John the brother of James, and led them up a high mountain by themselves. There he was transfigured before them. His face shone like the sun, and his clothes became as white as the light.

MATTHEW 17:1–2

This is the message we have heard from him and declare to you: God is light; in him there is no darkness at all. If we claim to have fellowship with him yet walk in the darkness, we lie and do not live by the truth. But if we walk in the light, as he is in the light, we have fellowship with one another, and the blood of Jesus, his Son, purifies us from all sin.

1 JOHN 1:5–7

Reflect On: Matthew 17:1–2 and 1 John 1:5–7.
Praise God: For there is no darkness in him.
Offer Thanks: For the grace to walk in the light.
Confess: Any tendency to make peace with habitual failings.
Ask God: To draw you more powerfully toward his light.

A few years ago, we hosted a young woman from South Africa who joined our family in late May for a year-long stay. I couldn't help smiling when she remarked how cold it was one warm spring afternoon. Then summer arrived, the temperature heated up, and Sarina began to feel right at home. The only thing that seemed alien to her was how intent everyone was on spending every minute of their free time outdoors—boating, gardening, golfing, biking, beachcombing. She didn't solve the puzzle until she lived through her first Michigan winter. Then she understood just how starved for warmth and light we northerners are by the time spring arrives.

I love all the images in Scripture that associate God with light. That association is strong and consistent, beginning in the first chapter of the Bible. The book of Genesis portrays God creating light when the earth was yet a formless void and "darkness was over the surface of the deep." Throughout Scripture, divine appearances are often marked by light. The psalmist describes a luminous God, wrapped in light as in a garment. Indeed, God is so bright that to look at him, as Moses did, was to have your own face shine with reflected glory. Later, the New Testament describes Jesus' dazzling transfiguration on the mountain top. The scene was so brilliant that the three disciples who were with him were literally awestruck, falling to the ground. Matthew's Gospel says of Jesus, "His face shone like the sun, and his clothes became as white as the light" (Matthew 17:2).

Whatever darkness still surrounds or resides in us, we need to remember that there is not a shred of darkness in our God. And we are to be pitied if we do not long to spend every day all day basking in his light. But how do we do it? To put it plainly, living in the light requires *effort impelled by grace*. At a minimum it means following the lighted path of God's commandments. But even more than laws, we are called to follow the world's true light, Jesus Christ, imitating his life as we are able. It's that simple—and that difficult.

Today, thank God for all the ways you have perceived his light at work in your life. Then examine your heart with respect to Exodus 20:1–17 and Matthew 22:34–40, which record his commandments. Before you go to bed tonight, pray the words of "Lead, Kindly Light," a hymn written by John Henry Newman:

> *Lead, Kindly Light, amid the encircling gloom*
> > *Lead thou me on!*
> *The night is dark, and I am far from home —*
> > *Lead thou me on!*
> *Keep thou my feet; I do not ask to see*
> *The distant scene — one step enough for me.*

I was not ever thus, nor pray'd that thou
  Shouldst lead me on.
I loved to choose and see my path, but now
  Lead thou me on!
I loved the garish day, and, spite of fears,
Pride ruled my will: remember not past years.

So long thy power hath blest me, sure it still
  Will lead me on,
O'er moor and fen, o'er crag and torrent, till
  The night is gone;
And with the morn those angel faces smile
Which I have loved long since, and lost awhile.

AT SEA. JUNE 16, 1833

Thursday

PRAYING THE NAME

You are the light of the world. A city on a hill cannot be hidden. Neither do people light a lamp and put it under a bowl. Instead they put it on its stand, and it gives light to everyone in the house. In the same way, let your light shine before others, that they may see your good deeds and praise your Father in heaven.

MATTHEW 5:14–16

Do everything without complaining or arguing, so that you may become blameless and pure, children of God without fault in a crooked and depraved generation, in which you shine like stars in the universe as you hold out the word of life.

PHILIPPIANS 2:14–16

Reflect On: Matthew 5:14–16 and Philippians 2:14–16.
Praise God: For his unswerving plan for the world.
Offer Thanks: For the high calling of God on your life.
Confess: Any apathy toward the poor and the oppressed.
Ask God: To increase your passion for the lost.

Westerners rarely if ever think about the meaning behind names. When expectant parents start shopping for names, they don't generally discuss the fact that Brian means "strength" or that Carlos means "expressive." They pick popular names, ones that sound pleasant or that remind them of friends and family. But naming customs vary. In China, where my daughters were born, a baby's given name is thought to express her destiny. Though I don't subscribe to that belief, I would be happy if it worked out that way for my children because Katherine Ailin means "Pure Light" and Luci means "Light." You could say that I am surrounded by light, at least in theory.

That is not a bad picture of what God intends for us—to live with him in paradise, to be surrounded by his light, hemmed in by his glory. That has always been his intention—to create a world where love is normative.

- In paradise there are no food pantries, foster homes, prisons, halfway houses, hospitals, or funeral homes because love is normative.
- In paradise there are no depressed, confused, broken, bitter, or lonely people because love is normative.
- In paradise there is no prejudice because love is normative.
- In paradise there are no wasting plagues, no howling wastelands because love is normative.
- In paradise there is no fear, only perfect peace and unbroken harmony.

Can you begin to comprehend the tragedy of our fall from grace?

But even though we are living in a fallen world, the light has not been extinguished. God is still with us, still wooing and calling us back into the light. And he invites us not simply to rest in his light but to become light bearers ourselves, bringing about his kingdom on earth. We are to be his hands, to express his heart, and to reproduce his character to our families, our coworkers, in hospitals, foster homes, and halfway houses. We are to roll back the darkness with the light of Christ's presence. That's the purpose for which you and I were created. Yet tragically our efforts are often halfhearted. We lose our sense of urgency for the world's grief. We get comfortable, busy, sated, dull. And the light in us wanes.

Pray today to know what in your life may be obstructing Christ's light. Then determine to do without it. Ask God to shine his face upon you and enable you to work for the coming of the light.

Friday

PROMISES ASSOCIATED WITH HIS NAME

What are you waiting for? The perfect mate, your next vacation, a coveted promotion, the kids to graduate from college, enough money to accumulate in your retirement account? Ask yourself that question because whatever you're waiting for is what you're living for.

At the deepest level, we need to remember that we are waiting for the second coming of Jesus Christ. That's when all the promises of the Bible will be perfectly fulfilled. We are waiting for him to bring justice to the oppressed, mercy to the suffering, strength to the weak. We are waiting for the time in which our hearts will no longer be assaulted by the headlines we read in the newspaper. We are waiting for a time in which death will lose its hold and the Lord God will be our everlasting light. And while we are waiting, this is also what we are living for.

Promises in Scripture

> The sun will no more be your light by day,
>   nor will the brightness of the moon shine on you,
> for the LORD will be your everlasting light,
>   and your God will be your glory.
> Your sun will never set again,
>   and your moon will wane no more;
> the LORD will be your everlasting light,
>   and your days of sorrow will end.
>
> ISAIAH 60:19–20

I did not see a temple in the city, because the Lord God Almighty and the Lamb are its temple. The city does not need the sun or the moon to shine on it, for the glory of God gives it light, and the Lamb is its lamp. The nations will walk by its light, and the kings of the earth will bring their splendor into it. On no day will its gates ever be shut, for there will be no night there. The glory and honor of the nations will be brought into it. Nothing impure will ever enter it, nor will anyone who does what is shameful or deceitful, but only those whose names are written in the Lamb's book of life.

REVELATION 21:22–27

Continued Prayer and Praise

Praise the One who is your light and your salvation. (Psalm 27:1)

Praise God for giving us a light bright enough for the entire world. (Luke 2:29–32)

Keep your love from growing cold. (Revelation 2:1–7)

Put on the armor of light. (Romans 13:12)

Pray for those living in the darkness of unbelief. (2 Corinthians 4:3–6)

Remember that God has called you into the light. (1 Peter 2:9–10; Ephesians 5:8–10)

Reflect on how Moses and Paul encountered God's light. (Exodus 34:29–35; Acts 9:1–22)

3

CHILD

יֶלֶד πᾶις

YELED, PAIS

The Name

A child was always at the heart of the biblical covenant. Already in the garden of Eden God promised that Eve's offspring would crush the head of the serpent, who beguiled her. Later God made a covenant with Abraham, promising that Sarah would bear him a child who would be the first of countless descendents. Then Isaiah spoke of a child who would be born of a virgin and be given the name "Wonderful Counselor, Mighty God, Everlasting Father, Prince of Peace." The New Testament tells of the fulfillment of that promise, and Jesus presents children as the model for his followers to emulate. The only way to enter the kingdom is with the humility and trust of little children.

Key Scripture

Joseph also went up from the town of Nazareth in Galilee to Judea, to Bethlehem the town of David, because he belonged to the house and line of David. He went there to register with Mary, who was pledged to be married to him and was expecting a child. While they were there, the time came for the baby to be born, and she gave birth to her firstborn, a son. She wrapped him in cloths and placed him in a manger, because there was no room for them in the inn.

LUKE 2:4–7

Monday

HIS NAME REVEALED

In those days Caesar Augustus issued a decree that a census should be taken of the entire Roman world. (This was the first census that took place while Quirinius was governor of Syria.) And everyone went to his own town to register.

So Joseph also went up from the town of Nazareth in Galilee to Judea, to Bethlehem the town of David, because he belonged to the house and line of David. He went there to register with Mary, who was pledged to be married to him and was expecting a child. While they were there, the time came for the baby to be born, and she gave birth to her firstborn, a son. She wrapped him in cloths and placed him in a manger, because there was no room for them in the inn.

And there were shepherds living out in the fields nearby, keeping watch over their flocks at night. An angel of the Lord appeared to them, and the glory of the Lord shone around them, and they were terrified. But the angel said to them, "Do not be afraid. I bring you good news of great joy that will be for all the people. Today in the town of David a Savior has been born to you; he is Christ the Lord. This will be a sign to you: You will find a baby wrapped in cloths and lying in a manger."

LUKE 2:1 – 12

Lord, you were cradled in human arms and laid in a manger. How can I begin to understand a gift so unexpected? That someone so great would allow himself to become so small? Help me to follow you, like a little child, laying aside my pretensions and admitting my need. Help me to love you, trust you, and lean on you today, and thank you for showing me the way into your kingdom.

Understanding the Name

Though the Israelites considered children a great blessing, they occupied the bottom rung of the social ladder. Entrusted with the solemn responsibility of teaching and disciplining them, parents were accorded nearly absolute authority over their children. To be a child was to be powerless, dependent, subservient. Yet even little children and young infants could receive wisdom from God and their lips could praise him. The prophet Isaiah spoke of a child, or *yeled* (YEL-ed), who would one day be born of a virgin and sit on David's throne. Luke's Gospel tells us that Mary, while she was yet betrothed, was expecting a child, or *pais* (PICE), and that she gave birth to him in Bethlehem.

Studying the Name

1. What images come to mind when you think of the child Jesus?

2. Why do you think Luke mentions that Jesus was born in Bethlehem and that he was Mary's son?

3. Why do you think God allowed his Son to be born in such humble circumstances and to be placed in a manger?

Tuesday

PRAYING THE NAME

For to us a child is born, to us a son is given.

ISAIAH 9:6

In a loud voice she [Elizabeth] exclaimed: "Blessed are you among women, and blessed is the child you will bear!"

LUKE 1:42

Reflect On: Isaiah 9:6 and Luke 1:26–45.
Praise God: For keeping his promise to his people.
Offer Thanks: That God's ways are so much higher than ours.
Confess: Your tendency to rely more on yourself than you do on God.
Ask God: For the grace to depend on him like children depend on their father and mother.

One of the reasons I find the gospel so convincing is that it's nothing I would have dreamed up. Think about it. God became human, a little baby who had to be fed, burped, and bathed. God allowed himself to get the flu, to be teased, to stub his toe like any other little kid. To be thought the illegitimate son of a teenage mother. To have for his main defense against an irate king a human father without an ounce of political pull. And that's just the beginning.

What if I had been God? Would I have devised an all-loving strategy to woo my people back to myself, developing a plan that would require weakness, humility, and dependency on the part of my child? I doubt it. My strategy would probably have involved more power than love because power seems less risky.

From a distance of two thousand years, it can be difficult to comprehend how shocking the incarnation was and still is. It's true that the Jewish people had been awaiting a child who would become Israel's deliverer, ushering in a golden age in which God's people would finally come out on top. No more oppression. No more bondage. Little wonder that every woman wanted to be that child's mother. But even in her wildest dreams, no Jewish woman would have thought that would have meant cradling God in her arms. God's gracious plan was beyond anything his people could have imagined.

The apostle Paul speaks of Christ's crucifixion as "the foolishness of God." But surely God's foolishness began when he allowed his Son to be born in a stable and laid in a manger. In fact, the life of Jesus was nothing but divine foolishness at work, trumping human wisdom and exposing it as folly.

Jesus puts it to his disciples like this: "Unless you change and become like little children, you will never enter the kingdom of heaven. Therefore, whoever humbles himself like this child is the greatest in the kingdom of heaven" (Matthew 18:3–4). Like everything else he demanded of his disciples, Jesus lived the pattern before he asked it of them. But what does it mean to become like little children?

Most children don't have much money. They don't have a lot of power. They often lack wisdom. And they aren't afraid to ask for help. Hasn't Jesus already made it plain? If you want to be big in God's kingdom, become small in this world. If you want to save your life, be willing to lose it.

Today, God is calling you to become like a little child, asking you to follow him with humility and trust. Decide to embrace his "foolish-seeming" plan for your life, confident that his strength will be perfected through your weakness. Guard against self-reliance and self-promotion. Try to find ways to humble yourself, committing yourself to following Christ in childlike trust and obedience.

Wednesday

PRAYING THE NAME

When they [the Magi] had gone, an angel of the Lord appeared to Joseph in a dream. "Get up," he said, "take the child and his mother and escape to Egypt. Stay there until I tell you, for Herod is going to search for the child to kill him."

So he got up, took the child and his mother during the night and left for Egypt, where he stayed until the death of Herod. And so was fulfilled what the Lord had said through the prophet: "Out of Egypt I called my son."

When Herod realized that he had been outwitted by the Magi, he was furious, and he gave orders to kill all the boys in Bethlehem and its vicinity who were two years old and under.

MATTHEW 2:13–16

Reflect On: Matthew 2:13–20.
Praise God: For never abandoning his plan to save us.
Offer Thanks: Because even as a child, Jesus shared our suffering.
Confess: Any tendency to hide your faith for fear of opposition.
Ask God: To increase your understanding of the gospel.

Christmas — it's not about a baby! That was the surprising message of a talk I listened to a few years back. I don't remember everything the speaker said, but I am certain he must have opened one too many Christmas cards depicting the Christ child as a cherubic babe, surrounded by velvety soft animals more suited to the pages of a children's book than a stable. He didn't want the celebration of the great feast of the incarnation to be reduced to something sentimental and saccharine. In fact, the Lord's birthday story is a dramatic and richly layered narrative that bears careful rereading. You could say it contains the DNA of the gospel, linking the child Jesus to Israel's past as well as to its future. It is like a seed that encapsulates the unfolding story of salvation — past, present, and to come.

For instance, Matthew's Gospel begins with a long genealogy linking Jesus to Abraham, Isaac, Jacob, David, and Solomon. Then, after recounting Jesus' birth and the visit of the Magi, the story shifts because already opposition to the Christ child is rising. An angel appears to Joseph in a dream, warning him that Herod is searching everywhere for Jesus, intending to murder him. So Joseph flees with Jesus and Mary to Egypt. Like Moses, the child Jesus is rescued only in the nick of time. Enraged that the Magi have left without telling him the precise location of the newborn king, Herod orders all the boys of Bethlehem two years old and under to be slaughtered, echoing Pharaoh's decree that every Hebrew male infant be drowned in the Nile River.

It's the Exodus story in miniature. From the very beginning, Jesus is linked to the suffering history of his people, to their exile and oppression. His life recalls the words of Hosea: "When Israel was a child, I loved him, and out of Egypt I called my son" (Hosea 11:1).

The nativity links Jesus not only to his people's past but also to their future. To shepherds tending their flocks outside Bethlehem, an angel proclaims: "I bring you news of great joy that will be for all the people. Today in the town of David a Savior has been born to you; he is Christ the Lord. This will be a sign to you: You will find a baby wrapped in cloths and lying in a manger" (Luke 2:10–12). The shepherds were amazed, telling everyone about him. They had seen their long-awaited Savior, the desire of all nations, the one who would one day refer to himself as the Good Shepherd.

So Christmas, the great feast of the incarnation, *is* about a baby after all. And *it's not* about a baby. It's about the great story of God's love as it stretched across the centuries toward its climax in the life of the child Jesus. No wonder Simeon held the boy in his arms when his parents brought him to the temple, speaking these words to Mary: "This child is destined to cause the falling and rising of many in Israel, and to be a sign that will be spoken against, so that the thoughts of many hearts will be revealed" (Luke 2:34–35).

Even as a child, Jesus created turbulence in the world. His mere existence demanded a response. Either love him or hate him, accept his message or try to quash it. Why then should we be surprised when we encounter opposition because of our faith? If we bear the image of

Christ within us, we will certainly cause offense to some. But many others will welcome the Jesus they see in us. Pray today that Christ will shine more brightly in your heart and in every heart that belongs to him because God wants to reveal his Son to a world that is dying to know him.

Thursday

PRAYING THE NAME

So Joseph also went up from the town of Nazareth in Galilee to Judea, to Bethlehem the town of David, because he belonged to the house and line of David. He went there to register with Mary, who was pledged to be married to him and was expecting a child. While they were there, the time came for the baby to be born, and she gave birth to her firstborn, a son. She wrapped him in cloths and placed him in a manger, because there was no room for them in the inn.

LUKE 2:4–7

Reflect On: Luke 2:1–20.
Praise God: For speaking to us through his Son.
Offer Thanks: For all the ways God has provided for you and your family, materially and spiritually.
Confess: Any failure to value God's Word enough to read it regularly.
Ask God: To nourish you through his Word.

Have you heard the story about the first grader who drew a picture of the nativity in his Sunday school class? After complimenting him on his artistic ability, his teacher inquired about the round figure lurking in the corner of his drawing. Surprised that she hadn't recognized him, the boy responded, "Oh, that's round John Virgin!"

At a distance of two thousand years, it can be easy to get some of the details wrong. How many of us, for instance, picture Mary riding a donkey into Bethlehem? But the Bible never tells us whether Mary walked or rode on an animal. The only donkeys in the story are the ones that populate our crèche sets. And what about the three Magi who worshiped the infant in the stable? The Bible never specifies how many Magi were there, though it does say they presented Jesus with three gifts. But at least we know they worshiped the infant in the stable, right? Sorry! Matthew's Gospel says Jesus was living in a house by the time the Magi arrived in Bethlehem. Some biblical scholars think he may have been a two-year-old by the time they caught up with him.

While none of these details significantly alter the meaning of the story, we sometimes miss details that do. Take the manger, for instance. There's no disputing the fact that the Bible says Mary placed her baby in a feeding trough shortly after his birth. This detail highlights the humble circumstances surrounding his birth. We know that. But how many of us have ever wondered if there's more to it—another reason why God's Son began his life in a feeding trough? Could God have been telegraphing a message, hoping we would understand that Jesus would become a source of nourishment for his people, feeding and sustaining us throughout our lives?

As you read Scripture today remember that Jesus wants to nourish you—to share his life with you. Take time to meditate on what you are reading, asking his Spirit to give you understanding. As you meditate on God's Word, remember that meditation simply means to ponder or to *chew on* something. Instead of going away hungry, ask God today to help you feed on his Word, to let it satisfy your longings and fill up your empty places.

Friday

PROMISES ASSOCIATED WITH HIS NAME

I was forty-six when I adopted my first child—not as old as the biblical Sarah but a far sight older than Mary, the teenage mother of Jesus. But no matter how old you are or how long you've waited, a child can be one of life's greatest blessings, opening you again to wonder, renewing your amazement at God's good plan for the future.

Little wonder that a child was God's first promise to the world. After Adam and Eve sinned, as they were being forced from their garden paradise, God made the greatest of all his promises, assuring them that Eve's offspring would one day crush the serpent whose temptation had pushed them out of Eden and into so much misery. No wonder Mary has sometimes been called the new Eve, her obedience a striking reversal of Eve's disobedience. And as for the Christ child—he has always been identified as the fulfillment of God's promise to crush Satan, our worst enemy, and to lead us back to paradise.

Promises in Scripture

So the LORD God said to the serpent, "Because you have done this,

> *"Cursed are you above all the livestock*
>   *and all the wild animals!*
> *You will crawl on your belly*
>   *and you will eat dust*
>   *all the days of your life.*
> *And I will put enmity*
>   *between you and the woman,*
>   *and between your offspring and hers;*
> *he will crush your head,*
>   *and you will strike his heel."*

GENESIS 3:14–15

Therefore the Lord himself will give you a sign: The virgin will be with child and will give birth to a son, and will call him Immanuel.

ISAIAH 7:14

Continued Prayer and Praise

Praise God for promising a child who would reign forever with his justice and righteousness. (Isaiah 9:6–7)

Strive to be the greatest in the kingdom of heaven. (Matthew 18:2–4; Luke 9:48)

4

BREAD OF LIFE

ἄρτος ζωῆς

ARTOS ZOES

The Name

Without bread no one in ancient Palestine would have survived for long. So it seems entirely reasonable for Jesus, in what has become known as the Lord's Prayer, to instruct his disciples to pray for their daily bread. Yet the Lord also challenged his followers not to work for food that spoils, announcing himself as the only food that would enable them to live forever.

In fact, Jesus was born in Bethlehem, which means "house of bread." After feeding five thousand people with only five loaves of bread and two fish, he shocked his listeners by declaring: "Unless you eat the flesh of the Son of Man and drink his blood, you have no life in you" (John 6:53). This week, as you seek to understand what it means that Jesus is the Bread of Life, ask him to show you exactly what it means to feed on him.

Key Scripture

"I am the bread of life. Your ancestors ate the manna in the wilderness, yet they died. But here is the bread that comes down from heaven, which people may eat and not die. I am the living bread that came down from heaven. Whoever eats of this bread will live forever. This bread is my flesh, which I will give for the life of the world."

JOHN 6:48–51

Monday

HIS NAME REVEALED

When they [Jesus' followers] found him on the other side of the lake, they asked him, "Rabbi, when did you get here?"

Jesus answered, "Very truly I tell you, you are looking for me, not because you saw the signs I performed but because you ate the loaves and had your fill. Do not work for food that spoils, but for food that endures to eternal life, which the Son of Man will give you. On him God the Father has placed his seal of approval. . . .

"I am the bread of life. Your ancestors ate the manna in the wilderness, yet they died. But here is the bread that comes down from heaven, which people may eat and not die. I am the living bread that came down from heaven. Whoever eats of this bread will live forever. This bread is my flesh, which I will give for the life of the world."

Then the Jews began to argue sharply among themselves, "How can this man give us his flesh to eat?"

Jesus said to them, "Very truly I tell you, unless you eat the flesh of the Son of Man and drink his blood, you have no life in you. Whoever eats my flesh and drinks my blood has eternal life, and I will raise them up at the last day. For my flesh is real food and my blood is real drink. Whoever eats my flesh and drinks my blood remains in me, and I in them. Just as the living Father sent me and I live because of the Father, so the one who feeds on me will live because of me. This is the bread that came down from heaven. Your ancestors ate manna and died, but whoever feeds on this bread will live forever."

JOHN 6:25–27, 48–58

Lord, I hunger and thirst for so many things that do not bring real life. Yet you speak of food that will enable me to live forever. Satisfy me with your body and your blood, the bread of your holy presence. Nourish and sustain me now and at the hour of my death. Amen.

Understanding the Name

Bread was baked daily in the ancient world. Made from a variety of grains (barley for the poor and wheat for those with money), it was usually shaped into small round loaves that looked more like rolls or buns than the large loaves of bread we eat today.

Because bread was a primary staple, it was also used in various aspects of worship. Cereal offerings took the form of loaves or cakes, and bread was also used as a firstfruit offering or a peace offering. The Bread of the Presence, consisting of twelve loaves of unleavened bread, symbolized the covenant between God and his people. Displayed in the temple sanctuary next to the Most Holy Place, it served as a constant reminder to the priests and the people that it was God who sustained the twelve tribes of Israel. Psalm 78:24–25 speaks of how God's people were fed in the wilderness:

> He [God] rained down manna for the people to eat,
>   he gave them the grain of heaven.
> Human beings ate the bread of angels;
>   he sent them all the food they could eat.

Bread also played an important role in the Feast of Unleavened Bread. In fact, the bread that was consumed at the Last Supper, as well as the bread Jesus shared with the two travelers in Emmaus, was probably unleavened bread since both meals occurred during Passover Week.

In John's Gospel, Jesus called himself *Artos Zoes* (AR-tos zo-ASE), the Bread of Life.

Studying the Name

1. Jesus knew that bread is one of life's necessities, so what did he mean by counseling his followers not to work for food that spoils? What are the implications for your life?

2. Various Christian denominations have interpreted Jesus' words about eating his flesh and drinking his blood differently. How have these words impacted your own spiritual journey?

3. Discuss the various ways in which it is possible for a person to "feed on Jesus."

Tuesday

PRAYING THE NAME

Jesus said, "Have the people sit down." There was plenty of grass in that place, and the men sat down, about five thousand of them. Jesus then took the loaves, gave thanks, and distributed to those who were seated as much as they wanted. He did the same with the fish.

When they had all had enough to eat, he said to his disciples, "Gather the pieces that are left over. Let nothing be wasted." So they gathered them and filled twelve baskets with the pieces of the five barley loaves left over by those who had eaten.

JOHN 6:10–13

Reflect On: John 6:1–15, 25–66.
Praise God: Who is able to take care of all your needs, both physical and spiritual.
Offer Thanks: For all the ways God has fed you.
Confess: Any tendency to settle for less than what Jesus offers.
Ask God: To renew your spiritual hunger.

I love the familiar story of how Jesus fed five thousand hungry people with only five loaves and two fish. A huge crowd had followed him to the far shore of the Sea of Galilee eager for miracles. But now they were tired and hungry, spread out on the grass like a great multicolored blanket. Except for a boy with five small loaves of bread and two small fish, no one had anything to eat. Taking the boy's bread in his hands, Jesus did what every Jewish father would have done at the beginning of a family meal. He gave thanks to God, broke the bread, and then began handing it out. And no one went away hungry. In fact there was so much food that his disciples collected twelve baskets of leftovers.

John's Gospel says the bread was made out of barley. It was poor man's bread, not the fine wheat bread of the rich. But it filled them up and made them glad. Astonished by the miracle, some in the crowd began to make the connection. This was like the manna that Moses and the Israelites fed on in the desert. God was giving them a sign. Surely this must be the longed-for Messiah! The rumors spread swiftly through the crowd.

Knowing what was in their hearts, that they wanted to make him king, Jesus withdrew into the mountains. But why? Why not soak up the admiration, the wide-eyed wonder of it all? Because Jesus wanted to do far more than feed bodies that were soon to perish. He wanted to nourish souls that could live forever. But the people only wanted more cheap bread. When his followers finally caught up with him, Jesus told them point blank:

"Stop working for food that spoils."
"Work for the forever food that I will give you."
"The work you need to do is to believe in me."
"I am the bread of life."
"When you fall down dead, I will make you stand up alive again
  on the last day."

It was too much for them. The crowd couldn't stomach it. That day, many of his followers fell away from him because they weren't hungry enough for the bread he offered—"This bread is my flesh, which I will give for the life of the world. . . . Unless you eat the flesh of the Son of Man and drink his blood, you have no life in you" (John 6:51, 53).

What about you? How hungry are you?

It's so easy to stuff ourselves with the world's cheap bread—with money, success, comfort, and pleasure—that we take the edge off our spiritual hunger. We fail to realize the dangers of living in an affluent, consumer-driven society in which we can be consumed by the things we desire. So many of us are like sponges, soaking up the world's good things with no space left for God.

If your spiritual appetite seems dull right now, ask Jesus for the grace to base your life not on the cheap bread of this world but on the bread he offers. Ask him to show you how to feed on him—on his life, his sacrifice, his Word, his promises. Then, to underline your prayer, consider fasting for a day. When you start to feel hungry, start praying. Tell Jesus, the Bread of Life, that you are hungry for more of him. Then remind him of his promise — that when you do the work of believing, he will do the work of feeding you.

#

PRAYING THE NAME

When he was at the table with them, he took bread, gave thanks, broke it and began to give it to them. Then their eyes were opened and they recognized him, and he disappeared from their sight. They asked each other, "Were not our hearts burning within us while he talked with us on the road and opened the Scriptures to us?"

LUKE 24:30–32

Reflect On: Luke 24:13–35.
Praise God: For revealing himself to us as bread that is broken.
Offer Thanks: For Christ's faithfulness to you.
Confess: Your lack of gratitude.
Ask God: To open your eyes to his goodness.

Remember the story about how Christ appeared to two of his disciples when they were walking to Emmaus, a town outside Jerusalem? It was a gloomy conversation, all about the tragedy that had unfolded three days earlier. Astonished by the stranger's seeming ignorance of the crucifixion of Jesus, the two travelers revealed their own ignorance by describing the death of the man who was walking right next to them.

Then the stranger began instructing them. How could they be so slow to understand? Jesus laid it out from start to finish, reminding them of all the Scriptures that applied to him from Moses straight through to Malachi.

When they arrived at their destination, the two travelers urged the stranger to stay with them. Again the roles were reversed. As the three sat down for their evening meal, the stranger began acting as the host, taking bread into his hands, giving thanks, breaking it, and then handing it to his guests. Suddenly, in the midst of thanksgiving and bread breaking, the two travelers knew exactly whom they were dining with—the same man who had fed the five thousand, who had called himself "the bread of life," who had died on a cross three days ago!

I wonder how many times we are like the two disheartened travelers. We act as if Jesus is a million miles away, though he's standing right beside us. Like the disciples on the road, we feel abandoned and bewildered, far from the God who promises to be with us always.

A friend of mine recently told me how discouraged she had been about her seven-year-old son. David was often impulsive and irritable and seemed clueless about how to get along with other kids. A loner at school, he could be a terror at home. She knew her son had a neurological disorder that contributed to his bad behavior. She had done everything she knew to help him, and she had prayed nonstop that God would heal him. Why hadn't he? Where was he? She was so hungry for a sense of Christ's presence, for tangible evidence that he cared about David and about her.

Suddenly her thoughts turned to the summer that was winding to a close. Despite David's difficulties, the last couple of months had been fun. She thanked God for the good times they'd had together as she recalled them one by one. Now that she thought about it, she realized David had been a lot calmer lately. There had been fewer bad episodes, fewer tantrums. Thank God for that! Maybe the new medicine was finally working. David had been eating and sleeping better too, come to think of it. And she was grateful for the neighborhood kids who had befriended him. David had spent nearly every day of the last month playing with them. The more my friend expressed her thankfulness to God, the more she found to be thankful for. Why hadn't she seen it before?

It's like that with most of us. We long for tangible evidence of God's love, but we fail to see it, in part because we have not learned to be thankful. It's not just that God likes to be thanked. It's that we *need* to thank him. Expressing our gratitude is like holding a little celebration in God's honor. It's a way of feeding on his goodness, reminding ourselves what he's done for us. Thankfulness opens our eyes to God's faithfulness, which in turn nourishes our faith. No wonder the word "Eucharist," a common name for the Christian commemoration of the Last Supper, comes from a Greek word meaning "thanksgiving."

Skipping gratitude is like skipping the meal God has prepared for us. Without it, we merely move on to the next need, feeling hungry and empty without the faith to believe that God will sustain us.

Not long ago, a friend confided in me that he no longer believed in God. To him all religions seemed like fairy tales concocted to make people feel better. I felt sad for him, realizing how tragic it is to watch a sunset, to listen to waves breaking against a shore, or to hold a child on your lap without having someone to thank.

If you are feeling hungry for God, spend some time right now thanking him for everything good in your life. It doesn't matter if your list is short. Just start thanking him for the good you can see. Then try to make gratefulness a habit. If you do, you will be surprised at how quickly your list will grow and how steady your sense of God's abiding presence will become.

Thursday

PRAYING THE NAME

Jesus said to them, "Very truly I tell you, unless you eat the flesh of the Son of Man and drink his blood, you have no life in you. Whoever eats my flesh and drinks my blood has eternal life, and I will raise them up at the last day. For my flesh is real food and my blood is real drink. Whoever eats my flesh and drinks my blood remains in me, and I in them. Just as the living Father sent me and I live because of the Father, so the one who feeds on me will live because of me. This is the bread that came down from heaven. Your ancestors ate manna and died, but whoever feeds on this bread will live forever."

JOHN 6:53–58

Reflect On: John 6:53–58 and Psalm 103.
Praise God: The source of all life.
Offer Thanks: For your daily bread.
Confess: Any tendency to live as though this world is all there is.
Ask God: To give you life everlasting.

I know someone who is dying, though you wouldn't know it to look at her. Her cheeks aren't sunken or sallow. She laughs frequently, sleeps well, has a hearty appetite, and tries to exercise regularly. She has two small children who drive her on alternate days either to delight or distraction. From the outside her life looks good. But she's dying, wasting away. Her body is deteriorating, wilting toward the earth that will one day swallow her whole. Still, you wouldn't know it if you passed her on the street. On a good day she might even be whistling. Even her friends don't know just how limited her days are. So how do I know she's dying? I know because the person I'm talking about is me.

But don't pity me, please. I've learned to deal with it, at least on some level. Most of the time I don't even think about it. In case you're wondering what I suffer from, I'll name the condition. It's called mortality, and it's an unstoppable epidemic.

The other night I dug out an old family movie and showed it to my children, who are considerably younger than I am. There was Uncle Tom, Aunt Betty, Uncle Warren, Grandpa and Grandma Spangler, Grandpa Dunbar, my dad, my cousin Judy, my sister Sue. We were water skiing, ice skating, blowing up balloons, grilling out, running races, kissing, unwrapping gifts, playing with the dog. The memories were warm and rich. But all at once they were tinged with grief as my children began asking: "Who's that? Is he alive? What happened to her? Is she dead?" Nearly every time the answer was yes — two of the children and all but three of the adults on the film, gone a long time ago.

I thought of the psalmist's words, "As for mortals, their days are like grass, they flourish like a flower of the field; the wind blows over it and it is gone, and its place remembers it no more" (Psalm 103:15–16). Humanity is like the soon-wilted grass. We are up to our necks in "grassness." But unlike grass, we bear the tragedy in our hearts, knowing how short life is.

So what can we do about it? Rather than trying to dodge the truth, why not take time today to deal with it head-on? Think about the ways death has already affected you. Then reflect on your own impending death. Let it sink in. Shed some tears if you must.

Then look at Psalm 103 again. Notice that it continues on a note of hope: "But from everlasting to everlasting the LORD's love is with those who fear him" (103:17). The psalmist cannot resist the qualifier. He says *but*, because there is more to the story, mitigating circumstances concerning our "grassness." The New Testament fills it out beyond his wildest imagination. In Jesus, God becomes flesh — everlasting love stretching across the widest of chasms — across death itself — and reaching toward us.

Remember today that Jesus is heaven's bread. He is the answer to our grief, the solution to our problem. Believe him. Listen to him. Feed on him so that his life will reverse death's curse. Then proclaim with the great apostle Paul: " 'Where, O death, is your victory? Where, O death, is your sting?' The sting of death is sin, and the power of sin is the law. But thanks be to God! He gives us the victory through our Lord Jesus Christ" (1 Corinthians 15:55–57).

PROMISES ASSOCIATED WITH HIS NAME

Imagine a scene in which all the people who have ever lived are standing one in front of the other. Then death enters the picture, snapping its steely cold fingers against the first person in line. One by one everybody collapses, like a long line of dominoes. The process goes on for centuries until one of the dominoes does the impossible — it stands back up again. Suddenly death's power has been challenged, disrupted, called into question.

That's what happened when Jesus was killed. Though death pressed down on him, it could not obliterate his life. As Peter assured his fellow Jews: "God raised him from the dead, freeing him from the agony of death, because it was impossible for death to keep its hold on him" (Acts 2:24).

Jesus, the greatest of all death's trophies, did what no human being had ever done before. He gave death the slip. And now he leads a revolt against sin and death, promising that the same divine power that raised him from the dead will raise us up as long as we have fed on him, the Living Bread come down from heaven.

Promises in Scripture

Then Jesus declared, "I am the bread of life. He who comes to me will never go hungry, and he who believes in me will never be thirsty."

JOHN 6:35

"I am the bread of life. Your ancestors ate the manna in the wilderness, yet they died. But here is the bread that comes down from heaven, which people may eat and not die. I am the living bread that came down from heaven. Whoever eats of this bread will live forever. This bread is my flesh, which I will give for the life of the world."

JOHN 6:48–51

Continued Prayer and Praise

Refuse to spend so much money on things that will never satisfy your hunger. (Isaiah 55:1–2)

Reflect on Jesus' words at the Last Supper. (Luke 22:7–22)

Remember the promise of hidden manna. (Revelation 2:17)

5

PHYSICIAN

ἰατρός

IATROS

The Name

Jesus, the greatest of all physicians, performed more healings than any other kind of miracle. Nothing stumped him—not blindness, craziness, lameness, deafness, or even death. Every ailment yielded to his undeniable power, and every healing served as evidence that his kingdom was breaking into our fallen world.

When you pray for healing for yourself or others, remember that God never sends sickness, though he sometimes allows us to become sick. Indeed, Scripture sees sickness and death as byproducts of sin. And it was to solve the sin problem that Jesus came into the world. When you pray for healing, remember that Jesus is always your ally, always wanting what is best for you and for those you care about.

Key Scriptures

The blind receive sight, the lame walk, those who have leprosy are cured, the deaf hear, the dead are raised, and the good news is preached to the poor.

MATTHEW 11:5

Jesus said to them, "Surely you will quote this proverb to me: 'Physician, heal yourself! Do here in your hometown what we have heard that you did in Capernaum.'"

LUKE 4:23

Monday

HIS NAME REVEALED

When John heard in prison what Christ was doing, he sent his disciples to ask him, "Are you the one who was to come, or should we expect someone else?"

Jesus replied, "Go back and report to John what you hear and see: The blind receive sight, the lame walk, those who have leprosy are cured, the deaf hear, the dead are raised, and the good news is preached to the poor."

MATTHEW 11:2–5

He [Jesus] went to Nazareth, where he had been brought up, and on the Sabbath day he went into the synagogue, as was his custom. And he stood up to read. The scroll of the prophet Isaiah was handed to him. Unrolling it, he found the place where it is written:

> "The Spirit of the Lord is on me,
>> because he has anointed me
>> to preach good news to the poor.
> He has sent me to proclaim freedom for the prisoners
>> and recovery of sight for the blind,
> to release the oppressed,
>> to proclaim the year of the Lord's favor."

Then he rolled up the scroll, gave it back to the attendant and sat down....

Jesus said to them, "Surely you will quote this proverb to me: 'Physician, heal yourself! Do here in your hometown what we have heard that you did in Capernaum.'"

"I tell you the truth," he continued, "no prophet is accepted in his hometown.

LUKE 4:16–24

Jesus, you are the great Physician, able to heal both body and soul. I praise you because no disease is beyond your healing power and no sin beyond your saving grace. Today I pray that you would heal me and make me whole and help me to live in a way that expresses my faith in you. Use me, Lord, to advance your healing work so that many others will learn of your compassion and your power.

Understanding the Name

The ancient Egyptians were among the first to practice medicine, learning how to fill teeth, stitch up wounds, set broken bones, and perform various kinds of surgery. Later on the Greeks developed a more empirical approach to medicine, while the Romans grew wealthy by developing specialties that focused on treating eyes, ears, teeth, or various gynecological disorders.

Though the Jews used physicians, they believed healing came ultimately from God. He was *Yahweh Rophe*, "the LORD Who Heals." What's more, their Divine Healer had given them a set of laws that included hygienic practices that contributed to their health and to their staying power as a people. Also, according to the Talmud, an authoritative collection of Jewish writings, every city had its own doctor who was licensed by city officials. The temple in Jerusalem also had its own physician, assigned to take care of the priests.

Jesus' healing miracles clearly reveal him as the greatest of all physicians. While he emphasized the importance of faith in the healing process, the Gospels do not support the teaching that a lack of healing always indicates a lack of faith. And though the New Testament sometimes directly links individual sin with sickness, it does not presume that every sickness is caused by individual sin. Rather, human beings become ill as the result of living in a fallen world.

It is interesting to note that the author of Luke's Gospel, which recounts many of Jesus' healing miracles, was himself a physician (see Colossians 4:14).

Studying the Name

1. Why do you think Jesus responded to John the Baptist in the way he did in Matthew 11:2–5? What does this say about his purpose for coming into the world?

2. Do you think Jesus still heals people today? Why or why not?

3. Have you experienced God's healing power in your own life? If so, how?

4. In Luke's Gospel, in a rather roundabout way, Jesus refers to himself as a "physician." Yet his words indicate that his work as a physician would not always be well received. What do you think he meant?

Tuesday

PRAYING THE NAME

Some men brought to him a paralytic man, lying on a mat. When Jesus saw their faith, he said to the man, "Take heart, son; your sins are forgiven."

At this, some of the teachers of the law said to themselves, "This fellow is blaspheming!"

Knowing their thoughts, Jesus said, "Why do you entertain evil thoughts in your hearts? Which is easier: to say, 'Your sins are forgiven,' or to say, 'Get up and walk'?" . . . So he said to the paralyzed man, "Get up, take your mat and go home." And the man got up and went home. When the crowd saw this, they were filled with awe; and they praised God, who had given such authority to human beings.

MATTHEW 9:2–8

Reflect On: Matthew 9:2–8.
Praise God: For his healing power.
Offer Thanks: For whatever health God has blessed you with.
Confess: Any sins that relate directly to your body—such as
                sexual sins, gluttony, sloth, or intemperance.
Ask God: To heal you, body, mind, and soul.

Imagine you are lying on a stretcher in the emergency room after having suffered a stroke. Though you cannot move, you are still aware of what's going on around you. Suddenly a doctor leans over you and, instead of injecting you with a clot-busting drug, takes hold of your hand, looks you in the eye, and says: "Cheer up! Your sins are forgiven." Wouldn't it sound crazy, like a colossal non sequitur?

That's how the story of the healing of the paralytic struck me on first reading. What does the man's need for healing have to do with his need for forgiveness? We know that ignorance regarding what causes disease has resulted in millions of deaths over the course of human history. As recently as two hundred years ago, physicians treated their patients by bloodletting, vomiting, purging, and starving them. Benjamin Rush, a physician friend of John Adams and a signer of the Declaration of Independence, routinely prescribed bloodletting as a treatment for yellow fever. George Washington died after physicians drained several pints of blood from his body in hopes of curing a throat infection. No wonder the seventeenth-century French dramatist Molière once quipped that most people die not from illness but from remedies.

But Jesus was not dealing in ignorance when he began to heal the paralyzed man by reading his heart and declaring his sins forgiven. He knew that every human being suffers from what might be called a kind of spectrum disorder. Think of it like this: On the low end of the spectrum is the common cold, then come allergies, then something like arthritis, then maybe cancer, and finally, on the extreme end of the spectrum, is the most dreaded condition of all—death. Jesus already knew what science can never discover—that every one of our afflictions is ultimately rooted in sin. Sin breaks our connection with God, the source of all wholeness and healing, distorting and obstructing his plan for the world.

When Jesus told the paralyzed man his sins were forgiven, he was acting not like an ignorant physician but like a skilled doctor who was not content to treat the man's symptoms without dealing with their root cause. After that the impossible happened. The man picked up his mat and walked home, praising God!

Jesus, our great Physician, is still at work, forgiving our sins, healing our bodies, and restoring our souls. Take time today to align yourself with his healing work by repenting of your sins. Then pray for those in your family, your church, or your neighborhood who are ill. Ask God to deal with the deep cause of their suffering, whether rooted in their own sin or in the sinful nature of our fallen world. Ask him to bring them complete healing—body, mind, and soul.

Wednesday

PRAYING THE NAME

Jesus went through all the towns and villages, teaching in their synagogues, preaching the good news of the kingdom and healing every disease and sickness. When he saw the crowds, he had compassion on them, because they were harassed and helpless, like sheep without a shepherd.

MATTHEW 9:35–36

Reflect On:　Matthew 9.
Praise God:　For his healing compassion.
Offer Thanks: For God's healing power.
Confess:　Any pride, which keeps you from asking for what you need.
Ask God:　To deepen your sense of dependence on him.

◌ↄ

Matthew's Gospel recounts fourteen spectacular miracles that displayed Jesus' healing power. Five of these appear in chapter 9:

- Jesus heals a paralytic.
- He heals a woman of chronic internal bleeding.
- He brings a dead girl back to life.
- He restores the sight of two blind men.
- He casts out a demon and enables a mute man to talk.

Jesus was an M.D., a physical therapist, a gynecologist, an ophthalmologist, and a psychiatrist all rolled up into one. He healed men, women, and children. He was a wonder worker whose healing power even brought the dead to life.

Pictures of Jesus as the meek and mild shepherd often fail to capture the incredible power of this man. Who else do you know that went around raising the dead? Surely someone with that much power must have created a stir whenever he walked into a room.

But despite his power not everyone was healed. To Pharisees who criticized him for dining with sinners he replied: "It is not the healthy who need a doctor, but the sick.... I have not come to call the righteous, but sinners" (Matthew 9:12–13). Can you hear the irony in his voice? He was saying that those who were too proud to admit their neediness would never know what he could do for them. They would never know his life-giving power to heal and to forgive. You have to ask before you can receive.

Then there's the matter of faith. He healed the paralytic when he saw the obvious faith of the friends who brought him; he told the woman who had the audacity to touch his garment that her faith had healed her; he touched the eyes of the blind men, telling them, "According to your faith will it be done to you" (Matthew 19:29). Time after time, wonder after wonder, Jesus healed and restored those who displayed two things—faith and humility. These two ingredients were catalysts for his power.

The next time you pray for healing, why not go out on a limb? Admit to yourself and to Christ just how desperate you are for him to touch you, body and soul. Then tell Jesus you believe in his power to heal you. Stop hedging your bets and qualifying your prayers. Ask him to glorify himself by making you a spectacle of his healing power and his great compassion. If in response you sense him asking you to do something to effect your healing, like asking others to pray for you, repenting of sin, changing your lifestyle, or seeking out the care of a specialist, do that as well. Don't limit the ways God can answer your prayer for healing grace.

Thursday

PRAYING THE NAME

*And a woman was there who had been subject to bleeding for twelve years,
but no one could heal her. She came up behind him and touched the edge of
his cloak, and immediately her bleeding stopped.*

"Who touched me?" Jesus asked.

*When they all denied it, Peter said, "Master, the people are crowding
and pressing against you."*

*But Jesus said, "Someone touched me; I know that power has gone out
from me."*

LUKE 8:43–46

Reflect On: Luke 8:43–48.

Praise God: For placing his Son, Jesus, in the midst of our struggles
and hurts.

Offer Thanks: For all the ways you have seen God's power at work in
your life.

Confess: Any tendency to mistrust God because of past
disappointments.

Ask God: To help you put your faith where it belongs — in him.

Catherine Marshall, best-selling author and widow of Senate Chaplain
Peter Marshall, was diagnosed in 1943 with tuberculosis. Doctors from
Johns Hopkins told the young mother she would need three to four
months of complete bed rest. As the mother of a three-year-old, she
couldn't imagine spending so much time in bed. She had no idea that
it would be two years before she would be back on her feet again.

Catherine spent hours reading Scripture and asking God the hard
questions of faith. Not surprisingly, one of her favorites had to do with
whether he still healed people. She had been told as a child that miracles had ceased with the early church. Yet healings had been so plen-
tiful in the Gospels. They seemed like Jesus' favorite kind of miracle,

an expression of his love and compassion for the crowds that always surrounded him. If this were so, how could Jesus refrain from healing people for two thousand years? She didn't believe he could or would. So both she and her husband prayed persistently for a miracle. But none came.

Finally, after a time of profound inner struggle, she prayed, telling God he could do whatever he wanted with her. She would accept his will even if it meant remaining an invalid for the rest of her life. God didn't have to explain himself to her, because she trusted him to love and provide for her no matter what happened. Her prayer marked a turning point. The same night, she had an experience that changed her life:

> In the middle of that night I was awakened. The room was in total darkness. Instantly sensing something alive, electric in the room, I sat bolt upright in bed. Past all credible belief, suddenly, unaccountably, Christ was there, in Person, standing by the right side of my bed. I could see nothing but a deep, velvety blackness around me, but the bedroom was filled with an intensity of power, as if the Dynamo of the universe were there. Every nerve in my body tingled with it, as with a shock of electricity. I knew that Jesus was smiling at me tenderly, lovingly, whimsically — as though a trifle amused at my too-intense seriousness about myself. His attitude seemed to say, "Relax! There's not a thing wrong here that I can't take care of."

Soon medical tests confirmed a remarkable improvement in her condition. And within six months, the doctors proclaimed Catherine Marshall completely well.

Her story reminds me of the woman in Scripture who had suffered for twelve years from vaginal bleeding. She spent all her money on physicians who couldn't do a thing for her. But she was healed the instant she touched Christ. I wonder if Catherine Marshall's prayer of faith, relinquishing her need for a miracle and affirming her complete trust in God, was what touched Christ, so much so that it attracted his healing power.

If you have been suffering physically or emotionally, ask for the grace today to put your faith in God rather than in a particular out-come. Tell the Lord you no longer expect him to explain himself to you and that you trust him to love you and provide for you no matter what.

Friday

PROMISES ASSOCIATED WITH HIS NAME

Wars, famines, poverty, and illness are obvious signs that we live in a broken world, one that is out of alignment with God's original intentions. Who but a Divine Physician could possibly heal us, bringing us body and soul back into alignment with his purposes?

Remember the woman with the issue of blood who pushed through the crowd in order to touch the hem of Jesus' garment? You might be interested to know that she touched a part of his robe called the *tzitzi-yot*, or tassels. Like other devout Jews, Jesus wore these in obedience to God's instructions to Moses: "Speak to the Israelites and say to them: 'Throughout the generations to come you are to make tassels on the corners of your garments with a blue cord on each tassel. You will have these tassels to look at and so you will remember all the commands of the LORD, that you may obey them'" (Numbers 15:38–39). So the sick woman touched the most sacred part of Jesus' garment. And she did this even though she knew that under the law her condition would have rendered her and whatever she touched ritually impure. But instead of being defiled by her touch, Jesus' proved the more contagious, rendering her whole and pure.

Jesus is still the source of our healing. If we humble ourselves and pray, if we seek him and turn from our sins, then we have reason to believe he will hear from heaven, forgive our sins, and heal our land.

Promises in Scripture

When I shut up the heavens so that there is no rain, or command locusts to devour the land or send a plague among my people, if my people, who are called by my name, will humble themselves and pray and seek my face and turn from their wicked ways, then will I hear from heaven and will forgive their sin and will heal their land.

2 CHRONICLES 7:13–14

Nevertheless, I will bring health and healing to it; I will heal my people and will let them enjoy abundant peace and security. I will bring Judah and Israel back from captivity and will rebuild them as they were before. I will cleanse them from all the sin they have committed against me and will forgive all their sins of rebellion against me. Then this city will bring me renown, joy, praise and honor before all nations on earth that hear of all the good things I do for it; and they will be in awe and will tremble at the abundant prosperity and peace I provide for it.

JEREMIAH 33:6–9

But for you who revere my name, the sun of righteousness will rise with healing in its wings. And you will go out and leap like calves released from the stall.

MALACHI 4:2

Continued Prayer and Praise

Ask God to increase your faith for healing. (Matthew 8:5–10; Mark 9:17–29; John 4:46–54)

Thank God for healing. (Luke 17:11–17)

Understand that miracles of healing are a sign of Christ's in-breaking kingdom. (Matthew 11:2–5)

Trust that God is with you in your weakness. (2 Corinthians 12:7–10)

Remember that God still heals. (James 5:14–16)

6

LAMB, LAMB OF GOD

ἀρνίον, ἀμνὸς τοῦ θεοῦ
Arnion, Amnos tou Theou

The Name

Most of us picture lambs as downy white animals frolicking in rolling green meadows or carried tenderly in the arms of their shepherd. Lambs represent gentleness, purity, and innocence. Though it is one of the most tender images of Christ in the New Testament, the phrase "Lamb of God" would have conjured far more disturbing pictures to those who heard John the Baptist hail Jesus with these words. Hadn't many of them, at one time or another, carried one of their own lambs to the altar to be slaughtered as a sacrifice for their sins, a lamb that they had fed and bathed, the best animal in their small flock? Hadn't the bloody sacrifice of an innocent animal provided a vivid image of the consequences of transgressing the Mosaic law? Surely, John must have shocked his listeners by applying the phrase "Lamb of God" to a living man.

When we pray to Jesus as the Lamb of God, we are praying to the One who voluntarily laid down his life to take in his own body the punishment for our sins and for the sins of the entire world.

Key Scripture

John saw Jesus coming toward him and said, "Look, the Lamb of God, who takes away the sin of the world!"

JOHN 1:29

78

Monday

HIS NAME REVEALED

> He was oppressed and afflicted,
>> yet he did not open his mouth;
> he was led like a lamb to the slaughter,
>> and as a sheep before her shearers is silent,
>> so he did not open his mouth.

ISAIAH 53:7

Now some Pharisees who had been sent questioned him, "Why then do you baptize if you are not the Christ, nor Elijah, nor the Prophet?"

"I baptize with water," John replied, "but among you stands one you do not know. He is the one who comes after me, the thongs of whose sandals I am not worthy to untie."

This all happened at Bethany on the other side of the Jordan, where John was baptizing.

The next day John saw Jesus coming toward him and said, "Look, the Lamb of God, who takes away the sin of the world! This is the one I meant when I said, 'A man who comes after me has surpassed me because he was before me.' I myself did not know him, but the reason I came baptizing with water was that he might be revealed to Israel."

Then John gave this testimony: "I saw the Spirit come down from heaven as a dove and remain on him. I would not have known him, except that the one who sent me to baptize with water told me, 'The man on whom you see the Spirit come down and remain is he who will baptize with the Holy Spirit.' I have seen and I testify that this is the Son of God."

The next day John was there again with two of his disciples. When he saw Jesus passing by, he said, "Look, the Lamb of God!"

JOHN 1:24–35

Jesus, perfect Offering for all my sins, help me to understand that sin extracts a deadly payment. Thank you for giving your life to deal with my debt. Forgive me for everything I've done to cause you suffering. Help me, Lamb of God, to rejoice in your love for me. Amen.

Understanding the Name

It is impossible to understand the title "Lamb of God" without understanding something about the practice of animal sacrifice in both Old and New Testaments. The sacrificial system provided a way for God's people to approach him even though they had violated the Mosaic law. When an animal was offered, its blood was shed and its flesh was then burned on the altar. When the animal was completely consumed by fire, the sacrifice was called a "holocaust." When only part of the animal was burned, it was considered a "peace offering," intended to restore communion with God. Those who offered sacrifices understood that the animal being sacrificed was a symbolic representation of themselves and their desire to offer their own lives to God. In fact, the sacrificial system of the Hebrew Scriptures represents God's way of instructing us about what it means to approach a holy God.

The lamb was the principal animal of sacrifice, and two were offered each day—one in the morning and one in the evening (Numbers 28:1–8). The offering was doubled on the Sabbath. Lambs (or other animals) were also sacrificed on the first day of the new month and on such feasts as Passover, Pentecost, Trumpets, Atonement, and Tabernacles. Lambs were also offered in cleansing ceremonies after a woman gave birth and after the healing of a leper.

To the Jews the lamb represented innocence and gentleness. Because the sacrifice was meant to represent the purity of intention of the person or people who offered it, lambs had to be without physical blemishes.

The New Testament uses two Greek words for Christ as "Lamb" or "Lamb of God": *Arnion* (AR-nee-on) and *Amnos Tou Theou* (am-NOS tou the-OU). The phrase "Lamb of God" is found only in John's Gospel, though Jesus is often referred to as "the Lamb" in the book of Revelation, where he is portrayed as the Lamb who, though slain, yet lives and reigns victorious. In fact, twenty-nine of the thirty-four

New Testament occurrences of "Lamb" occur in Revelation, a book so named, at least in part, because of what it reveals about who God is. The New Testament also refers to Christ's followers as lambs.

Because the temple was destroyed in AD 70, animal sacrifices could no longer be offered there. Most Jews today no longer eat lamb during the Passover meal or Seder. Instead, they place a roasted lamb shank bone on a Seder plate as a reminder of the sacrifice.

Studying the Name

1. Jesus refused to defend himself when dragged before the Jewish leaders and before Pilate and Herod. How does this relate to the passage from Isaiah? What does it say to you about Jesus?

2. Imagine that you are walking into the temple holding a young lamb in your arms. He is like a favorite pet, but now he is going to be sacrificed for your sins. How do you feel? Now imagine doing the same thing over and over because no one sacrifice can possibly take away your sins. What thoughts go through your mind?

3. What do you think of when you think of Jesus as the Lamb of God? How does this title relate to your life?

Tuesday

PRAYING THE NAME

If God is for us, who can be against us? He who did not spare his own Son, but gave him up for us all—how will he not also, along with him, graciously give us all things?

ROMANS 8:31

For you know that it was not with perishable things such as silver or gold that you were redeemed from the empty way of life handed down to you from your ancestors, but with the precious blood of Christ, a lamb without blemish or defect. He was chosen before the creation of the world, but was revealed in these last times for your sake. Through him you believe in God, who raised him from the dead and glorified him, and so your faith and hope are in God.

1 PETER 1:18–21

Reflect On: Romans 8:31–36 and 1 Peter 1:18–21.
Praise God: For his strong love.
Offer Thanks: That nothing in all creation can separate you from God's love.
Confess: Any tendency to identify yourself so closely with your sin that you have difficulty accepting God's forgiveness.
Ask God: To increase your gratitude for his forgiveness.

⌒

Since becoming a parent, I have come to realize that children are capable of asking the most profound theological questions. Take my seven-year-old. One of Luci's favorite questions is: "Where is God?" She cannot understand why she can't run up to him and throw her arms around him. Why doesn't this big God she hears about simply bend down, pick her up, and plant a kiss on her cheek? My oft-repeated answer—that God is everywhere but that he is a Spirit who cannot be seen—seems never to satisfy her. The other day, Luci posed the question again. Before I had a chance to trot out the same unsatisfactory answer, she asked another question: "Mom, is God mad at people?"

It occurred to me that Luci was wondering whether God's seeming remoteness was caused by his anger. Was he keeping his distance because he was upset with the way people were behaving? Without answering her first question, I found myself replying, "Honey, God has a problem, and it's a big one. He *loves* people but he *hates* sin. God is completely good and kind and loving, and he hates it when we aren't. How can he love us when he hates our sins? So God has decided to solve this big problem by getting rid of our sins rather than getting rid of us. That's why he sent his Son. Jesus took the punishment for all the wrong things we do. Jesus' death took away our sins, so that now, when God looks at us, he doesn't see the sin that he hates but only the people he loves. Does that make sense?" The smile on her face assured me it did.

Since then, I've found myself thinking about Jesus as the sacrifice who makes us whole. Have you ever wondered, at the outset of Jesus' public ministry, why John the Baptist hailed him as "the Lamb of God who takes away the sin of the world"? Why didn't John shout instead, "Hey, look, here comes the Messiah!" Or, "Look everybody, it's the Lion of Judah." Or, "It's the King of kings!" Instead of these powerful titles, John evokes a shocking image of Jesus as an innocent victim destined to become a bloody sacrifice.

The son of a priest, John would have been familiar with the sacrificial system. He would have heard the braying and the bleating of the innocent victims, would have seen the blood poured out, would have inhaled the pungent odor of burning animal flesh mingling with smoky incense in the temple. "Here comes Jesus, the marked man, the bloody sacrifice, the innocent Lamb who is going to be sacrificed for the sins of the whole world!"

The next time you think about Jesus as the Lamb of God, discard the image of a cuddly stuffed animal, the kind children like to carry around. Think rather of Jesus, the innocent victim who died because he loves you. Join me in thanking him because as far as the east is from the west, so far has he removed our transgressions from us. His sacrifice is so effective that when God looks at those who belong to him, he sees the Lamb who loves us, the one who has peeled sin's thick disfigurement from our souls, leaving now no barrier to God's love. No wonder Paul proclaimed so confidently that nothing—"neither death nor life, neither angels nor demons, neither the present nor the future ... nor anything else in all creation, will be able to separate us from the love of God that is in Christ Jesus our Lord" (Romans 8:38–39)! Because our names are written in the Lamb's Book of Life, we have become like magnets to which God's love is irresistibly drawn.

PRAYING THE NAME

Abraham took the wood for the burnt offering and placed it on his son Isaac, and he himself carried the fire and the knife. As the two of them went on together, Isaac spoke up and said to his father Abraham, "Father?"

"Yes, my son?" Abraham replied.

"The fire and wood are here," Isaac said, "but where is the lamb for the burnt offering?"

Abraham answered, "God himself will provide the lamb for the burnt offering, my son."

GENESIS 22:6–8

Reflect On: Genesis 22:6–13.
Praise God: For his mercy.
Offer Thanks: That God himself has provided the sacrifice that makes us whole.
Confess: Your need for a Savior.
Ask God: To open your eyes to what his Son has done for you.

~

A story is told of a young boy whose sister was suffering from a rare disease. Her only chance of recovery was to receive a blood transfusion from someone who had recovered from the disease. Her five-year-old brother was the perfect candidate. When the doctor explained the situation to the boy and asked him if he would be willing to give his blood to his sister, the boy hesitated for a moment, took a deep breath, and then said yes. During the transfusion, while lying in bed next to his sister, the boy smiled as he saw the color returning to her cheeks. Then, unaccountably, his face paled and he asked in a trembling voice, "Will I start dying right away?"

The story makes you want to smile and cry at the same time because you realize the boy's generosity and his mistake. He had been willing to give his last drop of blood if that meant his sister would live. His story reminds me of another story and another boy, one who nearly did give up his life. You probably remember it. It's the story of Abraham and Isaac and how the father was going to sacrifice the son. Do you remember the scene on Mount Moriah when Abraham was gathering wood for the burnt offering? Isaac turned to him and asked:

"Father?"

"Yes, my son?" Abraham replied.

"The fire and wood are here, but where is the lamb for the burnt offering?"

With poignant words, Abraham replied, "God himself will provide the lamb for the burnt offering, my son." And God did. At the last second, when the father was about to plunge the knife into his son, the angel of the Lord told Abraham to lay down his knife and spare the boy. Then Abraham noticed a ram that had been caught in the thicket and offered him in his son's place. God had provided, just as Abraham had unwittingly predicted he would.

But God's provision extends beyond that instant, beyond that father and that son. According to tradition, the temple in Jerusalem was built on Mount Moriah, where Abraham nearly sacrificed his son. And the temple was only a short walk from where Jesus, the only Son of the Father, was sacrificed for our sins.

The next time you are tempted to wallow in guilt over some sin or failing, remember that the Father has paid an impossibly high price to redeem you. Don't make the mistake of acting as if it wasn't enough. Instead, ask God's forgiveness and then turn your thoughts to the Lamb that he has provided. Praise Christ and thank him for being willing to spend his last drop of blood to save you.

Thursday

PRAYING THE NAME

"On that same night I will pass through Egypt and strike down every first-born—both men and animals—and I will bring judgment on all the gods of Egypt. I am the LORD. The blood will be a sign for you on the houses where you are; and when I see the blood, I will pass over you. No destructive plague will touch you when I strike Egypt. . . . "

Then Moses summoned all the elders of Israel and said to them, "Go at once and select the animals for your families and slaughter the Passover lamb. Take a bunch of hyssop, dip it into the blood in the basin and put some of the blood on the top and on both sides of the doorframe. Not one of you shall go out the door of his house until morning. When the LORD goes through the land to strike down the Egyptians, he will see the blood on the top and sides of the doorframe and will pass over that doorway, and he will not permit the destroyer to enter your houses and strike you down."

EXODUS 12:12–13, 21–23

Then I saw a Lamb, looking as if it had been slain, standing in the center before the throne, encircled by the four living creatures and the elders. . . . And they sang a new song, saying:

"You are worthy to take the scroll
and to open its seals,
because you were slain,
and with your blood you purchased for God
members of every tribe and language and people
and nation.
You have made them to be a kingdom and priests
to serve our God,
and they will reign on the earth."

REVELATION 5:6, 9–10

87

Reflect On: Exodus 12:12–13, 21–23; Revelation 5:6–10.

Praise God: For purchasing your soul with the currency of his Son's death.

Offer Thanks: Because God himself is your safety.

Confess: Any complacency about living your life for Christ.

Ask God: To help you approach each day with hope and trust.

⌒

A few years ago I woke in the middle of a wintry night to the unmistakable sound of someone creeping stealthily up the stairway. Aware that my children were too afraid of the dark to be roaming the house at 2:30 in the morning, I decided the best course of action was simply to confront whoever was lurking in the shadows. So with heart racing and hands trembling, I threw open my bedroom door. Startled by the boldness of my action, the intruders froze, staring straight at me. Oddly, the criminals were holding hands. Six-year-old Katie and four-year-old Luci were creeping up the stairs together. Close questioning revealed that my daughters had been searching the house for leprechauns and pots of gold, which they assured me could best be found in the middle of the night. (Don't ask who had been filling their heads with tales of leprechauns!)

Shaken by thoughts of how defenseless I would have been against a real intruder, I arranged to have a security system installed the next week. Whatever it cost, the sense of safety would be worth it. Now we could sleep in peace.

The book of Exodus talks about another kind of security system, one innocent of codes, wires, alarms, or warning signs but one far more effective than anything ever devised by human beings. Prior to their exodus from Egypt, God told Moses to instruct the Israelites to smear the doors of their houses with the blood of the Passover lamb. Any home so marked would be spared God's judgment. The angel of death would *pass over* it, visiting only the homes whose doors remained unmarked. In this last, most terrible plague, the Egyptians would lose their firstborn sons as punishment for resisting God's command to let his people go.

But why did God insist on a visible mark to distinguish between his people and the Egyptians? Couldn't he tell the difference? Of course, it was people and not God who needed this visible sign of God's protection. But what does this ancient story have to do with us today?

Last night I woke with a troubling thought foremost in my mind. I was thinking about death, about its inevitability, as though we are all riding a giant assembly line toward it. I thought about how nothing in this world is strong enough to halt its advance — not science, not money, not even love. From the best to the worst, from the youngest to the oldest, all of us are heading toward death. But instead of scrambling to get off the assembly line, because we know we can't, we act as though we aren't even on it, as though there's no such thing. And so we spend our time on the line chatting and laughing and planning and scheming and working to make life better, as though we are all going to live forever. I began thinking of all the things that had preoccupied me in the past week. They seemed trivial, even ridiculous, in light of my inevitable future.

But what do such gloomy thoughts have to do with any discussion of safety and security? Think of it like this: What if the Exodus story tells us something about our own future? What if it points to another Passover Lamb, to Jesus of Nazareth, who was himself killed shortly after celebrating a Passover meal with his disciples? What if it is his blood that marks us and sets us apart as God's people so that when the angel of death passes over us at the final judgment, we will experience not death eternally but life forever?

Indeed, belonging to Jesus, the Lamb of God, is the only security system capable of preserving us from death. It's the only thing powerful enough to get us off an assembly line that would otherwise lead to our destruction. Because of the death of the Lamb, we can live forever in perfect peace and joy. That is the hope we share, believing as we do that because Jesus lives in us, the Father will one day raise us up with him to a place that is eternally secure.

Take a moment to close your eyes and lift your heart to Jesus, the Lamb. Imagine him slain for you. Now picture him alive again and standing next to God's throne in heaven. What do you see? What does he say? How do you respond?

Friday

PROMISES ASSOCIATED WITH HIS NAME

"Handwriting without Tears"® is an innovative program that promises to make learning to write an easy and fun experience for children and those who teach them. Great as it is, I wish someone would develop a program entitled "Childhood without Tears." But how could they since every childhood inevitably holds its share of tears? And how could it be otherwise for imperfect people growing up on an imperfect planet?

One of my favorite lines in Scripture is the promise God makes near the end of the Bible. To those who have suffered because of their faith, he points to the day when "God will wipe away every tear from their eyes" (Revelation 7:17). Like a parent encouraging a child, he tells us that in the end all will be well. When the Lamb is on the throne, when every power in the universe is completely subject to him, God's own fingers will wipe away the last of our tears. Our life in this world is nothing but a long growing up, a time of testing that stretches and shapes us toward maturity so that we can become more Christlike. If we let him, God will use our suffering to etch his character in us. And in the end, no matter how deep our sorrow, it will be obliterated by the joy of seeing the Lamb face to face.

Promises in Scripture

> *Never again will they hunger;*
> > *never again will they thirst.*
> *The sun will not beat upon them,*
> > *nor any scorching heat.*
> *For the Lamb at the center of the throne will be their shepherd;*
> > *he will lead them to springs of living water.*
> *And God will wipe away every tear from their eyes.*

REVELATION 7:16–17

Then I heard a loud voice in heaven say:

> *"Now have come the salvation and the power*
>   *and the kingdom of our God,*
>   *and the authority of his Messiah.*
> *For the accuser of our brothers and sisters,*
>   *who accuses them before our God day and night,*
>   *has been hurled down.*
> *They triumphed over him*
>   *by the blood of the Lamb*
>   *and by the word of their testimony;*
> *they did not love their lives so much*
>   *as to shrink from death."*

REVELATION 12:10–11

Continued Prayer and Praise

Remember that Jesus is the Passover Lamb. (Exodus 12:2–47; 1 Corinthians 5:7b; and John 19:31)

Praise the great Lamb of God. (Revelation 7:9–10)

Be confident of the Lamb's final victory. (Revelation 17:12–14)

Realize that the church is the bride of the Lamb. (Revelation 19:6–9; 21:9–14)

7

KING OF KINGS

βασιλεὺς βασιλέων

BASILEUS BASILEON

The Name

The world has never seen a king like Christ, a ruler mightier than any earthly sovereign and more powerful than the unseen powers of the universe. Though he entered the world humbly, as an infant born in Bethlehem, Magi from the east still recognized him as the newborn king. Though his reign unfolds in hidden ways, he has promised to come again, at which time he will reveal himself unambiguously as "King of kings and Lord of lords." When you pray to Jesus, the King of kings, call to mind his mastery not only over human beings but over nature, disease, and death itself.

Key Scripture

On his robe and on his thigh he has this name written:

> KING OF KINGS AND LORD OF LORDS.

Revelation 19:16

Monday

HIS NAME REVEALED

As they approached Jerusalem and came to Bethphage on the Mount of Olives, Jesus sent two disciples, saying to them, "Go to the village ahead of you, and at once you will find a donkey tied there, with her colt by her. Untie them and bring them to me. If anyone says anything to you, tell him that the Lord needs them, and he will send them right away."

This took place to fulfill what was spoken through the prophet:

> "Say to the Daughter of Zion,
>   'See, your king comes to you,
> gentle and riding on a donkey,
>   on a colt, the foal of a donkey.'"

The disciples went and did as Jesus had instructed them. They brought the donkey and the colt, placed their cloaks on them, and Jesus sat on them. A very large crowd spread their cloaks on the road, while others cut branches from the trees and spread them on the road. The crowds that went ahead of him and those that followed shouted,

> "Hosanna to the Son of David!"
>
> "Blessed is he who comes in the name of the Lord!"
>
> "Hosanna in the highest!"

MATTHEW 21:1−9

I saw heaven standing open and there before me was a white horse, whose rider is called Faithful and True. With justice he judges and makes war. His eyes are like blazing fire, and on his head are many crowns. He has a name written on him that no one knows but he himself. He is dressed in a robe dipped in blood, and his name is the Word of God. The armies of heaven were following him, riding on white horses and dressed in fine linen, white and clean. Out of his mouth comes a sharp sword with which to strike down the nations. "He will rule them with an iron scepter." He treads the winepress of the fury of the wrath of God Almighty. On his robe and on his thigh he has this name written:

KING OF KINGS AND LORD OF LORDS.

REVELATION 19:11 – 16

Lord, my all-powerful King, I praise you for your humility. Help me to seek first your kingdom, forsaking my desire to build my own small kingdom. Infuse me with the values of your kingdom. Help me to love my enemies, do good to those who hate me, serve the poor, and spread the good news of the kingdom everywhere I go.

Understanding the Name

The Jewish people at the time of Christ longed for a coming king who would be descended from their great king, David. By hailing Jesus as the "Son of David," the large crowd who greeted him as he entered Jerusalem was using a popular title for the Messiah. They expected their messianic king to restore Israel's freedom and former glory. In the passage from Matthew's Gospel, Jesus fulfills the messianic prophecy of Zechariah 9:9 by riding into Jerusalem on a donkey, an animal that symbolized both peace and humility.

Today, Christ's kingdom unfolds in hidden ways as believers acknowledge him as King and Lord. But one day, when Christ comes again, his will be revealed as the greatest of all kingdoms. The passage from Revelation 19 presents Jesus riding not on a lowly donkey but on a magnificent white horse, as befits the greatest of all kings. Throughout the New Testament Jesus is variously referred to as "King," "King of the ages," "King of the Jews," "King of Israel," and "King of kings" — this last one translated from the Greek phrase *Basileus Basileon* (bas-si-LEUS ba-si-LE-own). Even today some Christian churches are called "basilicas," a phrase meaning "the hall of the king."

Studying the Name

1. Why do you think Scripture presents the reign of Jesus in two such different ways, as in the above passages?

2. Write a list of qualities that would describe the perfect king. Now compare and contrast these with the lives of today's rulers.

3. What do you think it means to have Jesus as your king? How have you experienced his reign in your life thus far?

4. What would life on earth look like today if Jesus' reign was perfectly established?

Tuesday

PRAYING THE NAME

Jesus replied, "Very truly I tell you, no one can see the kingdom of God without being born again."

"How can anyone be born when they are old?" Nicodemus asked. "Surely they cannot enter a second time into their mother's womb to be born!"

Jesus answered, "Very truly I tell you, no one can enter the kingdom of God without being born of water and the Spirit. Flesh gives birth to flesh, but the Spirit gives birth to spirit. You should not be surprised at my saying, 'You must be born again.' The wind blows wherever it pleases. You hear its sound, but you cannot tell where it comes from or where it is going. So it is with everyone born of the Spirit."

JOHN 3:3–8

Reflect On: John 3:3–8.

Praise God: For building a kingdom that will endure.

Offer Thanks: That God has called you into his kingdom.

Confess: Any tendency to try to pressure or force others to believe.

Ask God: To help you to spread the kingdom his way.

◌◌

Have you ever thought about the challenges of being a king—of presiding over a large group of people with differing temperaments, desires, needs, values, and interests? If you've ever been a parent, a teacher, a boss, or a building contractor, you know how difficult it can sometimes be to get people to act responsibly—like trying to get ducks to fly backwards or dogs to stop barking. Of course, one way to get people to behave is to force them.

Some nations have developed extreme measures for controlling their populations. One Islamic country has a law on the books that punishes nonconforming females with seventy-four lashes or a year in prison simply for violating its dress code. Secular regimes can be just as bad. North Korea, for instance, has a history of using food as a form of control, allotting rations according to political, social, or professional status. And when the Communist Party first came to power in China, it attempted to regulate every aspect of people's lives, even deciding which party members would be allowed to marry. In the early 1950s it also controlled how much time spouses could spend together, limiting cohabitation to one day a week. Even today, it tries to control birth rates by severely penalizing couples who give birth to more than one child.

This tendency to try to control people crops up even in free societies where filmmakers distort the truth to sway public opinion or political parties use lies and half-truths to influence elections. But God's kingdom, presided over by the most powerful ruler in the universe, operates on entirely different principles. Its integrity depends not on external force but on the internal, indestructible power of Christ's love. Our king begins by inviting, never compelling, us to join his kingdom. When we do, he reverses the outside-in formula whereby we are forced to conform, and, instead, begins to transform us internally by the power of his Spirit. It is the indwelling presence and power of the Spirit that enables us to become more Christlike.

As one early Christian writer put it, God "was determined to save us by persuasion, and not by compulsion — for there is no compulsion found with God. His mission was no pursuit or hounding of us, it was an invitation." In this way, step by step, Christ builds the only kind of kingdom that will last — the only kind worth living in forever.

Thank God today for the greatest of all invitations — to entrust your life to King Jesus, who calls you to live and reign with him forever. And while you are thanking him, remember that there is never any compulsion in Christ. We cannot pressure or coerce others into the kingdom. Only God's Spirit can enable a man or woman to be born again into God's kingdom. Each of us is called not to advance the kingdom by force but to spread it through the contagious power of Christ's love. Pray today that God will use your life as an eloquent invitation to bring others to himself, so that they may join you in praising him as King of kings and Lord of lords.

Wednesday

PRAYING THE NAME

Then the governor's soldiers took Jesus into the Praetorium and gathered the whole company of soldiers around him. They stripped him and put a scarlet robe on him, and then twisted together a crown of thorns and set it on his head. They put a staff in his right hand and knelt in front of him and mocked him. "Hail, king of the Jews!" they said. They spit on him, and took the staff and struck him on the head again and again. After they had mocked him, they took off the robe and put his own clothes on him. Then they led him away to crucify him.

As they were going out, they met a man from Cyrene, named Simon, and they forced him to carry the cross. They came to a place called Golgotha (which means The Place of the Skull). There they offered Jesus wine to drink, mixed with gall; but after tasting it, he refused to drink it. When they had crucified him, they divided up his clothes by casting lots. And sitting down, they kept watch over him there. Above his head they placed the written charge against him: THIS IS JESUS, THE KING OF THE JEWS.

MATTHEW 27:27–37

Reflect On: Matthew 27:27–37.
Praise God: For overcoming evil with good.
Offer Thanks: For the hope that Christ imparts to us.
Confess: Your fear of suffering.
Ask God: To help you put sin to death by the power of his Spirit.

Many churches, both Catholic and Protestant, celebrate the feast of Christ the King, a day originally set aside by Pope Pius XI in 1925 to counter the rising threat of Communism and Fascism. In spite of two world wars and a cold war that lasted for decades, we find that peace on earth still eludes us. Iraq is in the throes of a bloody insurgency. The Democratic Republic of Congo is embroiled in a conflict that has already killed six million people. The Israeli–Palestinian conflict continues unabated. Nuclear weapons proliferate. And terrorist violence continues ad naseum. Little wonder the future of our world seems at risk.

What are we to do in the face of such a future? Let it advance unhindered or fight it with every weapon in hand? Though it may at times be necessary for nations and peoples to take up arms to defend themselves, we must always remember that evil can never be defeated by evil. Retaliation will never win the peace. It will only produce more hatred and violence. Justice is worth fighting for; vengeance is not.

As Christians we must also remember what our Lord said to his disciples on the verge of his arrest. He told them to take heart because he had overcome the world! But how could they take heart when they saw him in chains? How could they believe he had overcome the world when he appeared so weak? No wonder they fled. They couldn't understand until after the resurrection that Jesus was intentionally reversing the usual formula whereby the strong dominate the weak. The strongest man who ever lived was allowing his body to be forced onto a cross, to suffer the violence of the crucifixion in order to defeat the world's evil.

As followers of Christ the King, we too must suffer a kind of necessary violence, a violence directed against our sin and against the sinful instincts of our fallen nature that make us want to repay hatred with hatred. Instead, we must allow Christ to overthrow our selfishness so that he can ascend the throne of our hearts. When he reigns there, he enables us to reproduce the pattern of his life, even to the extreme of loving our enemies. As the apostle Paul says:

Do not repay anyone evil for evil. Be careful to do what is right in the eyes of everybody. If it is possible, as far as it depends on you, live at peace with everyone. Do not take revenge, my friends, but leave room for God's wrath, for it is written: "It is mine to avenge; I will repay," says the Lord. On the contrary:

> *"If your enemy is hungry, feed him;*
> *if he is thirsty, give him something to drink.*
> *In doing this, you will heap burning coals on his head."*

Do not be overcome by evil, but overcome evil with good.

ROMANS 12:17–21

No matter how brutal the world may become, we must resist the temptation to fight evil with evil. We are called instead to forcefully advance Christ's kingdom by overcoming evil with good, hatred with love. Let us pray to have Christ's mind about the various conflicts that beset our world, asking Jesus to impart his wisdom to leaders of nations and peoples. Let us commit ourselves to loving others by actively working on behalf of the world's poor, praying for the grace to act justly, to love mercy, and to walk humbly before our God.

Thursday

PRAYING THE NAME

Our Father in heaven,
hallowed be your name,
your kingdom come,
your will be done
    on earth as it is in heaven.

MATTHEW 6:9–10

Then he said to his disciples, "The time is coming when you will long to see one of the days of the Son of Man, but you will not see it. People will tell you, 'There he is!' or 'Here he is!' Do not go running off after them. For the Son of Man in his day will be like the lightning, which flashes and lights up the sky from one end to the other. But first he must suffer many things and be rejected by this generation.

LUKE 17:22–25

Reflect On: Matthew 6:9–10 and Luke 17:22–25.
Praise God: Because he is a perfect Ruler.
Offer Thanks: That Christ has promised to come again.
Confess: Any complacency in your relationship with Christ.
Ask God: To stir up your longing for his coming again in glory.

King Farouk of Egypt once wryly predicted the end of his reign, remarking that "in a few years there will be only five kings in the world—the king of England and the four kings in a pack of cards." But Farouk, the last real king of Egypt, was leaving out the greatest King of all.

This year as Christmas approached, I wanted to avoid making the same mistake. But what does Christmas have to do with acknowledging Jesus as King? In many churches throughout the world, Advent is observed as a season in which we prepare spiritually to celebrate

Christ's first coming. It is also a season to prepare our hearts for his second coming, when every knee will bend and every tongue will confess that he indeed is King and Lord.

I wanted to find a way to make Advent a central part of our family's celebration of Christmas. To do this, I had to make some practical decisions. A few years ago, I was surprised to learn that my grandparents never trimmed their Christmas tree until the night before Christmas. Apparently, it was a common practice back then. So that was the first order of business. Resist the urge to decorate and shop and party as though Christmas had arrived the day after Thanksgiving. No more nonstop Christmas music. No more franticness. Let the season's meaning unfold in calmness.

Despite the protests of my children who saw everyone else's decorations going up, I was determined that Advent would not become an endangered species in our house. I did allow them one concession, but it played perfectly into my Advent scheme. I made the traditional candy house, the delectable one my mother had made for me as a child, placing it as always in a prominent spot in the living room. And as always I reminded them of rule number one: no eating—not one bite—until Christmas morning. There were the usual murmured complaints, but I knew my children were learning the Advent discipline of waiting with eager expectation.

For my part, I made no superhuman efforts to observe the season, but simply made sure I finished most of my Christmas shopping before Thanksgiving. Then I prayed a little more. In the morning and evening I read Scriptures that expressed a longing for the Messiah, for peace on earth, for captives to be set free, for the lion and lamb to lie down together. I read about the Bright Morning Star and the Light of the World. And I read the news—the kidnappings, the beheadings, the battles, the political wrangling, and the poisoning of a political opponent. I read about the man in a wheelchair who had frozen to death in our city because of people's carelessness—and I interceded with anguish for Christ to set things right, to bring justice and peace, forgiveness and mercy. I prayed with longing and tears that he would come with his power and his wisdom to reign over us.

Christmas is now two days away. Advent is nearly past. I am glad for the baby born in Bethlehem, but I am longing for the greatest of kings. I see how broken the world is, how broken I am, without him. As I have prayed in the weeks leading up to Christmas, I find my thoughts returning to the day in which the World Trade Towers collapsed. I remember sitting in a hospital room with my daughter, who was about to undergo a medical test. We sat transfixed in front of the TV, watching as New York came under attack—planes crashing, people jumping out of buildings, the city devastated. We watched the Pentagon burning. It seemed surreal, so sudden and impossible—the financial heart and the power center of the greatest country on earth both under attack. Like everyone else who watched, it changed our perception of the world completely.

Since then, I have not found it difficult to believe in Christ's sudden coming. In an instant, in a flash, in the twinkling of an eye, at the last trumpet—the dead will be raised imperishable and we will all be changed, and the greatest of all kings will ascend his throne.

Maranatha, come, Lord Jesus!

Friday

PROMISES ASSOCIATED WITH HIS NAME

What are you worried about? Do you need clothes or food or a roof over your head? *I own the cattle on a thousand hills.* Are you worried about your marriage, your career, your children? *I am compassionate toward all I have made.* Are you anxious because you don't have today what you need for tomorrow? *I open my hand to satisfy the desires of every living thing.* Are you sick or sorrowful? *For you who revere my name, the sun of righteousness will rise with healing in its wings.* Are you lonely or fearful? *I am with you always, to the very end of the age.* These are the promises of our great and faithful King. Pray for the grace today to seek first his kingdom and his righteousness, and all these things will be added to you as well.

Promises in Scripture

"And why do you worry about clothes? See how the lilies of the field grow. They do not labor or spin. Yet I tell you that not even Solomon in all his splendor was dressed like one of these. If that is how God clothes the grass of the field, which is here today and tomorrow is thrown into the fire, will he not much more clothe you, O you of little faith? So do not worry, saying, 'What shall we eat?' or 'What shall we drink?' or 'What shall we wear?' For the pagans run after all these things, and your heavenly Father knows that you need them. But seek first his kingdom and his righteousness, and all these things will be given to you as well."

MATTHEW 6:28–33

Do you not know that the wicked will not inherit the kingdom of God? Do not be deceived: Neither the sexually immoral nor idolaters nor adulterers nor male prostitutes nor homosexual offenders nor thieves nor the greedy nor drunkards nor slanderers nor swindlers will inherit the kingdom of God. And that is what some of you were. But you were washed, you were sanctified, you were justified in the name of the Lord Jesus Christ and by the Spirit of our God.

1 CORINTHIANS 6:9–11

Continued Prayer and Praise

Prepare for the King's return. (Matthew 24:9 – 14; Luke 19:11 – 26; 1 Timothy 6:11 – 16; 2 Peter 1:5 – 11)

Inherit the kingdom. (Matthew 25:31 – 43)

Praise the greatest of all kings. (Revelation 11:15; 15:1 – 4; 17:12 – 14)

8

PRINCE OF PEACE

שַׂר שָׁלוֹם

SAR SHALOM

The Name

Who hasn't longed for peace, living in a world that is so often full of strife? The Hebrew word for peace, however, means much more than the absence of conflict or the end of turmoil. *Shalom* conveys not only a sense of tranquility but also of wholeness and completion. To enjoy *shalom* is to enjoy health, satisfaction, success, safety, well-being, and prosperity. Though the New Testament does not directly call Jesus the Prince of Peace, this title from Isaiah has traditionally been associated with him as the One who brings peace to the world. Furthermore, Paul assured the Ephesian Christians saying of Jesus, "He himself is our peace" (Ephesians 2:14). When you pray to *Sar Shalom*, you are praying to the One who is the source of all peace. To live in peace is to live in his presence.

Key Scripture

> *For to us a child is born,*
> > *to us a son is given,*
> > *and the government will be on his shoulders.*
> *And he will be called*
> > *Wonderful Counselor, Mighty God,*
> > *Everlasting Father, Prince of Peace.*
> >   ISAIAH 9:6

Monday

HIS NAME REVEALED

The people walking in darkness
    have seen a great light;
on those living in the land of the shadow of death
    a light has dawned....
For to us a child is born,
    to us a son is given,
    and the government will be on his shoulders.
And he will be called
    Wonderful Counselor, Mighty God,
    Everlasting Father, Prince of Peace.
Of the increase of his government and peace
    there will be no end.
He will reign on David's throne
    and over his kingdom,
establishing and upholding it
    with justice and righteousness
    from that time on and forever.

ISAIAH 9:2, 6–7

His [John's] father Zechariah was filled with the Holy Spirit and prophesied....

"And you, my child, will be called a prophet of the Most High;
    for you will go on before the Lord to prepare the way for him,
to give his people the knowledge of salvation
    through the forgiveness of their sins,
because of the tender mercy of our God,
    by which the rising sun will come to us from heaven
to shine on those living in darkness
    and in the shadow of death,
to guide our feet into the path of peace."

LUKE 1:67, 76–79

Jesus, my life was in chaos until you entered it. Thank you for the forgiveness that brought me peace. Deepen my sense of your presence by keeping me close to you. Teach me to become a peacemaker — loving justice, doing right, and leading others along the path of peace.

Understanding the Name

Though the Hebrew title *Sar Shalom* (SAR sha-LOME) does not appear in the New Testament, Zechariah calls it to mind with words that echo Isaiah 9. Both passages speak of a people living in darkness and in the shadow of death. And both speak of a child who will bring peace to God's people. Shortly after Christ was born, we hear angels proclaiming: "Glory to God in the highest heaven, and on earth peace to those on whom his favor rests" (Luke 2:14).

In Greek the word for peace is *eirene*. Like the Hebrew concept of *shalom*, the New Testament portrays peace as much more than the absence of conflict. Mark's Gospel, for instance, links healing and peace by capturing Jesus' words to a woman he has just healed. He tells her to "go in peace" (Mark 5:34). The New Testament further develops our understanding of peace by revealing Jesus as the source of all peace. Though we were alienated from God because of our sins, Jesus reconciled us, making peace through his blood. Peace with God produces peace with others and peace within ourselves. When Christ's kingdom is fully established, all strife will cease, and those who belong to him will enjoy forever the fullness of peace — health, wholeness, well-being, tranquility, satisfaction, safety, prosperity, and perfect contentment.

Studying the Name

1. What does the word "peace" mean to you? How does this differ from the biblical idea of *shalom*?

2. Why is the "Prince of Peace" a fitting title for Jesus? Can you think of incidents in his life that display his peace?

3. What do you think it means to walk in "the path of peace"?

4. Ask yourself whether you are experiencing Christ's peace in your life. How can you participate more deeply in his peace?

Tuesday

PRAYING THE NAME

On the evening of that first day of the week, when the disciples were together, with the doors locked for fear of the Jews, Jesus came and stood among them and said, "Peace be with you!" After he said this, he showed them his hands and side. The disciples were overjoyed when they saw the Lord. . . .

A week later his disciples were in the house again, and Thomas was with them. Though the doors were locked, Jesus came and stood among them and said, "Peace be with you!" Then he said to Thomas, "Put your finger here; see my hands. Reach out your hand and put it into my side. Stop doubting and believe."

JOHN 20:19–20, 26–27

Therefore, as God's chosen people, holy and dearly loved, clothe yourselves with compassion, kindness, humility, gentleness and patience. Bear with each other and forgive whatever grievances you may have against one another. Forgive as the Lord forgave you. And over all these virtues put on love, which binds them all together in perfect unity.

Let the peace of Christ rule in your hearts, since as members of one body you were called to peace.

COLOSSIANS 3:12–15

Reflect On: John 20:19–20, 26–27 and Colossians 3:12–15.
Praise God: Who is the source of all peace.
Offer Thanks: To Christ our peace.
Confess: Any failure to forgive.
Ask God: To help you live in peace with others.

In my church it is customary midway through the service to turn to your neighbor and offer "a sign of peace"—usually a handshake and the greeting: "Peace be with you." One Sunday morning, a lively little girl altered the formula slightly. With pigtails bobbing and pink cheeks shining, she grabbed my hand, intoning loudly and sincerely: "PEACE

AND QUIET BE WITH YOU!" As the mother of two small children, I couldn't help but find her greeting attractive, expressing as it does the wish of every parent.

Not that I want to meddle with the traditional phrase, "Peace be with you," which comes straight from the Bible and is still the typical greeting in modern Israel. Like the Jews of Jesus' day, modern Israelis often greet each other with the words *Shalom aleikhem* [sha-LOME a-LAY-khem]! The Gospels record Jesus using this ordinary greeting but under extraordinary circumstances. *Shalom aleikhem!* "Peace upon you!" were the first words he spoke to startled disciples, cowering behind locked doors after his crucifixion. Instead of rebuking them for abandoning and betraying him when he was arrested, he blessed them with *shalom*. A week later he invited Thomas, the doubting disciple, to touch his wounds, to probe the separated flesh in his hands and side so that he too could believe that Jesus had risen from the dead.

Indeed, it is the wounds of Christ that bring us peace. This may sound like poetry until you begin to picture just how hideous the crucifixion was. A naked man nailed to a set of crossbeams and then slowly tortured to death in full view of the public. Jesus hung on the cross for three hours, making himself the target of God's wrath against all the pettiness, self-righteousness, bickering, meanness, anger, gossip, gluttony, greed, jealousy, lies, drunkenness, child abuse, infidelity, lust, rape, murder, and destruction that we humans have wreaked upon the world. The cross was our punishment, the payback for our sins. But Christ, loving us and being unwilling to let us suffer a punishment we could not survive, transformed an instrument of torture into one of victory. Through it he both upheld God's justice and healed our relationship with a holy God.

No matter what we have done, how agitated or frantic we feel, or how chaotic life has become, Christ says to us today: *Shalom aleikhem!* "Peace upon you." Peace be with you in your relationship with God, with others, and with yourself. May his peace settle into your soul and rule in your heart. May it become the loom on which your life is woven, clothing you with his compassion, kindness, humility, gentleness, and patience. Repent of what you have done wrong. Forgive as you have been forgiven. And let the one who is called the Prince of Peace rule in your heart.

Wednesday

PRAYING THE NAME

The fruit of righteousness will be peace;
the effect of righteousness will be quietness and confidence
forever.
My people will live in peaceful dwelling places,
in secure homes,
in undisturbed places of rest.

ISAIAH 32:17–18

Finally, brothers, whatever is true, whatever is noble, whatever is right,
whatever is pure, whatever is lovely, whatever is admirable — if anything
is excellent or praiseworthy — think about such things. Whatever you have
learned or received or heard from me, or seen in me — put it into practice.
And the God of peace will be with you.

PHILIPPIANS 4:8–9

Reflect On: Isaiah 32:17–18 and Philippians 4:8–9.
Praise God: For showing us the path to peace.
Offer Thanks: For the peace you have enjoyed.
Confess: Any tendency to rationalize behaviors that transgress
                God's law.
Ask God: To make you someone who spreads peace, not chaos.

Five years ago, we bought a house in a charming area of the city, full
of older homes, tenderly cared for. The streets are wide and peaceful,
lined with trees that have grown strong over decades. The neighborhood is tight-knit and so friendly that it feels as though we are living
in a time warp, back in the tranquil 1950s.

That perception shattered one sultry summer night. It took a while
to clear the sleep from my head after I heard the noise. Three o'clock

in the morning—I could see the digital readout on the clock. Had I dreamt that loud bang or had something happened? I closed my eyes and rolled over, too tired to draw a conclusion. Then I heard groans coming from the street below. Stumbling out of bed, I stood at the open window, staring down. A minivan lay crumpled against a tree directly across the street. Soon the darkness was punctuated by sirens and flashing lights. Two young men were placed on stretchers and bundled into an ambulance. A third screamed in pain as firemen used the "Jaws of Life" to extricate him from the vehicle, mangling the passenger door in the process. That night I prayed for the injured with silent anguish, standing next to neighbors who had gathered on the street.

We learned the next day that the van had been stolen. The three young thieves had come careening the wrong way down our one-way street at God-knows-what speed. They hadn't had seat belts on and one was thrown onto the street while another was tossed around in the back compartment of the car. Only the tree had kept the car from ramming into my neighbor's house. Fortunately, though the three were banged up, they would recover. But what if they had killed themselves or someone else? What if the accident had occurred in the middle of the day with young children playing outside? It wasn't the first time a car had been stolen in our neighborhood. Suddenly our beautiful tree-lined street no longer seemed like the safe enclave we thought it was.

A year later, the only sign that anything unusual happened on our street was the large bare patch on the tree where the bark was ripped off. So far it shows no signs of healing. Perhaps it will stay that way, a reminder that evil, despite its allure, is essentially stupid. Pursuing our impulses regardless of God's instructions is like throwing ourselves headlong into a tree.

You and I may never be tempted to go joyriding, but what about other temptations—like stretching the truth to gain an advantage, or constantly yelling at our kids, or flirting with someone else's spouse, or spending more money than we have, or spouting off just because we feel like it? What happens when these behaviors become common-place in our society—in businesses, churches, government, and media? Inevitably, such moral failures will diminish the peace. Sometimes they will even destroy it.

God has already shown us the path of peace. We need to walk in it and pursue it with all our hearts, remembering the counsel of the prophet Isaiah, who reminds us that "the fruit of righteousness will be peace; the effect of righteousness will be quietness and confidence forever" (Isaiah 32:17).

Take some time today to pray for yourself and for your neighbors. Ask Christ to work in all hearts so that all may experience his peace.

Thursday

PRAYING THE NAME

As he [Jesus] approached Jerusalem and saw the city, he wept over it and said, "If you, even you, had only known on this day what would bring you peace — but now it is hidden from your eyes. The days will come upon you when your enemies will build an embankment against you and encircle you and hem you in on every side. They will dash you to the ground, you and the children within your walls. They will not leave one stone on another, because you did not recognize the time of God's coming to you."

LUKE 19:41–44

For the creation was subjected to frustration, not by its own choice, but by the will of the one who subjected it, in hope that the creation itself will be liberated from its bondage to decay and brought into the glorious freedom of the children of God.

We know that the whole creation has been groaning as in the pains of childbirth right up to the present time. Not only so, but we ourselves, who have the firstfruits of the Spirit, groan inwardly as we wait eagerly for our adoption as sons, the redemption of our bodies.

ROMANS 8:20–23

Reflect On: Luke 19:41–44 and Romans 8:20–23.
Praise God: For his promised redemption.
Offer Thanks: For the ways you have experienced God's mercy rather than his judgment.
Confess: Any tendency to rationalize your sins.
Ask God: To bring good out of evil, spreading the gospel of peace throughout the world.

∞

Dilip Sivakumar has always made his living from the sea. After spending much of his life on the water, he rarely has trouble navigating. "Once I see the shore, I see a certain tree, the roof of my house, then I know the currents and I get in," he said. In December of 2004, he and his younger brother were fishing, twenty miles offshore. "We could tell something strange was happening," he said about the sea. Things were so strange, in fact, that this seasoned fisherman had trouble locating his village when he scanned the horizon. "I could see the trees, but I couldn't see any buildings. I thought, *Am I lost?*" Then the truth set in. His village on the south coast of Sri Lanka had been destroyed. There was nothing left to find. It had been devastated by the tsunami that had developed in the Indian Ocean, claiming the lives of perhaps 225,000 people. That day, Dilip lost more than half the members of his extended family. Multiply his grief a million and a half times (the number of people displaced from their homes by the tsunami) and you get a tragedy of enormous proportions.

While this region of the world suffered so horribly, the rest of us stayed glued to our television sets, unable to comprehend the extent of the devastation even though we saw the bodies, bloated and decomposing on the beach, even though we heard the cries of those whose children were ripped from their arms by the ruthless seas. The stories continue, horrifying and bizarre. In one village, nine women claimed to be the mother of a lone orphan. The husband of one of the women threatened that he and his wife would commit suicide if they were not awarded the child while another woman threatened murder. Finally, through DNA testing, the baby was reunited with his true parents.

In addition to claiming lives, this natural disaster has challenged the faith of people around the world. How could a loving God allow it? Is he angry? Weak? Uncaring? Where is the protection we thought he owed us by virtue of our religious beliefs and practices? Does he even exist?

These questions deserve our respect. The world's grief is strong and deep. But as I have tried to make sense of the tragic circumstances, I have discovered one thing about natural disasters. They are not all that natural, at least in terms of God's original design. Scripture tells us that in the beginning, creation was a place of natural order, peace, and harmony. In fact the word "peace" as it is used in the Bible contains within it the notion of completion. When God's work is complete, things are as they should be.

But sin has spoiled the peace, disrupted life, and caused fractures and divisions within the natural world. As a result our universe, though it is beautiful, has also become treacherous. Life is not as it should be. As St. Paul so vividly put it, all creation groans, awaiting the day when it too will be delivered from its bondage to death and decay.

I do not believe that a wrathful God presided over the tsunami in the Indian Ocean. But God may have watched and wept as Jesus wept over Jerusalem when he envisioned the death and destruction his people would one day suffer at the hands of the Roman army. He wept because they did not know what made for peace.

No matter how broken our world is, it is still right to call God loving, still right to hail Jesus as the Prince of Peace. During his life on earth he calmed the storm, walked on the water, healed the sick, and brought the dead to life. These are signs that he intends to restore God's plan for creation, to bring it to completion by inaugurating and establishing the new creation. One day Jesus Christ will enable the lion and the lamb to lie down together, making the world what it should be. A place where there is no more death, no more decay, no more illness or suffering or sorrow. A place where sin cannot be found and peace will reign from sea to sea. Until then, we must help those who suffer and console those who grieve. We must pray for peace and work for peace and refuse to accept a world that is less than it should be and less than it will be. And as we pray, let us remember that Jesus not only brings us peace, he is our peace.

Friday

PROMISES ASSOCIATED WITH HIS NAME

Peace is meant to be a shield, guarding us against the onslaught of anxiety and fear that stands ready to attack our faith and erode our confidence in God. It is like a down payment, a sign of the blessed life Jesus has promised. Because this peace is not rooted in circumstances, others may find it puzzling. In fact, Christ's peace is often most evident in the midst of difficulty. Paul tells us to actively seek this peace. We do this not by anxiously trying to control our lives but by surrendering our needs to God in prayer and by remembering to live with rejoicing, thankful for what he has already done. Furthermore, peace comes as a byproduct of righteousness—and righteousness comes from living in accordance with the Spirit.

Promises in Scripture

> You will keep in perfect peace
> those whose minds are steadfast,
> because they trust in you.

> ISAIAH 26:3

> This is what the LORD says—
> your Redeemer, the Holy One of Israel:
> "I am the LORD your God,
> who teaches you what is best for you,
> who directs you in the way you should go.
> If only you had paid attention to my commands,
> your peace would have been like a river,
> your righteousness like the waves of the sea."

> ISAIAH 48:17–18

Those who live according to the sinful nature have their minds set on what that nature desires; but those who live in accordance with the Spirit have their minds set on what the Spirit desires. The mind controlled by the sinful nature is death, but the mind controlled by the Spirit is life and peace.

ROMANS 8:5–6

Rejoice in the Lord always. I will say it again: Rejoice! Let your gentleness be evident to all. The Lord is near. Do not be anxious about anything, but in everything, by prayer and petition, with thanksgiving, present your requests to God. And the peace of God, which transcends all understanding, will guard your hearts and your minds in Christ Jesus.

PHILIPPIANS 4:4–7

Continued Prayer and Praise

Pray for the peace of Jerusalem. (Psalm 122:6–7; Isaiah 66:10–13)

Try to be a peacemaker. (Matthew 5:9)

Praise the one who is able to impart peace to your heart. (John 14:1–27; 16:33)

Seek peace, which is a fruit of the Spirit. (Galatians 5:19–26)

Thank Christ for making peace through his blood. (Colossians 1:15–23)

Let the peace of Christ rule in your hearts. (Colossians 3:12–15)

9

CHRIST, MESSIAH

Χρίστος מָשִׁיחַ

CHRISTOS, MASHIACH

The Name

Most of us are so familiar with the title "Christ" that we tend to consider it part of Jesus' personal name. But what exactly does it mean? Like "Messiah," "Christ" means the "anointed one." The phrase "anointed one" refers to someone who has been set apart for a special mission. That was how the first Christians thought about Jesus. As Israel's Messiah, he was the greatest of all kings, the one called and empowered to destroy God's enemies and extend his kingdom throughout the earth. His mission was to put an end to our deepest troubles—to rebellion, sin, and death. When we pray to Jesus Christ, we are praying to the Messiah, the Anointed One, whose mission involves calling the world back to God through the power of his love.

Key Scripture

Therefore let all Israel be assured of this: God has made this Jesus, whom you crucified, both Lord and Christ.

ACTS 2:36

Monday

HIS NAME REVEALED

"Listen to this: Jesus of Nazareth was a man accredited by God to you by miracles, wonders and signs, which God did among you through him, as you yourselves know. This man was handed over to you by God's set purpose and foreknowledge; and you, with the help of wicked men, put him to death by nailing him to the cross. But God raised him from the dead, freeing him from the agony of death, because it was impossible for death to keep its hold on him.....

"God has raised this Jesus to life, and we are all witnesses of the fact. Exalted to the right hand of God, he has received from the Father the promised Holy Spirit and has poured out what you now see and hear....

"Therefore let all Israel be assured of this: God has made this Jesus, whom you crucified, both Lord and Christ."

When the people heard this, they were cut to the heart and said to Peter and the other apostles, "Brothers, what shall we do?"

Peter replied, "Repent and be baptized, every one of you, in the name of Jesus Christ for the forgiveness of your sins. And you will receive the gift of the Holy Spirit."

ACTS 2:22–24, 32–33, 36–38

Jesus, my Messiah, I praise you for triumphing over the powers of sin and death. Thank you for allowing yourself to be raised up on a cross and then raised from the grave. Cover me with your forgiveness, and fill me with your Spirit so that my one purpose will be to glorify you now and forever. Amen.

Understanding the Name

Many ancient peoples believed that oil rubbed onto the body could impart strength, health, and beauty. Since oil was a staple of life in biblical times, used for lighting, cooking, medicine, cosmetic purposes, hygiene, and hospitality, it served as a symbol of both wealth and joy.

An abundance of oil was evidence of God's pleasure. Scarcity symbolized his displeasure.

Oil was also used for sacred purposes, such as consecrating altars and vessels for worship, indicating that they had been set apart for the Lord's purposes. People could also be anointed and set apart. Though some of Israel's high priests were anointed when they took office, Israel's kings, especially those descended from David, were anointed rather than crowned. According to rabbinic tradition, oil (olive oil mixed with spices like cinnamon, calamus, and myrrh) was poured on their heads in a circle to form a crown. This anointing signified the king's right to rule. It meant that God had blessed him with authority, strength, and honor.

When the prophet Samuel anointed David as king, David was also given the gift of the Spirit and accorded the Lord's special protection. In time, oil became a symbol for the Holy Spirit, who imparts divine favor, power, and protection. The English word "christen" ("to anoint") comes from the Greek verb *chrio* ("to anoint").

The New Testament identifies Jesus as Christ, the "Anointed One," no less than 530 times. Jesus, however, was not anointed with oil but with the Holy Spirit at his baptism in the Jordan River. The early Christians understood that Jesus was the Christ — the Messiah, or *Mashiach* (ma-SHEE-ach) — in a unique sense. Like no king before him, he was called to heal the rift between God and his people. Christ fulfilled his mission as the ideal king in a completely unexpected way, confounding his contemporaries, who expected the Messiah to be a powerful earthly king who would deliver Israel from its enemies. In order to avoid being forced into playing this political role, Jesus avoided the title of Christ or Messiah throughout most of his life. Finally, shortly before his death, he answered the high priest's question: "Are you the Christ, the Son of the Blessed One?" with the startling confession: "I am."

Studying the Name

1. Describe in your own words what it means to say that Jesus was anointed, or set apart for God's service.

2. Why do you think the Acts 2 passage speaks about the need for repentance and being baptized in the name of Jesus Christ?

3. What do you think it means for believers to be anointed or set apart for Christ's service? How have you experienced this anointing in your own life?

4. What do you think it means to receive the gift of the Holy Spirit?

Tuesday

PRAYING THE NAME

"Who do you say I am?"

Simon Peter answered, *"You are the Christ, the Son of the living God."*

Jesus replied, *"Blessed are you, Simon son of Jonah, for this was not revealed to you by flesh and blood, but by my Father in heaven. . . ."*

From that time on Jesus began to explain to his disciples that he must go to Jerusalem and suffer many things at the hands of the elders, chief priests and teachers of the law, and that he must be killed and on the third day be raised to life.

Peter took him aside and began to rebuke him. *"Never, Lord!"* he said. *"This shall never happen to you!"*

Jesus turned and said to Peter, *"Get behind me, Satan! You are a stumbling block to me; you do not have in mind the things of God, but merely human concerns."*

MATTHEW 16:15 – 17, 21 – 23

Reflect On: Matthew 16:13 – 23.
Praise God: Because his thoughts are higher than ours.
Offer Thanks: For Christ's willingness to suffer.
Confess: Any tendency to settle for less than what Christ
                       desires for you.
Ask God: To give you his mind and heart.

How ironic that Peter's 20/20 vision clouded so quickly. Having identified Jesus as the Christ, Peter recoiled the moment Jesus spoke about suffering and death. How could the man on whom he had pinned his hope talk about defeat? How could the Messiah save Israel by lying in a grave? Peter can hardly be faulted for failing to realize that the way to victory would be down and not up, and that the way to life would run straight through death.

Like the rest of the Jews who were looking for Israel's deliverance, Peter was guilty of trying to reshape Jesus into the Messiah he wanted, not the Messiah he needed. His failure to see that the main problem was not external dominance but the internal oppression of sin made him like a doctor who performs cosmetic surgery when what a patient really needs is a quadruple bypass. Jesus, the most perceptive of physicians, wasn't interested in merely alleviating human suffering. He wanted his people to live forever. And to do that, he was willing to lay down his life in order to himself become their medicine.

I wonder how many of us make Peter's mistake, even with the benefit of hindsight. We know that Jesus came to deliver us by dying on a cross and then rising from the dead. But do we realize that after having gone to such an extreme, Christ is not about to let us settle for the surface goods we so ardently desire?

I confess to taking voyeuristic pleasure in a television show about extreme makeovers. It's astonishing to see what liposuction, plastic surgery, makeup, hair dye, and expensive clothing can do for people. But I can't help thinking that such transformations aren't really all that extreme. After all, they don't alter who people are under the skin. I wonder too what could motivate people to expose themselves in this way on national television.

Then it occurs to me to wonder about my own priorities. How much time do I spend thinking about quick fixes that would improve my life? How about a little more money? Or what if I could teach my children to respond to my every request with: "Yes, Mama, whatever you say, Mama?" Or what if I could retire early and travel the world? Wouldn't all these things make my life better? Maybe, but maybe not. Sometimes getting what you want is more of a curse than a blessing.

Jesus, it would seem, specializes not in the quick fix but in the kind of extreme makeover that transforms us and the world from the inside. Such changes take time. Though Christ blesses us in this life, his goals for us stretch far beyond it. That's one reason we won't always get what we pray for.

Instead of the success I desire, I may need to endure a time of humiliation and loss. Or instead of controlling my children, I may need to learn how to guide them into greater maturity. Or rather than granting me early retirement, Christ may reveal new ways for me to serve.

What do you want Jesus to do for you today? Make a wish list. Then ask him to show you what you truly need rather than what you simply want. Write down what you hear. Ask Christ for the grace to transform your mind so that you can begin to make his priorities yours. Then praise him for being the Messiah you need rather than merely the Messiah you want.

Wednesday

PRAYING THE NAME

"God raised him [Jesus Christ] from the dead, freeing him from the agony of death, because it was impossible for death to keep its hold on him. . . .

"Therefore let all Israel be assured of this: God has made this Jesus, whom you crucified, both Lord and Christ."

When the people heard this, they were cut to the heart and said to Peter and the other apostles, "Brothers, what shall we do?"

Peter replied, "Repent and be baptized, every one of you, in the name of Jesus Christ for the forgiveness of your sins."

ACTS 2:24, 36–38

Dear friends, do not be surprised at the painful trial you are suffering, as though something strange were happening to you. But rejoice that you participate in the sufferings of Christ, so that you may be overjoyed when his glory is revealed.

1 PETER 4:12–13

Reflect On: Acts 2:22–38 and 1 Peter 4:12–13.
Praise God: For the promise of eternal life.
Offer Thanks: For the way God has enabled you to endure difficulty.
Confess: Any habit of complaining or any unbelief leading to despair.
Ask God: To give you the grace to persevere to the end.

What if somebody managed to concoct a vitamin that enabled you to live forever? Its only drawback was that it didn't start working until all your vital signs had shut down. In other words, you would need to die once before coming back to life.

Or what if you had a choice of riding out a storm in either a 1,200-foot cruise ship that despite its size could not withstand the storm, or a small lifeboat that registered every swell of the sea but was designed to be self-bailing, self-righting, and nearly unsinkable—able to right itself eight seconds after capsizing?

Wouldn't the choice be obvious in both cases?

These are the crudest of images to explain how Jesus saves us. Belonging to him does not insulate us from suffering and death. But it does mean that Christ will be faithful to his mission by raising us to live with him forever. When Jesus himself was crucified, it was as though death opened its mouth too wide, unaware that it was attempting the impossible, trying to swallow life itself. No wonder Paul remarks that "it was impossible for death to keep its hold on him." So it makes sense that when Christ lives within us through faith, we inherit a kind of spiritual buoyancy that cannot be destroyed by death.

But blending our lives with Christ's is not like swallowing a pill. Being "in Christ" means that we are called to draw our strength from him in order to reproduce the pattern of his life on a smaller scale. With him and in him, we too will suffer, die, and rise. I confess that I like the last bit, about rising, but I shrink back from the part about suffering and dying.

Nine years ago an executive from CBS News negotiated a ten-year lease for the right to broadcast from a hotel that overlooks St. Peter's Square. She wanted cameras to capture the drama of Pope John Paul II's death the moment it happened. But the pope nearly outlived her lease at the hotel. As one editor remarked, "I have been interviewed for obituaries on the pope for the last ten years and he's outlived everybody, even some of his biographers."

What is so remarkable is not that Pope John Paul II had a corner on longevity but that this once-vigorous man made a point, not of hiding his suffering but of giving the world a close-up view of his decline from Parkinson's disease. In a time when many are advocating euthanasia as a way for people to die with dignity, the pope used his illness to show the world how to face suffering with dignity and courage, believing that life is a gift from God. To those who say his illness should have ended his papacy, he merely replied: "Did Christ come down from the Cross?"

The point is not that the pope thought he was Christ but that he believed Christ lived within him and that he needed to obediently imitate the Lord by living with hope and trust in the midst of suffering. As one of his biographers so aptly remarked prior to his death, "The world is watching a man live out, to the end, one of the convictions that has shaped his life and his impact on history: the conviction that the light of Easter is always preceded by the darkness of Good Friday, not just on the calendar but in the realm of the spirit."

What kind of suffering have you faced and how have you faced it? If you are like me you may have sometimes responded to difficulty with complaining, evasion, and near despair. But Christ calls each of us to face it with courage, trust, and hope, confident that as we share in his sufferings, we will one day share in his glory.

Thursday

PRAYING THE NAME

There was given me a thorn in my flesh, a messenger of Satan, to torment me. Three times I pleaded with the Lord to take it away from me. But he said to me, "My grace is sufficient for you, for my power is made perfect in weakness." Therefore I will boast all the more gladly about my weaknesses, so that Christ's power may rest on me. That is why, for Christ's sake, I delight in weaknesses, in insults, in hardships, in persecutions, in difficulties. For when I am weak, then I am strong.

2 CORINTHIANS 12:7–10

Forgetting what is behind and straining toward what is ahead, I press on toward the goal to win the prize for which God has called me heavenward in Christ Jesus.

PHILIPPIANS 3:13–14

Reflect On: 2 Corinthians 12:7–12; Philippians 3:7–14.
Praise God: For revealing his power in human weakness.
Offer Thanks: That God has called you heavenward.
Confess: Any tendency to rely on your own strength.
Ask God: To encourage you to keep running the race.

∞

If you had to choose one word to sum up your Christian life, what would it be? Joy? Grace? Love? Peace? Power? Much as I am tempted to claim one of these for my own, I have to be honest. The word that most captures me is "weakness," though I didn't always think so. My favorite childhood song, in fact, went like this: "Anything you can do, I can do better. I can do anything better than you." As with most people, however, reality eventually intruded on my fantasy.

Over the years, Christ has graciously revealed my need of him, not once but many times. Through painful experience I have begun to realize that I am not strong enough to stay spiritually afloat for even a second should God withdraw his sustaining hand. The powers and the principalities are too much for me, to say nothing of my flesh. Left alone, my sinful reactions to life would destroy me. But thank God I have not been left alone. He has held me up, above the raging waters and the roaring seas. He has loved me when I could not love myself, preserved me when I could not preserve myself.

Not long ago, after enduring a time of difficulty, I joined my voice with others singing a familiar Easter hymn. As the congregation belted out the lyrics, the joy I felt was palpable:

> *Jesus Christ is risen today, Alleluia!*
> *Our triumphant holy day, Alleluia!*
> *Who did once, upon the cross, Alleluia!*
> *Suffer to redeem our loss, Alleluia!*
>
> *Hymns of praise then let us sing, Alleluia!*
> *Unto Christ, our heavenly King, Alleluia!*
> *Who endured the cross and grave, Alleluia!*
> *Sinners to redeem and save, Alleluia!*
>
> *Sing we to our God above, Alleluia!*
> *Praise eternal as his love, Alleluia!*
> *Praise him, all you heavenly host, Alleluia!*
> *Father, Son, and Holy Ghost.*

Easter, of course, is the great celebration of Christ's victory. It recognizes that Jesus, God's "Anointed One," finished the job he came to do. Like him, we are called to finish well by reproducing the pattern of his life until it is time for us to leave this world.

As we sang the Easter hymn, I suddenly found myself thinking about my own funeral, wishing I could be there to preach at it, though I am no preacher. I had a picture of myself standing jubilant in front of family and friends, a smile spreading wide across my face, one arm raised in victory. I had done it—remained faithful to the end! Though I had nearly fainted on the way, I had managed to cross the finish line. I had won the race. And if I could do it, they could too. God alone had carried me across, and he would carry them as well. I wanted to shout out the words of St. Paul, telling them how my weakness had been Christ's opportunity.

Of course, I know that such a celebration is premature. But I look forward to it in hope. And as I do, I cry out to God for grace, reminding him that my weakness forms the perfect backdrop for his strength. And as I pray, I remind myself once again that I can do all things in Christ who strengthens me.

PROMISES ASSOCIATED WITH HIS NAME

What is the one word every young person wants to hear, especially from a parent? I'll give you a clue. It starts with "y" and ends with "s." It has only three letters, and it is the opposite of *no*. "Yes, you can have the car tonight." "Yes, you can go to the concert." "Yes, you can sleep as late as you like." Yes, yes, yes … human beings love this word. So it makes perfect sense that Paul equates it with Jesus, saying that Christ is the positive answer to every promise God has made. "Yes, I forgive you." "Yes, I am with you." "Yes, I love you and will never let you go." Jesus Christ, now and forever — God's resounding *yes* to everyone who asks.

Promises in Scripture

But as surely as God is faithful, our message to you is not "Yes" and "No." For the Son of God, Jesus Christ, who was preached among you by me and Silas and Timothy, was not "Yes" and "No," but in him it has always been "Yes." For no matter how many promises God has made, they are "Yes" in Christ. And so through him the "Amen" is spoken by us to the glory of God. Now it is God who makes both us and you stand firm in Christ. He anointed us, set his seal of ownership on us, and put his Spirit in our hearts as a deposit, guaranteeing what is to come.

2 CORINTHIANS 1:18–22

But Christ has indeed been raised from the dead, the firstfruits of those who have fallen asleep. For since death came through a man, the resurrection of the dead comes also through a man. For as in Adam all die, so in Christ all will be made alive.

1 CORINTHIANS 15:20–22

Continued Prayer and Praise

Reflect on the prophecies. (Psalm 22; 69:20–21; Isaiah 52; Zechariah 9:9; Luke 24:45–48)

Understand his role. (Psalm 72:1–8; Isaiah 11:1–9)

Guard against false messiahs. (Matthew 24:24; Philippians 2:5–11; 1 John 2:18–24)

Reflect on his anointing. (Luke 4:14–21; John 12:1–7)

Remember, nothing can separate you from the love of Christ. (Romans 8:32–37)

Clothe yourself in Christ. (Galatians 3:26–28)

IO

RABBI, RABBOUNI, TEACHER

ῥαββί, ῥαββουνί, διδάσκαλος
RHABBI, RHABBOUNI, DIDASKALOS

The Name

In Jesus' day, the name "rabbi" or "teacher" was normally reserved for someone who had studied under another rabbi for many years. Jesus offended the religious leaders of his day by ignoring this system. Instead of apprenticing himself to a rabbi, he simply laid down his carpenter tools and called twelve ordinary men to become his disciples. Unlike other rabbis, who merely passed on the teaching of the rabbi under whom they had studied, Jesus spoke with an authority that startled many of his listeners.

Two thousand years later, we are called to become his disciples, to stay as close to him as a disciple would to a rabbi, studying his life, examining his teaching, and allowing his Spirit to remake us in his image. When you pray to Rabbi Jesus, remember that you are praying to the only Teacher who is all-wise, all-good, and all-powerful, able to transform not only your mind but also your heart.

Key Scripture

[Jesus said to his disciples] "But you are not to be called 'Rabbi,' for you have only one Master."

MATTHEW 23:8

Monday

HIS NAME REVEALED

"But you are not to be called 'Rabbi,' for you have only one Master."

Matthew 23:8

Jesus knew that the Father had put all things under his power, and that he had come from God and was returning to God; so he got up from the meal, took off his outer clothing, and wrapped a towel around his waist. After that, he poured water into a basin and began to wash his disciples' feet, drying them with the towel that was wrapped around him.

He came to Simon Peter, who said to him, "Lord, are you going to wash my feet?"

Jesus replied, "You do not realize now what I am doing, but later you will understand."

"No," said Peter, "you shall never wash my feet."

Jesus answered, "Unless I wash you, you have no part with me...."

When he had finished washing their feet, he put on his clothes and returned to his place. "Do you understand what I have done for you?" he asked them. "You call me 'Teacher' and 'Lord,' and rightly so, for that is what I am. Now that I, your Lord and Teacher, have washed your feet, you also should wash one another's feet. I have set you an example that you should do as I have done for you. I tell you the truth, no servant is greater than his master, nor is a messenger greater than the one who sent him. Now that you know these things, you will be blessed if you do them.

John 13:3–8, 12–17

Jesus, my Rabbi and Lord. On the night before you died, you painted a picture by your words and deeds of what it means to be your disciple. Help me to advance in wisdom, love, and grace as your disciple. Give me opportunities to follow you by serving those around me. Help me to seek hidden and humble ways to do your will.

Understanding the Name

In ancient Israel all education was religious education, and Scripture was the sole textbook. Understanding it was vital, because long life, success, and happiness flowed from living in accordance with the laws of God. But the Jews did not believe that ordinary people were equipped to understand and apply Scripture without the guidance of a teacher. Gradually, scribes, who devoted their lives to copying and understanding the Mosaic law, became their primary instructors. Lacking access to the temple after the Exile, the Jews began meeting together for prayer and instruction in places that became known as synagogues. Eventually, schools formed around these synagogues, where boys began to be educated between the ages of five and seven.

In the first century, "Rabbi" (ra-BEE, a Hebrew word) came to be used as a title for scribes or theologians trained in the Law. (*Rabbouni* [ra-BOU-nee] is an expanded Hebrew form that means "my rabbi.") Scribes were also known as "teachers of the law." The King James Version of the Bible calls them "lawyers."

"Rabbi" is literally translated "my great one" and can also be translated as "my master" or "my teacher." During the first century it was customary for a rabbi to take disciples, who would be bound to him for life. After spending several years with their rabbi studying Scripture and the oral and written traditions surrounding it, the disciples would in turn become rabbis through the laying on of hands.

By Jesus' day, the scribes held considerable power in Jewish society, serving not only as religious educators but as judges. The majority were members of the party of the Pharisees. Many of them, as Jesus pointed out, were consumed with the desire for public acclaim and positions of honor. Over time, the scribes added so many rules and regulations to the Law that Jesus faulted them for placing heavy burdens on the people without lifting a finger to help them.

Though Jesus' disciples called him "rabbi," which must have incensed the scribes because of his lack of formal training, there is no evidence he was ever ordained. Unlike most rabbis, who merely taught what they had learned from another rabbi, Jesus taught with his own authority, as though his wisdom came from above—a fact remarked upon by many who heard him. Jesus counseled his disciples never to seek the honorific title "rabbi." He alone was to be their Teacher and Master.

Another word for teacher in the New Testament is the Greek word *didaskolos* (di-DAS-ka-los). Jesus was an enormously popular teacher who drew crowds wherever he went, using questions, discussions, proverbs, symbolic actions, parables, and even miracles in order to teach people the way to live. The content of his teaching is most powerfully and eloquently evident in the story of his life.

Studying the Name

1. Why do you think Jesus cautioned his disciples in Matthew 23:8 against the title "rabbi"?

2. Why do you think Jesus washed his disciples' feet the night before his death, making this one of the last lessons he would leave them prior to his crucifixion?

3. Describe ways in which you have experienced people in leadership serving you.

4. How would your life be different if you understood that your primary identity consisted of being a disciple of Rabbi Jesus?

Tuesday

PRAYING THE NAME

"But you are not to be called 'Rabbi,' for you have only one Master and you are all brothers. And do not call anyone on earth 'father,' for you have one Father, and he is in heaven. Nor are you to be called 'teacher,' for you have one Teacher, the Christ. The greatest among you will be your servant. For whoever exalts himself will be humbled, and whoever humbles himself will be exalted."

MATTHEW 23:8–12

Reflect On: Matthew 23:8–12.
Praise God: For sending his Son to be our Teacher.
Offer Thanks: For the clear teaching of Christ in the Scriptures.
Confess: Any disregard for the teaching of Jesus.
Ask God: To give you a greater hunger to understand and practice your faith.

The other day my daughter asked whether she could invite her third-grade teacher home to watch a favorite movie with her. I found myself explaining that teachers aren't in the habit of making after-school play dates with their students. Still, relationships between students and teachers seem much less formal these days. One of my brothers is a teacher who every summer calls his upcoming fifth graders to tell them how much he is looking forward to having them in his class. When I was in school, kids would have fainted if a teacher had ever called them on the phone.

But as long as two thousand years ago in a place called Palestine, students and rabbis were extremely close. In fact, when a rabbi took disciples, they were linked to him for life, living in his house for several years without paying room and board in exchange for performing various kinds of personal service. The idea was to live and breathe the master's teaching—to learn not only what he knew but also who he was, so that they could replicate both his knowledge and his character. But it was hardly a relationship of equals. Hungry for praise, some rabbis demanded that their disciples show them even greater deference than a son would show a father. The rabbis Jesus criticized weren't exactly models of humility.

Jesus, by contrast, hadn't served as anyone's understudy. A carpenter who hailed from the backwater of Galilee, he had simply quit his trade and called twelve not very impressive men to follow him in what was clearly a rabbi-disciple arrangement. The scribes and Pharisees were offended—and threatened. Who did this Jesus think he was? And how was he able to back up his teaching with so many signs and wonders? Furthermore, he didn't talk nice—at least about them. By his words and actions, Jesus challenged the values that had shaped their lives and consolidated their power. In fact he warned his disciples against falling into the pattern of being called "Rabbi," pointing out that they were all brothers and that he alone was to be their Master and Teacher.

Jesus wasn't discounting the benefits of learning from the examples or the teaching of others. But he was warning his disciples against following or becoming self-important teachers who led others astray by their focus on externals.

Our call, like that of the disciples, is centered, not on externals, not on adhering to a set of laws or regulations, but on following a person—Jesus. That's why faith is such an adventure. We are called to keep moving, growing, learning, becoming. We are lifelong disciples, bound to Jesus in a unique way, serving him daily and relying on him to provide for our needs just as the rabbis of old did for their disciples.

Today as you seek Rabbi Jesus in prayer, thank him for calling you. Tell him that everything you most want to learn in this life can only be found in him and through him, your Teacher and your Lord.

Wednesday

PRAYING THE NAME

They came to Bethsaida, and some people brought a blind man and begged Jesus to touch him. He took the blind man by the hand and led him outside the village. When he had spit on the man's eyes and put his hands on him, Jesus asked, "Do you see anything?"

He looked up and said, "I see people; they look like trees walking around." Once more Jesus put his hands on the man's eyes. Then his eyes were opened, his sight was restored, and he saw everything clearly.

MARK 8:22–25

Reflect On: Mark 8:22–25 and John 9:1–3.

Praise God: Because there are no shadows in him.

Offer Thanks: For the ways Jesus continues to reveal himself to you.

Confess: Any tendency to ignore the difficult teachings of Christ.

Ask God: To open your eyes to your need for grace.

♋

One golden afternoon when my daughter was a toddler, barely able to speak, she peered over the edge of a railing at the Grand Canyon and uttered the single word that captures our common response to such grandeur. "Wow!" she said. After that she was speechless. In the face of such splendor, anything more would have been redundant.

Unless our responses have been blunted by skepticism or dulled by overfamiliarity, many of us respond to the miracles of Jesus in a similar way. We are wowed by stories of how he healed lepers, walked on water, calmed storms, and multiplied bread. Surely such miracles provide clear evidence of his divinity. But there is more to the story of these miraculous events.

Hundreds of years ago, St. Augustine commented on our tendency to miss the deeper meaning of the miracles, advising believers to "ask the miracles themselves what they tell us about Christ, for they have a tongue of their own, if it can only be understood. Because Christ is the Word of God, all the acts of the Word become words to us. The miracle which we admire on the outside also has something inside which must be understood."

If Jesus is our Rabbi, surely he teaches us not only through his parables and sayings but also through his actions. Take the incident in Mark's Gospel in which Jesus gradually heal a blind man. But why couldn't Jesus get the job done with a single touch? Didn't he have the power? The answer may lie, not in any lack of divine power but in a lack of human readiness. Perhaps Jesus healed the blind man in stages in order to reveal a deeper point — to show us that our own healing often happens in stages as well.

To be converted to Christ is first of all to be healed of our spiritual blindness — but not completely. We are still only half-seeing, only partially perceiving the truth about God and about us. Knowing we can only bear so much light, Jesus never forces us to see the whole truth but only enables us to see it as we are willing and able. Despite our faith, most of us still resist the gospel at some level. We tolerate and sometimes even cherish the shadows precisely because the Good News is also Bad News for the sins we still harbor — our pride, pettiness, and greed.

Today as you ponder the miracle of how Christ healed the blind man from Bethsaida, ask him to touch the eyes of your soul so that they may open wide to the truth of the gospel. Pray for the faith to see and the grace to learn.

Thursday

PRAYING THE NAME

Jesus replied, "The hour has come for the Son of Man to be glorified. I tell you the truth, unless a kernel of wheat falls to the ground and dies, it remains only a single seed. But if it dies, it produces many seeds. The man who loves his life will lose it, while the man who hates his life in this world will keep it for eternal life. Whoever serves me must follow me; and where I am, my servant also will be. My Father will honor the one who serves me."

JOHN 12:23–26

He told them another parable: "The kingdom of heaven is like a mustard seed, which a man took and planted in his field. Though it is the smallest of all your seeds, yet when it grows, it is the largest of garden plants and becomes a tree, so that the birds of the air come and perch in its branches."

MATTHEW 13:31–32

Reflect On: John 12:23–26 and Matthew 13:31–32.
Praise God: For his ability to bring good out of evil.
Offer Thanks: For the ways Christ has called you to bear fruit.
Confess: Any tendency to lose heart when life gets difficult.
Ask God: To increase your spiritual vision.

Throughout my professional life, I have found myself coaching authors on the importance of storytelling, trying to convince them that showing is often more powerful than telling. Occasionally an author objects, fearing that telling stories will somehow "dumb down" his or her writing. But human beings crave stories, just as we crave art and music. Good stories compel us in ways that simple statements of fact or truth often do not. They connect to us at every level—emotionally, intellectually, and spiritually.

Jesus was the last person to overlook the power of a story well told. His favorite form of storytelling was the parable, a form described by William Barclay as "a sword to stab men's minds awake." Drawn from everyday life, Jesus' parables convey spiritual messages that often both reveal and hide the truth. Once, when his disciples asked him the meaning of a particular parable, he replied: "The knowledge of the secrets of the kingdom of God has been given to you, but to others I speak in parables, so that, 'though seeing, they may not see; though hearing, they may not understand' " (Luke 8:10). The "secrets of the kingdom" can only be grasped by hearts that are open to faith and truth.

One of the most popular of Jesus' parables is that of the mustard seed. With its thick-stemmed branches, the mustard plant is an enormous herb, growing to a height of ten to fifteen feet. A favorite nesting place for birds who eat the seeds, its seeds were ground into a paste or powder and used as a spice or medicine. So when Jesus compared the advance of his kingdom to the smallest of seeds that grows into the tallest of plants, he immediately created a vivid and encouraging image for his disciples. He and his followers were the small beginning that would grow into the greatest kingdom the world had ever known—a kingdom that would nurture, heal, and shelter all who would take refuge there.

Jesus intended this comparison to impart vision to disciples who needed it. At first it may have seemed easy to be his disciples—when the crowds wanted to proclaim him king. But what about when the opposition grew stiff, when other rabbis denounced him, when Pharisees linked him to Beelzebub, the prince of demons? Wouldn't his disciples, called to walk the downward path along with their rabbi, need the encouragement of this parable?

The parable of the mustard seed must have bolstered the disciples' faith, helping them see what was taking place in the spiritual realm despite the reverses they suffered in the natural realm. It is a parable that is still fresh thousands of years later, for to follow this Rabbi means that we too will walk the downward path. Like the first disciples, we need encouragement to remain faithful when we are tempted to despair.

Perhaps your efforts to serve Jesus seem small or insignificant. You may have encountered opposition as you have tried to do his will. Or perhaps the opposition is indirect. You may be facing declining health, financial trouble, conflict at work, strife at home, a child or a parent who is ill. Whatever difficulties confront you, Jesus is calling you to plant your hope, not in the circumstances of this life, but in the soil of his faithfulness. Pray today that he will open your eyes to the way he is advancing his kingdom in and through you, blessing you with greater fruitfulness than you can imagine.

Friday

PROMISES ASSOCIATED WITH HIS NAME

Promises in Scripture

Every Christian is called to become a lifelong student of the greatest of all teachers. But following Jesus is far different from following some ancient teacher like Aristotle or Confucius. Our Teacher is still alive, still speaking, still writing his lessons into our lives. In addition to guiding us through Scripture, and through those who lead and teach in the body of Christ, he has also given us his Spirit to instruct us moment by moment, day by day. Advancing in wisdom and grace as his students requires no special aptitude, no remarkable intellectual gifting. It requires only humility, faithfulness, and trust. With these, the least gifted among us may become greatest in the kingdom of God.

"If you love me, you will obey what I command. And I will ask the Father, and he will give you another Counselor to be with you forever—the Spirit of truth. The world cannot accept him, because it neither sees him nor knows him. But you know him, for he lives with you and will be in you. I will not leave you as orphans; I will come to you."

JOHN 14:15–18

"Now I am going to him who sent me, yet none of you asks me, 'Where are you going?' Because I have said these things, you are filled with grief. But I tell you the truth: It is for your good that I am going away. Unless I go away, the Counselor will not come to you; but if I go, I will send him to you. . . .

"I have much more to say to you, more than you can now bear. But when he, the Spirit of truth, comes, he will guide you into all truth. He will not speak on his own; he will speak only what he hears, and he will tell you what is yet to come. He will bring glory to me by taking from what is mine and making it known to you. All that belongs to the Father is mine. That is why I said the Spirit will take from what is mine and make it known to you."

JOHN 16:5–7, 12–15

If any of you lacks wisdom, he should ask God, who gives generously to all without finding fault, and it will be given to him.

JAMES 1:5

Continued Prayer and Praise

Pray that Christ will open your eyes. (Psalm 119:18)

Realize that following Jesus involves not merely learning his ways but doing his will. (Matthew 7:21–29)

Make a complete commitment to your Teacher. (Matthew 19:16–21)

Remember two things. (Matthew 22:36–40)

Train yourself by reading Scripture. (2 Timothy 3:16)

II

WORD

λόγος

Logos

The Name

Though God has always revealed himself in some way, the incarnation is the clearest, most compelling revelation of who God is — of his holiness, love, and power. Because Jesus is one with the Father, he is uniquely able to communicate God's heart and mind. As *Logos*, or "the Word," everything about Jesus — his teaching, miracles, suffering, death, and resurrection — speaks to us of God. Our destiny depends on how well we listen. Will we believe, or will we turn a deaf ear to the message of God's love? When you pray to Jesus as the Word, you are praying to the One whose voice calls us from death to life and from darkness to light.

Key Scripture

The Word became flesh and made his dwelling among us. We have seen his glory, the glory of the One and Only, who came from the Father, full of grace and truth.

JOHN 1:14

Monday

HIS NAME REVEALED

In the beginning was the Word, and the Word was with God, and the Word was God. He was with God in the beginning.

Through him all things were made; without him nothing was made that has been made....

He was in the world, and though the world was made through him, the world did not recognize him. He came to that which was his own, but his own did not receive him. Yet to all who received him, to those who believed in his name, he gave the right to become children of God—children born not of natural descent, nor of human decision or a husband's will, but born of God.

The Word became flesh and made his dwelling among us. We have seen his glory, the glory of the One and Only, who came from the Father, full of grace and truth.

JOHN 1:1–3, 10–14

Jesus, you are the One and Only Word made flesh, speaking your love and your light into the world's thick darkness. Reshape my life through your message of mercy. Give me ears to hear and a heart to do your will. Make me eager and able to proclaim your Word in season and out, confident in your life-giving power and in your enduring love.

Understanding the Name

John's Gospel begins by calling Jesus the *Logos* (LO-gos), the "Word." Though *Logos* was a term used in Greek philosophy, John echoes a Hebrew mindset by using it to refer not to a rational principle or an impersonal force but to the One who created the universe by speaking it into existence. Unlike the prophets, who merely *spoke* God's word, Jesus *is* God's dynamic, creative, life-giving Word.

Furthermore, John says, "The Word became flesh and made his dwelling among us" (John 1:14). The Greek for "made his dwelling" is linked to the word for "tent" or "tabernacle." Jewish readers would have immediately recognized this as a reference to the Tent of Meeting, in which God's glory dwelt prior to the building of the temple in Jerusalem. Jesus, the Word made flesh, became a man so that through his miracles, teachings, and way of life we could perceive God's glory. He is the Word calling out to us, healing our deafness and bringing us back to God.

No wonder Jesus responded to Philip by saying: "Don't you know me, Philip, even after I have been among you such a long time? Anyone who has seen me has seen the Father. How can you say, 'Show us the Father'? Don't you believe that I am in the Father, and that the Father is in me?" (John 14:9–10). We are to respond to Jesus, the Word, with both faith and faithfulness, reproducing Christ's life so that the Word may become flesh in us.

Studying the Name

1. Compare Genesis 1:1–5 with John 1:1–5. Why do you think John begins his Gospel this way?

2. John says that though "the world was made through him, the world did not recognize him" (John 1:10). Do you think this is still true today? Why or why not?

3. What does it mean to "believe in his name" (John 1:12)?

4. Read John 1:14. What do you think it means to see God's glory?

Tuesday

PRAYING THE NAME

In the beginning was the Word, and the Word was with God, and the Word was God. He was with God in the beginning. Through him all things were made; without him nothing was made that has been made. In him was life, and that life was the light of all people.

JOHN 1:1–4

Reflect On: John 1:1–4.
Praise God: For his all-powerful Word.
Offer Thanks: For Christ's words to you.
Confess: Any lack of faith in the Word of God.
Ask God: To increase your love of Scripture.

✑

I have a friend who is so attracted to numbers that she thinks of them as having distinct personality traits. Take the number six, for instance. A compulsive talker, six, she informs me, always dominates the weaker-minded seven, who does whatever six tells him to. The number eight, on the other hand, is hard to pin down. He's the creative, playful type, always chuckling over some private joke.

My friend's description of the antics, personalities, and various relationships among numbers is fascinating, especially to a math-challenged person like myself, who invariably prefers words to numbers. To me, words have always presented themselves in living color. For instance, I see the word "open" as white with a green tinge. "Can" is sea-green and "No" is a deep purple/blue. Clearly, both my friend and I are a little weird. But our different fascinations help explain why she grew up to become a statistician and I a writer.

Much as I love words, I also know that human words, in addition to being beautiful, can also be deceptive, treacherous, and empty. We can talk a blue streak without saying a single thing. By contrast, God's Word is "living and active. Sharper than any double-edged sword, it penetrates even to dividing soul and spirit, joints and marrow; it judges the thoughts and attitudes of the heart" (Hebrews 4:12). God's Word has the power not just to communicate his purpose but to accomplish whatever he intends. It never returns to him empty. When God speaks, things happen. Read the first page of Genesis if you doubt it:

And God *said*, "Let there be light," and there was light.
And God *said*, "Let the water under the sky be gathered to one place, and let dry ground appear." And it was so.
God *said*, "Let the land produce vegetation." And it was so.

The world was created by God *speaking* it into existence. Jesus, the Word of God, the second person of the Trinity, was thus present at the world's beginning. But the perfect world that God created was soon corrupted through sin. Jesus came to earth to recreate the world, restoring it to God's original purpose. Miracles happened when he spoke. Storms ceased, the lame walked, people were delivered from demons, and the dead were raised. These were signs that a world deformed by sin was being reshaped by God's all-powerful Word. Listen to the record of the Gospels:

Jesus *said* to the waves, "Quiet! Be still!" Then the wind died down and it was completely calm.
Jesus *said* to the paralytic, "Get up, take your mat and go home." And the man got up and went home.
Jesus *rebuked* the evil spirit. "You deaf and mute spirit," he said, "I *command* you, come out of him and never enter him again." The spirit shrieked, convulsed him violently and came out.
Jesus *called* in a loud voice, "Lazarus, come out!" The dead man came out.

Jesus is still speaking, still reshaping the world, one person at a time. As his followers, we need to study and pray over his words. We need to listen carefully and expectantly for his voice. Try spending ten to fifteen minutes today meditating on John 1:1–4 and Genesis 1:1–5. May God's Spirit nourish your mind and heart as you listen for the voice of the Lord.

Wednesday

PRAYING THE NAME

Very truly I tell you, whoever hears my word and believes him who sent me has eternal life and will not be judged but has crossed over from death to life. Very truly I tell you, a time is coming and has now come when the dead will hear the voice of the Son of God and those who hear will live. For as the Father has life in himself, so he has granted the Son to have life in himself.

JOHN 5:24–26

Let the word of Christ dwell in you richly.

COLOSSIANS 3:16

Reflect On: John 5:24–26.
Praise God: For opening your ears to his Word.
Offer Thanks: For all the ways God has spoken through Jesus.
Confess: Any heedlessness of God's Word.
Ask God: To help you hide his Word in your heart.

I have never been good at memorizing Scripture. I had a friend who used to commit entire books of the Bible to memory while I struggled to memorize one short psalm. Once, when I was thirty-five, I made the mistake of remarking to an elderly woman that I was too old to memorize Scripture. "Nonsense," was her quick comeback. "I didn't start memorizing Bible passages until I was sixty-five." Since she knew an awful lot of them by heart, my handy excuse was pretty quickly demolished.

Surely even the least mnemonically gifted among us (that's me) could memorize a few brief Scripture passages, committing to memory some of the most powerful words ever spoken. Here's one to start with: "A time is coming and has now come when the dead will hear the voice of the Son of God and those who hear will live" (John 5:25).

This assurance is given to us by Jesus, the last, most perfect Word of God, who tells us that if you hear his Word and believe in the Father who sent him, there is nothing you cannot survive—no tragedy, financial crisis, emotional problem, illness, betrayal, disappointment, or accident. Nothing can ever tear you away from Christ. Even death, the most final of all calamities, cannot destroy your hope, because Jesus, the all-powerful Word of God, assures you that he will call you out of your grave. His is the voice that spoke the world into being, that healed the sick and delivered those in torment. And his is the voice that you will certainly hear on the very last day calling your name.

Today, as you ponder this promise of Jesus, try committing John 5:24–26 to memory. As you do, pray for faith and for the grace to let the truth sink in so that it becomes a source of joy, strengthening you in the midst of life's ever-present challenges.

Thursday

PRAYING THE NAME

The Word became flesh and made his dwelling among us. We have seen his glory, the glory of the One and Only, who came from the Father, full of grace and truth.

JOHN 1:14

And we also thank God continually because, when you received the word of God, which you heard from us, you accepted it not as the word of men, but as it actually is, the word of God, which is at work in you who believe.

1 THESSALONIANS 2:13

Reflect On: John 1:14 and 1 Thessalonians 2:13.
Praise God: For his living, active Word.
Offer Thanks: For the freedom to read and study the Bible.
Confess: Any negligence of God's Word.
Ask God: To make you hungry for his Word.

I remember my first Bible. I loved running my fingers across the grain of its rich, red leather binding, elegantly stamped in gold, with lavish end papers featuring a Renaissance portrait of Jesus. Inside the words of Christ were printed in the requisite red ink on thin, gilded pages. Though I prized it as the most beautiful book I had ever seen, I don't remember reading it — not ever. It seemed too massive, too otherworldly, and much too difficult. It never occurred to me that God could speak to me through this ancient, holy book.

Years later I began to read it, hungry for a sense of God's presence in my life. Since then I have read through the Bible several times. To be honest, I haven't found it easy or always pleasant. Often I have had to force myself through the long genealogies and the endless records of wars and disasters. But imperfect as my efforts have been, I have been richly rewarded. The more I read, the more I see. Connections get made. Lights go on. God speaks. Often, when I am facing some difficult or puzzling situation, God reminds me of a Scripture passage I have read. And it makes all the difference — like when I adopted my first child.

I remember sitting in a hotel room in China, holding my daughter on my lap as I explored every inch of her nine-month-old body. That's when I felt the lump. It was small and hard and lodged in the back of her neck. What was this? A tumor? I wanted to rush her home to our pediatrician for a battery of tests, but we couldn't leave China until the adoption was complete. And that would take ten more days. So I prayed, asking God to heal my baby and deal with my anxiety.

Instantly, I recalled words Jesus had spoken to his disciples: "Which of you, if his son asks for bread, will give him a stone? Or if he asks for a fish, will give him a snake? If you, then, though you are evil, know how to give good gifts to your children, how much more will your Father in heaven give good gifts to those who ask him!" (Matthew 7:9–11). I felt reassured, as though God were telling me that my daughter was going to be all right. He had not given me a stone — a burden of grief I could not carry — but a child, who would live and grow. When our pediatrician finally did examine her, he merely diagnosed a swollen lymph node, a common enough occurrence in young children fighting an infection. Since then, through all the ups and downs that inevitably accompany parenthood, I have held on to this Scripture, sometimes as though for dear life.

Then came my second child. It wasn't immediately apparent that something was wrong. But my little girl didn't take her first step until she was two. And she barely spoke at three. Then the diagnosis: mild cerebral palsy and a severe speech disorder. Her progress was painstaking and slow, especially when it came to speech. In the midst of a season of discouragement, God spoke to me through the words of the apostle Paul: "And let us not be weary in well doing: for in due season we shall reap, if we faint not" (Galatians 6:9 KJV). I love that part about not fainting because it captured how I felt, as though I might faint, as though I wasn't up to the task, as though I couldn't be the mother she needed me to be. Now I hold on to this Scripture, letting it motivate me while believing that a harvest of good things will someday come from the efforts I am making now to help my daughter as she struggles to overcome her disability. Whenever I start to feel discouraged, I aim that passage like a laser gun straight at my fears.

These kinds of experiences have convinced me of the importance of reading Scripture whether I feel like it or not. Opening myself to God's Word is a way of investing myself in the conversation God wants to have with me. It is a way of clearing the channel for communication, of giving him room to speak while I listen.

I believe that God wants to speak to every one of his children through the words of Scripture. If you have been letting your Bible languish on the shelf, maybe it's time to start reading it on a regular basis. If you don't own a Bible, consider buying a modern translation with study notes that will help you understand the text. And as you read, pray. Ask Jesus, the Word made flesh, to communicate his heart and mind to you. He is eager to speak. Be eager to listen. Decide to base your life on his Word. Lean all your weight on it. It will hold you, nourish you, challenge you, and change you. If you let it, God's Word will become flesh in you.

PROMISES ASSOCIATED WITH HIS NAME

Imagine a family in which the people are incapable of communicating at any level — not a touch, a glance, or a word ever passes between them. Wouldn't they cease to be a family? How would the parents care for their children or for each other? How would the children know they were loved? Each child would be left alone to figure out how to live in this world.

We can be thankful that God has not left us orphans but that he has brought us into his own family, communicating his love in the most eloquent and powerful way possible through Jesus, the Word made flesh. Through his actions and his words, Jesus is the perfect expression of the Father's love. As members of God's family, we need to hear his Word and obey it just as children in a human family need to listen to and obey their parents. Without obedience, we become like fools who look in a mirror and then forget what they look like, don't remember whom they belong to. Obedience shapes us into the likeness of Jesus, the Word, so that we can experience the full blessing of being part of God's family.

Promises in Scripture

As Jesus was saying these things, a woman in the crowd called out, "Blessed is the mother who gave you birth and nursed you."

He replied, "Blessed rather are those who hear the word of God and obey it."

LUKE 11:27–28

Do not merely listen to the word, and so deceive yourselves. Do what it says. Those who listen to the word but do not do what it says are like people who look at their faces in a mirror and, after looking at themselves, go away and immediately forget what they look like. But those who look intently into the perfect law that gives freedom and continue in it — not forgetting what they have heard but doing it — they will be blessed in what they do.

JAMES 1:22–25

Continued Prayer and Praise

Live in obedience to God's Word. (Deuteronomy 30:14)

Let God's Word be your light in the darkness. (Psalm 119:105)

Remember that God's Word will not return to him empty. (Isaiah 55:10–11)

Be hungry for the Word. (Matthew 4:1–4)

Never be ashamed of Christ's words. (Mark 8:38)

Remember that Christ's words will never pass away. (Mark 13:31)

Let the seed of God's Word grow in your heart. (Luke 8:4–15)

Preach the Word, in season and out of season. (2 Timothy 4:1–5)

Listen to Jesus. (Hebrews 1:1–4)

Envision the final triumph of the Word. (Revelation 19:11–15)

12

CORNERSTONE, CAPSTONE

ἀκρογωνιαῖος λίθος

AKROGONIAIOS LITHOS

The Name

Stones were used for building altars, homes, palaces, and temples. When "capstone" or "cornerstone" is mentioned in the Bible, it refers to a particularly important stone that held two rows of stones together in a corner, one that stabilized the structure at the foundation, or one that formed the keystone over an arch or at the top of a roof parapet. In order to hold the structure together, the cornerstone had to be perfectly fitted for the task, both strong and well shaped. A flawed or poorly cut stone would compromise the building's integrity.

Jesus is the Cornerstone or Capstone to which we are joined as living stones. Together we form a spiritual house in which God can dwell. As the foundation stone on which God is building his kingdom, Jesus is strong enough to hold everything together. He is also the fitting conclusion to all God's work. When you pray to him as the Cornerstone, you are praying to the One on whom you can base your life.

Key Scripture

Jesus looked directly at them and asked, "Then what is the meaning of that which is written:

> " 'The stone the builders rejected
> has become the capstone '?"

LUKE 20:17

Monday

HIS NAME REVEALED

He went on to tell the people this parable: "A man planted a vineyard, rented it to some farmers and went away for a long time. At harvest time he sent a servant to the tenants so they would give him some of the fruit of the vineyard. But the tenants beat him and sent him away empty-handed. He sent another servant, but that one also they beat and treated shamefully and sent away empty-handed. He sent still a third, and they wounded him and threw him out.

"Then the owner of the vineyard said, 'What shall I do? I will send my son, whom I love; perhaps they will respect him.'

"But when the tenants saw him, they talked the matter over. 'This is the heir,' they said. 'Let's kill him, and the inheritance will be ours.' So they threw him out of the vineyard and killed him.

"What then will the owner of the vineyard do to them? He will come and kill those tenants and give the vineyard to others."

When the people heard this, they said, "May this never be!"

Jesus looked directly at them and asked, "Then what is the meaning of that which is written:

> " 'The stone the builders rejected
> has become the capstone '?

"Everyone who falls on that stone will be broken to pieces, but he on whom it falls will be crushed."

The teachers of the law and the chief priests looked for a way to arrest him immediately, because they knew he had spoken this parable against them. But they were afraid of the people.

LUKE 20:9–19

Lord, Jesus, you are the cornerstone on which God is building. I pray that you will help me to build my life on you in a way that makes me a vital, living stone, so that I may be part of God's dwelling place on earth.

Understanding the Name

When Jesus quoted the passage from Psalm 118:22, referring to the stone the builders rejected, he was pointing to his rejection by the Jewish nation and its leaders. But despite their rejection, God's purposes could not be thwarted. In fact, the master builder would make Jesus, through his death and resurrection, the *Akrogoniaios Lithos* (ah-kro-go-nee-EYE-os LI-thos), capstone or cornerstone, on which he would build. The New Testament portrays the whole community of believers as a holy temple in which God dwells. To those who reject Jesus and his saving message, he will be not a cornerstone but a stone of stumbling, because rejection of God's chosen one inevitably brings judgment.

As an interesting side note, the royal name was often inscribed on the cornerstone, and among the ancient Canaanites before the time of Joshua, the laying of the foundation stone was often accompanied by human sacrifice. Tragically, a number of skeletons, especially those of small babies in earthen jars, have been found at various sites.

Studying the Name

1. Why do you think Jesus' comments about "the stone the builders rejected" immediately follows the parable of the vineyard?
2. What do you think it means to build your life on Jesus as the Cornerstone?
3. What does it mean that Jesus is a stone that people will fall on?

Tuesday

PRAYING THE NAME

"Then the owner of the vineyard said, 'What shall I do? I will send my son, whom I love; perhaps they will respect him.'

"But when the tenants saw him, they talked the matter over. 'This is the heir,' they said. 'Let's kill him, and the inheritance will be ours.' So they threw him out of the vineyard and killed him.

"What then will the owner of the vineyard do to them? He will come and kill those tenants and give the vineyard to others."

When the people heard this, they said, "May this never be!"

Jesus looked directly at them and asked, "Then what is the meaning of that which is written:

" 'The stone the builders rejected
has become the capstone'?

"Everyone who falls on that stone will be broken to pieces, but he on whom it falls will be crushed."

LUKE 20:13–18

What then shall we say? That the Gentiles, who did not pursue righteousness, have obtained it, a righteousness that is by faith; but Israel, who pursued a law of righteousness, has not attained it. Why not? Because they pursued it not by faith but as if it were by works. They stumbled over the "stumbling stone."

ROMANS 9:30–32

Reflect On: Luke 20:9–19 and Romans 9:30–32.

Praise God: Whose plans and purposes endure forever.

Offer Thanks: That God did not give up on us.

Confess: Any tendency to water down the gospel or reduce it to a list of dos and don'ts.

Ask God: To renew your faith in Jesus.

Imagine that you own a large and prosperous vineyard. You decide to enlist tenant farmers to work the land in exchange for a portion of the harvest. That way you can all prosper together. The sloping, well-drained fields produce a fine crop of grapes year after year. Trouble is, you have yet to see even one grape. The three men you sent to collect your portion of the harvest have returned one after the other, empty-handed. Worse yet, they still bear the scars of their beatings.

But you do not give up easily. So you risk one more man. This time you send the best man you have, the one closest to your heart. If he can't talk sense into those surly, stiff-necked tenant farmers, no one can. After all, he is your son. They should listen to him as though they were listening to you. But instead of listening, the farmers do the unthinkable. They murder the son you love in hopes of claiming the vineyard as their own.

Shortly after September 11, 2001, the president of the United States accused Islamic terrorists of hijacking not just American planes but the religion of Islam itself, distorting it to serve their purposes. Two thousand years earlier, Jesus made a similar claim, using radically different images, but ones that would instantly connect with his audience. Jesus' story echoed a stinging prophecy from Isaiah:

> The vineyard of the LORD Almighty
>   is the house of Israel,
> and the people of Judah
>   are the vines he delighted in.
> And he looked for justice, but saw bloodshed;
>   for righteousness, but heard cries of distress. . . .
> The LORD Almighty has declared in my hearing:
> "Surely the great houses will become desolate,
>   the fine mansions left without occupants."
>
> ISAIAH 5:7, 9

Jesus was pointing a finger straight at the chief priests and teachers of the law, who had hijacked the faith and led God's people astray through their hypocritical behavior and legalistic teachings. Instead of acting as the servant leaders they were supposed to be, they had created a form of religion that advanced not God's agenda but their own. In his love and mercy, God had already sent multiple prophets to call them back, but they rejected each one. In a final, grand act of mercy, God sent his Son. But they hated him, seeing not a Savior, but only someone who threatened their power, who undermined their control. Thus, Jesus became for them the threat they feared.

Fully aware of their desire to kill him, Jesus provoked them further by quoting the words of Psalm 118:22: "The stone the builders rejected has become the capstone." And then, "Everyone who falls on the stone will be broken to pieces" (Luke 20:18). He himself was the cornerstone of what God was doing in the world. But he was also a stone of stumbling, a rock of offense for those who failed to believe in him. For a time he would seem to be the one who would be broken, but his brokenness would result in triumph. And sooner or later everyone who opposed him would be brought to ruin.

The same is true today. Many forces are at work in the world and within our own fallen natures to twist and distort the gospel. There are those who would try to hijack it for their own purposes, using it for a bully pulpit, making of it a caricature that is easily rejected by the rest of the world, or watering it down to make it more palatable. How sad when Christians themselves reduce the faith to a set of rules and regulations, conforming outwardly to religious conventions while their hearts are filled with unbelief. How sad when believers fail to preach the whole gospel because they fear offending someone.

If we really believe that we have needed saving and that we have been saved, our lives should say so, because faith has led a revolution in our souls. Of all people we have the most to be grateful for, the most to be excited about, the most to celebrate, for Christ, the cornerstone on which God is building up his kingdom, is leading his church. He is our rock forever.

PRAYING THE NAME

> The LORD Almighty is the one you are to regard as holy,
>   he is the one you are to fear,
>   he is the one you are to dread,
> and he will be a sanctuary;
>   but for both houses of Israel he will be
> a stone that causes men to stumble
>   and a rock that makes them fall.
> And for the people of Jerusalem he will be
>   a trap and a snare.
>
> ISAIAH 8:13–14

Jesus left the temple and was walking away when his disciples came up to him to call his attention to its buildings. "Do you see all these things?" he asked. "I tell you the truth, not one stone here will be left on another; every one will be thrown down."

MATTHEW 24:1–2

Reflect On: Isaiah 8:13–14 and Matthew 24:1–2.

Praise God: For dwelling with us.

Offer Thanks: That God is a refuge for you.

Confess: Any patterns of self-reliance that keep you from relying on God.

Ask God: For the grace to be a refuge for others.

                ∽

I remember listening to a call-in radio program a few days after the September 11 attacks on New York and Washington. A woman residing in Southern California called to say that she had decided to move to a remote region in Canada where she hoped her family would be safe. It seemed an extreme response, even more extreme than shelling out a few hundred dollars for a gas mask, as some people were doing at the time. I thought back to the bomb shelter that childhood friends had built during the Cold War when people feared Russia would launch a nuclear attack on the United States. Tucked into the side of a hill and stocked with provisions, it made a neat little refuge from tornadoes, if not from atomic bombs.

Every age and place seems to hold its share of danger and trouble. Who hasn't at one time or other looked for refuge, for a place in which to shelter until danger passes? For the Israelites the Jerusalem temple seemed to be just such a place. After all, it was where God had placed his name, where he had chosen to dwell. Hadn't God long ago promised that he himself would be a sanctuary to Israel?

But the promises of God swing one way for the faithful and another for the faithless. As Isaiah had prophesied, God would be a sanctuary for those who followed him but a stone of stumbling for those who did not. Jesus himself wept over Jerusalem, foreseeing a time when it would be overrun by its enemies, when one stone would not stand upon another, because its people had failed to recognize God's coming to them.

In AD 30 Jesus predicted the temple's destruction. His words must have sounded ridiculous to those accustomed to worshiping in such a magnificent structure. How could God not be pleased with it? After all, it had taken forty-six years to build, and the work was still not complete. Herod had spared no expense on the massive building project. Constructed of white marble, its eastern front was covered with plates of gold that reflected the rays of the rising sun. Yet forty years after Jesus' prediction, the temple was destroyed. The Romans burned it to the ground when they overran Jerusalem in AD 70, and the six thousand people who had sought refuge inside the temple perished as well. It has never been rebuilt.

The New Testament clearly presents Jesus as the cornerstone of the new and living temple that God is building. As Christ's followers, we are living stones, integral parts of a structure that is being built to last forever. Together we form the temple in which God dwells. Joined to Christ as the cornerstone and to our brothers and sisters, we are living stones cemented together by bonds of faith. In this way, we both find and become a place of refuge.

If this is God's intention, what then is our experience? Do we draw strength and hope from Christ and from those who love him, standing firm in our faith when life is difficult? Or do we revert to old habits and patterns of behavior that make it clear we are pinning our hopes, not on God, but on our relationships, our sense of prosperity, our success? What if the stock market crashes next week? What if a spouse is diagnosed with a chronic and debilitating illness? What if a child dies? Where will we find refuge when everything in this world collapses? Let's ask God today to give us a vision for what it means both to take refuge in him and to become a refuge for others as we link our lives to his in faith.

Thursday

PRAYING THE NAME

Unless the LORD builds the house,
its builders labor in vain.

PSALM 127:1

Therefore everyone who hears these words of mine and puts them into prac-
tice is like a wise man who built his house on the rock. The rain came down,
the streams rose, and the winds blew and beat against that house; yet it did
not fall, because it had its foundation on the rock. But everyone who hears
these words of mine and does not put them into practice is like a foolish man
who built his house on sand. The rain came down, the streams rose, and the
winds blew and beat against that house, and it fell with a great crash.

MATTHEW 7:24–27

Reflect On: Matthew 7:24–27.
Praise God: Because he cannot be shaken.
Offer Thanks: For all the ways Christ has steadied you in times of
               trouble.
Confess: Any fear you may have about the future.
Ask God: To increase your confidence in his love and care.

A few years ago I signed up for a calculus course. I had little choice
in the matter since it was a prerequisite for an MBA program I was
pursuing at the time. Worse yet, before I took calculus, I had to take
trigonometry; and before I took trigonometry, I had to take Algebra
II. I began to realize that studying math has a lot in common with
building pyramids. You have to lay the foundation precisely, proceed-
ing step by step. If you don't understand concepts sequentially, in their
proper order, you won't be able to proceed to the next level. There's no
fudging, no skipping things. It's not like taking a literature course. You

can enjoy reading Jane Austen, for instance, regardless of whether you have ever read Shakespeare. In mathematics as in pyramid building, all the blocks have to be carefully laid out, one on top of the other in proper alignment.

This principle of building a strong foundation underlies much of life. Build your house on a sandy cliff and it may one day come toppling down. Build your marriage on distorted expectations and it may not last. Build your investments on faulty information and they may soon amount to nothing. The truth is, we often do not know how sound anything is until it is tested by various kinds of stress and trouble. But how on earth can we withstand all the troubles that may assail us in a lifetime? We can't possibly plan for every contingency — or can we?

Jesus tells us there is a way. But it is not a way that squares with our own intuition about how the world works. It has nothing to do with building on our personal strengths, insights, or efforts. Self-reliance isn't a strategy for ultimate success. Nor can we build on the institutions of this world, however good they might be — marriage, family, higher education, work. If we want to build something that in the end will last, there is only one way. Forsake ourselves and follow Christ. We put our faith in Jesus and express that faith daily through what Eugene Peterson has called (borrowing a phrase from the philosopher Nietzsche) "a long obedience in the same direction." That's how our lives become joined to the One who is the tested cornerstone, perfectly shaped, solid, and strong.

Friends of mine lived on the top floor of a high rise in Mexico City. In the early morning of September 19, 1985, they awoke to a massive earthquake (8.1 on the Richter scale). Their building swayed crazily, like a length of wire that had been twanged by a giant hand. Though more than eight hundred buildings — hospitals, hotels, schools, businesses — collapsed, killing more than ten thousand people, their building held. They were fortunate, blessed in an extraordinary way.

When I think of how God holds us when we build our lives on his Son, I think of that building. There will be times when we will feel shaken to the core, perhaps even terrified as my friends were. Belonging to Jesus does not make us immune to tragedy. But basing our lives on him through faith will enable us to stand rather than collapse in the face of unbearable pressure. Our standing will have nothing to do with luck but everything to do with where we are standing—on the cornerstone, tested and true.

Ask yourself today whether you need to shift your priorities in order to stand more squarely with Christ. As you let God's Spirit probe your heart, take up the words to the old hymn "How Firm a Foundation":

> *How firm a foundation, ye saints of the Lord,*
> *Is laid for your faith in his excellent word!*
> *What more can he say than to you he hath said,*
> *You, who unto Jesus for refuge have fled?*
>
> *Fear not, I am with thee, O be not dismayed,*
> *For I am thy God and will still give thee aid;*
> *I'll strengthen and help thee, and cause thee to stand*
> *Upheld by my righteous, omnipotent hand.*
>
> *The soul that on Jesus has leaned for repose,*
> *I will not, I will not desert to its foes;*
> *That soul, though all hell should endeavor to shake,*
> *I'll never, no never, no never forsake.*

Friday

PROMISES ASSOCIATED WITH HIS NAME

When I was four, I spent much of my time wondering how things worked. I tried hard to understand, for instance, how people made footprints in cement. An older, wiser child assured me it wasn't that difficult. You only had to press your foot into the cement when it was wet. So I poured water on the sidewalk, stamped hard on the cement, and got nothing for my efforts but a sore foot.

In a way the truth about salvation isn't that difficult either, though we often misunderstand it to our hurt. We cannot quite believe that the good news is as good as it is. So we try to add to it. Instead of trusting in Christ's forgiveness when we repent, we beat ourselves up until enough time has elapsed for us to finally *feel* forgiven. Or we let worry eat away at our faith because we think that more depends on us than depends on Christ. Our misguided notions produce nothing but a sore heart.

Let's get it straight today. The cornerstone of our faith is this: If we confess with our mouths, "Jesus is Lord," and believe in our hearts that God raised him from the dead, we will be saved.

Promises in Scripture

So this is what the Sovereign LORD says:

"See, I lay a stone in Zion,
    a tested stone,
a precious cornerstone for a sure foundation;
    the one who trusts will never be dismayed."

ISAIAH 28:16

If you confess with your mouth, "Jesus is Lord," and believe in your heart that God raised him from the dead, you will be saved.... "Everyone who calls on the name of the Lord will be saved."

ROMANS 10:9, 13

Continued Prayer and Praise

Rely on the Lord, who is your rock and refuge. (Psalm 18:2)

Praise Jesus, who has become the cornerstone. (John 2:13–20)

Recall that there is only one foundation. (1 Corinthians 3:11)

Remember that you are no longer your own. You are a living stone, being built into a spiritual house. (1 Peter 2:4–9)

Repent so that times of refreshing may come from the Lord. (Acts 3:1–4:12)

Pray for God's chosen people to believe in his Son. (Luke 19:41–44)

13

BRIGHT MORNING STAR

ἀστὴρ λαμπρὸς πρωϊνός
ASTER LAMPROS PROINOS

The Name

In the last chapter of the book of Revelation, Jesus calls himself the "bright Morning Star." In ancient times, the morning star was thought of as a herald of the new day, signaling the dawn of hope and joy. The brightest object in the sky aside from the sun and moon, it is a fitting type for Christ, who ushers in a new day for the entire world. When you call on Jesus, the Bright Morning Star, you are calling on the One from whom all darkness flees.

Key Scripture

"I am the Root and the Offspring of David, and the bright Morning Star."

REVELATION 22:16

HIS NAME REVEALED

I see him, but not now;
I behold him, but not near.
A star will come out of Jacob;
a scepter will rise out of Israel.

NUMBERS 24:17

"Behold, I am coming soon! My reward is with me, and I will give to everyone according to what he has done. I am the Alpha and the Omega, the First and the Last, the Beginning and the End.

"Blessed are those who wash their robes, that they may have the right to the tree of life and may go through the gates into the city. Outside are the dogs, those who practice magic arts, the sexually immoral, the murderers, the idolaters and everyone who loves and practices falsehood.

"I, Jesus, have sent my angel to give you this testimony for the churches. I am the Root and the Offspring of David, and the bright Morning Star."

REVELATION 22:12–16

Lord, you are the brightest of all stars. With your light, chase away the world's darkness and the shadows that linger in my life. Help me to await your coming with hope and confidence and to long eagerly for the new day that will never end, the day in which your kingdom will be finally and fully established.

Understanding the Name

What the Bible refers to as the morning star is actually the planet Venus, known since prehistoric times. As the second planet from the sun, it is also one of the hottest. A relatively young planet, it is Earth's closest neighbor and is often called our sister planet. Because of its appearance in the eastern sky before dawn, it was thought of as the harbinger of sunrise. The title *Aster Lampros Proinos* (as-TAIR lam-PROS pro-i-NOS) presents a powerful and beautiful image of the One who is also known as "the light of the world."

Studying the Name

1. Jesus says that he is coming soon. In what ways do you think his second coming will differ from his first?

2. Describe your attitude toward the second coming—fear, doubt, hope, joy? Why do you feel the way you do?

3. What kinds of people is Jesus describing in the passage from Revelation?

Tuesday

PRAYING THE NAME

After Jesus was born in Bethlehem in Judea, during the time of King Herod, Magi from the east came to Jerusalem and asked, "Where is the one who has been born king of the Jews? We saw his star in the east and have come to worship him."

MATTHEW 2:1–2

"I, Jesus, have sent my angel to give you this testimony for the churches. I am the Root and the Offspring of David, and the bright Morning Star."

REVELATION 22:16

Reflect On: Matthew 2:1–12 and Revelation 22:16.
Praise God: For shining his light into our world.
Offer Thanks: For the ways God has shed his light on you.
Confess: Any hidden sins, which fester in the darkness.
Ask God: To make you eager for the new life he gives you.

"Light therapy" is the treatment of choice for a depressive condition called Seasonal Affective Disorder, commonly known as SAD. Though the diagnosis may sound trendy, anyone who lives in a climate that gets only a little winter sunlight is not likely to doubt it. Many of us would be the first to patronize a restaurant like the one in Helsinki, Finland, that from October to March serves bright light with breakfast. Every morning the Café Engel places light boxes throughout the restaurant so that, along with Danish and coffee, patrons can get their fix of light.

It seems obvious that our bodies are wired for light. Without enough of it, some of us are prone to weight gain, irritability, anxiety, sleeplessness, and stress. But it's not only our bodies that suffer in the darkness. Our souls long for the light as well. Perhaps that's why the story of Jesus is associated with light from start to finish.

Remember the brilliant star that led Magi from the east to the child Jesus in Bethlehem? Some scholars think the "star" was the light produced by the conjunction of Jupiter and Saturn, which happened three times in 7 BC. Such a celestial event would have been of particular interest at that time because Jupiter was commonly associated with kingly rule and Saturn with the Jewish people. To the Magi, the star of Bethlehem was a sign that a glorious kingdom was about to dawn.

So the life of Jesus begins with a "star," and you can say that it also ends with a star, because in the last chapter of the Bible the risen Lord calls himself the "bright Morning Star," a reference to the planet Venus, the brightest object in the predawn sky except for the moon — the sure sign that dawn will soon break over the world.

Two thousand years later, we can echo the words of the Magi concerning the newborn king: "We have seen his star when it rose and have come to worship him" (Matthew 2:2). Because of Jesus, a new day, bright with promise, has dawned on the entire world. Or, to put it another way, Jesus is the most powerful light therapy ever invented. He is the One who destroys our darkness by the light of his presence.

This week, try imprinting this name on your heart by choosing a day to rise early. As you watch the sun come up, you may even spot Venus rising in the east. In those predawn moments, praise the risen Christ, the Bright Morning Star, who has come to shine his light on you.

Wednesday

PRAYING THE NAME

I see him, but not now;
I behold him, but not near.
A star will come out of Jacob;
a scepter will rise out of Israel.

NUMBERS 24:17

He [Jesus] replied, "When evening comes, you say, 'It will be fair weather, for the sky is red,' and in the morning, 'Today it will be stormy, for the sky is red and overcast.' You know how to interpret the appearance of the sky, but you cannot interpret the signs of the times."

MATTHEW 16:2–3

Reflect On: Numbers 24:17 and Matthew 16:2–3.
Praise God: For giving us signs of his presence.
Offer Thanks: For all the ways God has guided you.
Confess: Any confusion that comes from taking your eyes off Jesus.
Ask God: To help you stay the course by fixing your eyes on him.

Have you ever wondered how ancient mariners were able to navigate without using a compass? One trick was to watch the flight paths of birds. Norse sailors knew that a seabird with a full beak was heading to its rookery on land while a bird with an empty beak was probably heading out to sea in search of food.

The Phoenicians, like many seafaring peoples that followed, were sophisticated enough to rely on the sky to get them through the treacherous seas. By watching the sun in its path, they knew whether they were heading east or west. They could also locate their position by gazing at the night sky, aware as they were that individual stars appear at fixed distances above the horizon at any particular location and time of year. Even today, satellites use a similar technique, marking their position in space by using "star trackers," instruments that use groups of stars as reference points.

But what does any of this have to do with Christ as the bright Morning Star? Remember that the morning star was considered the harbinger of dawn. When Jesus called himself the bright Morning Star, he was saying that he is our reference point—the sign that a new day is dawning on the world. Scripture tells us that this will be a day that will never end. Its light will be so steady, strong, and fixed that darkness will finally be banished from the earth. No more sin, no more sorrow, no more tears. If the first coming of Jesus is like the star that announces the dawn, his second coming will be like lightning, bringing the swift fulfillment of his kingdom.

Like the ancient mariners, who were able to read the skies, we need to remember to look up, to lift our faces to the Bright Morning Star, because it is only when Jesus is our reference point that we understand our true location in space and time.

Jesus faulted the religious leaders of his day for failing to interpret the signs of the times. Let us pray today for the grace to be like wise seafarers, joyful when they saw the morning star rising in the east.

Thursday

PRAYING THE NAME

We did not follow cleverly invented stories when we told you about the power and coming of our Lord Jesus Christ, but we were eyewitnesses of his majesty. For he received honor and glory from God the Father when the voice came to him from the Majestic Glory, saying, "This is my Son, whom I love; with him I am well pleased." We ourselves heard this voice that came from heaven when we were with him on the sacred mountain.

And we have the word of the prophets made more certain, and you will do well to pay attention to it, as to a light shining in a dark place, until the day dawns and the morning star rises in your hearts.

2 PETER 1:16 – 19

Reflect On: 2 Peter 1:16 – 19.
Praise God: For bringing you into the light of his presence.
Offer Thanks: Because God has a unique purpose for your life.
Confess: Any tendency to resist God's purpose because of fear
                or insecurity.
Ask God: To strengthen your hope.

I graduated from college during the midst of a recession. Armed with a combined degree in psychology, sociology, and political science, my resume didn't place me at the top of any employer's wish list. For the first few months, the best job I could find was at a small spring and wire factory serving the auto industry. The work was so monotonous I thought I would lose my mind. And I wasn't the only one. Every night when the bell rang, workers stampeded to the exits to see who could be the first out. Worse yet, the day started before sunrise and ended after sundown. The daily commute in the darkness seemed like a metaphor for my life. In contrast to friends who had landed promising jobs in San Francisco, Los Angeles, Washington, DC, New York, and Dallas, I felt futureless. Stuck in the Midwest with a meaningless job—I couldn't have scripted a more depressing start to the rest of my life.

Back then I didn't realize my life was a story God was writing. As far as I knew, I had grabbed the pen right out of his hand, refusing to believe he even existed. I was intent on enjoying life on my terms, determined to write my life the way I wanted it to be. Trouble was, I seemed to be suffering from writer's block.

Looking back, I realize God hadn't entirely let go of the script. He was using the shadows—my insecurity and fears—to drive me toward his light. When I finally admitted the truth—that I was headed nowhere unless God led the way—I felt my fear about the future suddenly lift. I didn't have to face it alone. God was real and he cared about me. Instead of being depressed, I felt excited. Life had a purpose—my life had a purpose. I had ideas about where I was headed and how to get there. In the midst of my conversion I felt suddenly transported from midwinter darkness to midsummer light.

William D. Watley, pastor of St. James A.M.E. Church in Newark, New Jersey, captures the kind of transformation I am talking about:

> We usually think of stars as nighttime luminaries, but the morning star announces the beginning of a new day. Who can testify that "since I met Jesus, it's a new day now"? I used to be bound by the devil, but since I met Jesus, it's a new day now. I used to have low self-esteem and was in a constant self-destruct mode, but since I met Jesus, it's a new day now. I've put down my blues guitar and picked up a tambourine of praise. It's a new day now. People and things that used to upset me don't bother me anymore. It's a new day now. Fear that used to paralyze me and guilt that used to beat me up have lost their hold upon me. It's a new day now. Glory, glory hallelujah since I laid my burden down—it's a new day now.

It is a new day for anyone who belongs to Christ. We still have problems. We still struggle. But good stories never develop without conflict. The truth is that Christ has set us on a new course, infusing our lives with his light, his presence, and his purpose.

Join me today in hailing Jesus, our Bright Morning Star, the one who fills us with expectation for a day that will never end, when darkness and death will be words we barely remember. Together, let us lift up our hands, throw away our caution, and shout aloud: "Glory, glory hallelujah! It's a new day now!"

Friday

PROMISES ASSOCIATED WITH HIS NAME

Some things never change. Imagine what bedtime must have been like a few thousand years ago. The children are snugly tucked into their corner of the cave. "Dad," a terrified voice cries out, "something's crawling up my leg!" "This bearskin is scratchy!" "Mom, she's hitting me. Make her stop!" And then the inevitable: "I'm thirsty. Can I have another drink of glog ... pleeeease!" The chorus continues until their weary-to-the-bone cave parents finally assert their authority and everything is quiet but for the rustle of a few bat wings.

Little people always seem to resist the ending of the day. Come to think of it, I sometimes stay up way past my bedtime. Maybe the problem is a primeval fear of the darkness — we resist closing our eyes lest we will never open them again. I wonder, did human beings panic when they saw the sun go down for the very first time? Were they heartened by a brilliant white light hanging low in the western sky? If so, they were probably gazing at the evening star, which just so happens to be the second planet from the sun. Yes, Venus is both the morning and the evening star, a steady brightness that reminds us of the One who lights up our darkness and chases away our gloom.

Promises in Scripture

> If I say, "Surely the darkness will hide me
>   and the light become night around me,"
> even the darkness will not be dark to you;
>   the night will shine like the day,
>   for darkness is as light to you.
>
> PSALM 139:11–12

> In that day the deaf will hear the words of the scroll,
>> and out of gloom and darkness
>> the eyes of the blind will see.
> Once more the humble will rejoice in the LORD;
>> the needy will rejoice in the Holy One of Israel.
>
> ISAIAH 29:18–19

Continued Prayer and Praise

Hold fast to Christ and he will give you the morning star.
(Revelation 2:26–28)

Remember that Jesus is the radiance of God's glory. (Hebrews 1:3)

Be glad because Jesus shines on those living in darkness. (Luke
1:67–79)

14

LION OF THE TRIBE OF JUDAH

אַרְיֵה לְמַטֵּה יְהוּדָה
λέων ἐκ τοῦ φυλῆς Ἰουδα

ARYEH LAMMATTEH YEHUDAH,
LEON EK TOU PHYLES IOUDA

The Name

Only once in the New Testament is Jesus described as a lion. The book of Revelation (named in part for what it reveals about Christ) portrays the risen Jesus as the only one worthy to open the scroll that contains the ultimate unfolding of God's purposes for the world. The apostle John perceived Jesus as both Lion and Lamb, who through his death and resurrection becomes the ultimate victor and conqueror. When you pray to Jesus as the Lion of the Tribe of Judah, you are praying to the One with the power to banish all fear, to the One who watches over you with his fierce protecting love. You are also praying to the One who is judge of the living and the dead.

Key Scripture

I wept and wept because no one was found who was worthy to open the scroll or look inside. Then one of the elders said to me, "Do not weep! See, the Lion of the tribe of Judah, the Root of David, has triumphed. He is able to open the scroll and its seven seals."

REVELATION 5:4–5

Monday

HIS NAME REVEALED

Judah, your brothers will praise you;
>   your hand will be on the neck of your enemies;
>   your father's sons will bow down to you.
You are a lion's cub, O Judah;
>   you return from the prey, my son.
Like a lion he crouches and lies down,
>   like a lioness—who dares to rouse him?
The scepter will not depart from Judah,
>   nor the ruler's staff from between his feet,
until he comes to whom it belongs
>   and the obedience of the nations is his.

GENESIS 49:8–10

Then I saw in the right hand of him who sat on the throne a scroll with writing on both sides and sealed with seven seals. And I saw a mighty angel proclaiming in a loud voice, "Who is worthy to break the seals and open the scroll?" But no one in heaven or on earth or under the earth could open the scroll or even look inside it. I wept and wept because no one was found who was worthy to open the scroll or look inside. Then one of the elders said to me, "Do not weep! See, the Lion of the tribe of Judah, the Root of David, has triumphed. He is able to open the scroll and its seven seals."

Then I saw a Lamb, looking as if it had been slain, standing in the center of the throne, encircled by the four living creatures and the elders. The Lamb had seven horns and seven eyes, which are the seven spirits of God sent out into all the earth. He went and took the scroll from the right hand of him who sat on the throne. And when he had taken it, the four living creatures and the twenty-four elders fell down before the Lamb. Each one had a harp and they were holding golden bowls full of incense, which are the prayers of God's people. And they sang a new song, saying:

"You are worthy to take the scroll
   and to open its seals,
because you were slain,
      and with your blood you purchased for God
      members of every tribe and language and people and nation.
You have made them to be a kingdom and priests to serve our God,
      and they will reign on the earth."

Revelation 5:1 – 10

Jesus, you are the Lion of the Tribe of Judah. Thank you for your fierce love and your strong protecting power. Come with your might and rule over us. Defeat your enemies and ours, extending your reign throughout the universe.

Understanding the Name

Today, lions can be found in sub-Saharan Africa and in northwest India. But in biblical times lions also roamed the region of the world now comprised of Israel, Syria, Iran, Iraq, Greece, and Turkey. From ancient times their images have graced thrones, palaces, gates, and temples, including the temple in Jerusalem. First Kings indicates that King Solomon's throne was adorned with twelve lions, symbolizing his greatness and power. And Ezekiel pictures the cherubim with lion's heads.

Throughout the Bible, the lion appears as a symbol of might, and it is hardly surprising that Israel's enemies are sometimes depicted as lions. In the New Testament, Peter calls the devil a roaring lion and warns believers that he is constantly on the prowl, looking for someone to devour.

Though lions are sometimes a symbol of evil, they are also used as symbols of God's people. Near the end of his life, the patriarch Jacob prayed a blessing over his twelve sons. When it came time to bless Judah, he compared him to a lion—hence the phrase "the Lion of the Tribe of Judah" (*Aryeh Lammatteh Yehudah* in Hebrew, pronounced ar-YEH la-mat-TEH ye-hou-DAH, or *Leon ek tou Phyles Iouda*, in Greek, pronounced LE-own ek tou fu-LAIS YOU-dah). Jacob's prediction that the scepter would not depart from Judah has been traditionally applied to the Messiah.

In the Hebrew Scriptures, Yahweh is sometimes depicted as a lion who roars in judgment against the nations and against his own faithless people. But he is also depicted as a mighty lion who fights fiercely on behalf of his people. Revelation depicts the risen Christ as the mightiest of all victors. He is the Lion of the Tribe of Judah, the one found worthy to open the scrolls of history, meaning that he is in charge of history and of how the world's destiny unfolds.

Studying the Name

1. Why do you think the book of Revelation portrays Jesus as both Lion and Lamb?

2. In the Bible "seven" is considered a sacred number, symbolizing perfection or completeness, while a "horn" symbolizes power. What does this say to you about how the Lamb is portrayed in Revelation 5?

3. How have you experienced and understood both the "lamblike" and "lionlike" nature of Jesus in your own life?

4. If you could choose one adjective to describe this passage from Revelation, what would it be and why? Would you call it bizarre, moving, perplexing, enlightening, or something else?

Tuesday

PRAYING THE NAME

> *When a trumpet sounds in a city,*
>> *do not the people tremble?*
> *When disaster comes to a city,*
>> *has not the* LORD *caused it?*
> *Surely the Sovereign* LORD *does nothing*
>> *without revealing his plan*
>> *to his servants the prophets.*
> *The lion has roared—*
>> *who will not fear?*
> *The Sovereign LORD has spoken—*
>> *who can but prophesy?*
>>> AMOS 3:6–8

Whoever believes in the Son has eternal life, but whoever rejects the Son will not see life, for God's wrath remains on him.

JOHN 3:36

Reflect On: Amos 3:6–8 and John 3:36.
Praise God: For his power and his mercy.
Offer Thanks: Because you are no longer under God's wrath.
Confess: Any tendency to take mercy for granted.
Ask God: To reveal his love and mercy to friends and family members.

When it comes to using nature imagery to describe God, it is not surprising that Scripture pictures him sometimes as a great and mighty Lion. This image seems fitting, in harmony with the notion of his majesty and power. But it also fits an image of God that many people have grown up with, picturing him as a scowling, angry, impossible-to-please God.

But where on earth did this idea of a grumpy, implacable, even frightening God come from? Is it simply a psychological projection, the result of the emotional distance many of us feel from the father figures in our lives, or is there more to it? I would argue that this image of God is constructed from multiple sources: from our own wounded and guilt-ridden psyches but also from demonic distortions of God's character and even from the Bible itself.

It is hardly surprising, given our fallen condition, that many of us instinctively sense the gap between who we are and who we were meant to be. From there it is not difficult to imagine a disappointed and disgruntled Creator scowling down at us from lofty heights. And then there's the devil, ever intent on distorting God's image, painting the Lord according to his own likeness—prone to divine temper tantrums.

But what about the Bible? Doesn't an honest reading of Scripture, particularly the Old Testament, reveal a God who is often spoken of in terms of his wrath? Isn't this the God described as a mighty Lion, roaring in judgment against the nations and against his own faithless people? Before we reach too hasty a conclusion about a supremely irritable Supreme Being, we should at least try to understand the meaning of the Greek word *orge*, translated as "wrath" in the New Testament. When Scripture talks about God's *orge*, it is not talking about the emotion of anger as we experience it. God's wrath is not primarily an emotion but rather a divine work of judgment that results when people adamantly resist him. God's wrath is his holy resistance to everything that is unholy.

Fortunately God has given us his Son to be both Lion and Lamb. As the Lamb he has taken the brunt of God's wrath, bearing it away so that we can experience God's mercy. But as the Lion he stands in judgment on all who persist in opposing God. As one commentator has pointed out, whoever accepts God's mercy is freed from his wrath. But whoever rejects mercy remains under wrath.

Today, as we contemplate Jesus, the Lion of the Tribe of Judah, let us thank him for going to the divine extreme of the cross in order to enable us to stop resisting the God who made us. Let us remember that we will be one day be judged according to how well we have responded to his grace, allowing it to shape our lives. Today, let us kneel before his majesty, determined to repent of our sins and to intercede for those who yet oppose him—family and friends who are still ignorant of his love and clueless of his mercy.

Wednesday

PRAYING THE NAME

The LORD will roar from Zion
  and thunder from Jerusalem;
  the earth and the sky will tremble.
But the LORD will be a refuge for his people,
  a stronghold for the people of Israel.

JOEL 3:16

And when Jesus had cried out again in a loud voice, he gave up his spirit.

At that moment the curtain of the temple was torn in two from top to bottom. The earth shook and the rocks split. The tombs broke open and the bodies of many holy people who had died were raised to life. They came out of the tombs, and after Jesus' resurrection they went into the holy city and appeared to many people.

When the centurion and those with him who were guarding Jesus saw the earthquake and all that had happened, they were terrified, and exclaimed, "Surely he was the Son of God!"

MATTHEW 27:50–54

Reflect On: Joel 3:16 and Matthew 27:50–54.
Praise God: For the greatest of all victories.
Offer Thanks: For the specific victories Christ has won in your life.
Confess: Any tendency to forget what God has done for you.
Ask God: To increase your hope.

The Lincoln Park Zoo in Chicago boasts a collection of some of "the world's rarest, most beautiful big cats, including African lions, Amur tigers, leopards from Asia and Africa, jaguars from South America and snow leopards from the Himalayas." I remember strolling through the lion house several years ago, feeling a bit depressed as I watched a magnificent lion pacing restlessly in his cage. He had forepaws powerful enough to break a zebra's back, eyes keen enough to hunt by starlight, hearing so sharp that he could detect prey as much as a mile away. All were useless to him in that caged environment. I stared and the huge maned head stared back at me. Then suddenly, this great, sad beast opened his mouth and let out the most earsplitting, heartrending sound imaginable. I was so startled that I nearly hit the vaulted ceiling above me, and no wonder since a lion's roar can be heard from five miles away!

The Gospels tell us that Jesus cried out just before his death. John's Gospel supplies the words: "It is finished!" These are not the last gasping words of a dying man. No, the Gospels say that Jesus cried out in a loud voice and then gave up his spirit! It was a shout of triumph, the raised fist of victory! Jesus had gone willingly to the cross, fulfilling every detail of the mission the Father had given him. Having won the struggle for our souls, it was as though the great Lion of Judah had roared from the cross itself.

No wonder the earth shook, the curtain of the temple ripped apart, and people rose up from their graves! Jesus, the conquering Lion, could be neither caged nor killed. Through his victory he has made a way for sin to be forgiven, for death's power to be rolled backward. By dying Christ shows us the lengths to which God's love will go. By rising he shows us the heights to which God's power will stretch.

The cry of Jesus on the cross still reverberates, still heralds the news of what God has done for us. As believers we need to shape our lives toward that victory, even when we feel defeated. We need to remember that no matter what or who is against us, God is still for us. The Lion of the Tribe of Judah is reigning from his throne, protecting us, purifying us, and using even the worst of circumstances to our advantage.

Today as we consider what Jesus has done, let us lift our voices in praise of the One who humbled himself and became obedient to death—even death on a cross! Let us remember that God has exalted him to the highest place of all and given him the name that is above every name, that at the name of Jesus every knee should bow, in heaven and on earth and under the earth, and every tongue confess that Jesus Christ is Lord, to the glory of God the Father. Amen.

PRAYING THE NAME

The wolf will live with the lamb,
    the leopard will lie down with the goat,
the calf and the lion and the yearling together;
    and a little child will lead them.
The cow will feed with the bear,
    their young will lie down together,
    and the lion will eat straw like the ox.
The infant will play near the hole of the cobra,
    and the young child put his hand into the viper's nest.
They will neither harm nor destroy
    on all my holy mountain,
for the earth will be full of the knowledge of the LORD
    as the waters cover the sea.

ISAIAH 11:6–9

Then one of the elders said to me, "Do not weep! See, the Lion of the tribe of Judah, the Root of David, has triumphed. He is able to open the scroll and its seven seals."

    Then I saw a Lamb, looking as if it had been slain, standing in the center of the throne, encircled by the four living creatures and the elders.

REVELATION 5:5–6

Reflect On: Isaiah 11:6–9 and Revelation 5:5–6.
Praise God: For revealing himself in Jesus.
Offer Thanks: For the Lord's lionlike care and protection.
Confess: Any dividedness in your heart toward doing God's will.
Ask God: To help you lean on his strength and protection.

How is it possible that children in the same family can grow into adults with diametrically opposing views of their family of origin? One brother recalls his parents as warm and caring while another characterizes them as cold and unloving. There could be multiple reasons why this is so, but certainly one explanation is that the brothers' temperaments and personalities have significantly shaped their experience of relationships within the family. The compliant older brother did whatever he could to please, while the stubborn younger brother responded to parental direction with obstinate resistance.

Something similar happens when it comes to our perceptions of God. Some people see him as a loving God full of mercy while others see him as cold and distant, harsh and punitive. To some degree our perception of him depends on our response to him. Will we love him, expressing our love through obedience, or will we hold him in contempt by disregarding his commandments and his intentions for our lives? Even in the best of us, our experience of God remains fractured and divided so that we sometimes experience him one way and sometimes another.

The preacher William Watley captures our various experiences of Jesus as both Lion and Lamb:

> Jesus as Lion and Lamb means that he has more than one way of approaching us and addressing our situation. When we have sinned and fallen short of God's glory, we don't need a lion of condemnation and judgment attacking us and ravaging our spirit. When we are already feeling like a nobody, we don't need a stern lion beating us up and making us feel worse. We need a gentle word from the Lord. We need a word of comfort and encouragement. We need the Lamb to speak tenderly and tell us, "Come to me, all you that are weary and are carrying heavy burdens, and I will give you rest" (Matthew 11:28). Justice says that we deserve a lion to slay us, but mercy says, "I'm going to send a lamb and let you know that you have another chance."
>
> But when we get comfortable with being miserable; when we start feeling so sorry for ourselves and are tempted to stay down; when we've been down so long that getting up doesn't even cross

our minds (or if it does, it seems like an impossibility), then we don't need a lamb comforting us in our misery. We need the Lion with power to pull us up....

As Lion and Lamb, Jesus understands our weaknesses but relates to our strength, and he loves us with all our contradictions.

I have always been drawn to Isaiah's portrait of a future era of perfect peace in which the whole earth will be joined together in harmony with God. Even nature's opposites—the lion and the lamb—will lie down together without a trace of fear or animosity. Think about it. No more sibling rivalry, no more arguments with your spouse, no more competition with coworkers, no more church splits, no more political infighting, no more crime, no more terrorist attacks or suicide bombings. The peace we experience will be profound, threading its way through every living thing. Even our various perceptions of God will be reconciled. The Lion God will lie down with the Lamb God, and we will experience not his fierce anger but his powerful safeguarding protection perfectly joined to his immense, sacrificial love.

Today as you seek God's face, praise him for his strength and ask him to reveal his lionlike love and his fierce, protecting care.

PROMISES ASSOCIATED WITH HIS NAME

Have you ever thought about how surprising God is? Wouldn't it be completely natural if Scripture were to cast him as some kind of superman, as a new and improved version of a human being? But Scripture isn't natural. It is a supernatural disclosure of God and his plans for us, one that would not have occurred to us in a million years. Who could have imagined God on a cross, who is a King and Servant, a Lion and a Lamb, a God whose justice is trumped by his mercy? Aren't you glad that God's ways are not your ways and that his thoughts are as far above yours as the heavens are above the earth? Today, as you meditate on the Lion of the Tribe of Judah, let him expand your notion of who he is and how he thinks about you. Begin by thanking him for calling you out of the anguish and exile of sin into his loving and merciful protection.

Promises in Scripture

> "I will not carry out my fierce anger,
>> nor will I turn and devastate Ephraim again.
> For I am God, and not a human being—
>> the Holy One among you.
>> I will not come against their cities.
> They will follow the LORD;
>> he will roar like a lion.
> When he roars,
>> his children will come trembling from the west.
> They will come trembling
>> like birds from Egypt,
>> like doves from Assyria.
> I will settle them in their homes,"
>> declares the LORD.

HOSEA 11:9–11

> *A king's rage is like the roar of a lion,*
> *but his favor is like dew on the grass.*
>
> PROVERBS 19:12

> *The wicked man flees though no one pursues,*
> *but the righteous are as bold as a lion.*
>
> PROVERBS 28:1

Continued Prayer and Praise

Recall his great power. (Psalm 106:8)

Remember that the Lord is a Lion who does battle for his people. (Isaiah 31:4–5)

15

LORD

κύριος

KYRIOS

The Name

Christianity's earliest confession of faith consisted of three short but incredibly powerful words: *Jesus is Lord!* The early Christians believed that the Father had placed Jesus, by virtue of his death and resurrection, at the apex of time and eternity—higher than any power or person in the universe. It is no wonder that Paul was "convinced that neither death nor life, neither angels nor demons, neither the present nor the future, nor any powers, neither height nor depth, nor anything else in all creation, will be able to separate us from the love of God that is in Christ Jesus our Lord" (Romans 8:38–39). Both those who love him and those who oppose him will one day call Jesus "Lord." In the end, even the devil will be forced to acknowledge him. As you bow your head in prayer before the sovereign Lord, remember that you are placing your life—the worst of your disappointments, the most protracted of your struggles, the wildest of your dreams—squarely in his hands. Knowing Jesus as Lord will lead you to a deeper experience of his presence and his power.

Key Scripture

> *Therefore God exalted him to the highest place*
> *and gave him the name that is above every name,*
> *that at the name of Jesus every knee should bow,*
> *in heaven and on earth and under the earth,*
> *and every tongue confess that Jesus Christ is Lord,*
> *to the glory of God the Father.*

PHILIPPIANS 2:9–11

HIS NAME REVEALED

Your attitude should be the same as that of Christ Jesus:

> Who, being in very nature God,
>   did not consider equality with God something to be grasped,
> but made himself nothing,
>   taking the very nature of a servant,
>   being made in human likeness.
> And being found in appearance as a man,
>   he humbled himself
>   and became obedient to death—even death on a cross!
> Therefore God exalted him to the highest place
>   and gave him the name that is above every name,
> that at the name of Jesus every knee should bow,
>   in heaven and on earth and under the earth,
> and every tongue confess that Jesus Christ is Lord,
>   to the glory of God the Father.

PHILIPPIANS 2:5–11

Lord, you emptied yourself so that I could be filled. You made yourself nothing so that I could be something. You descended to the lowest place so that I could be raised to the highest. Come and take all of me, leaving no part of me beyond your care, bereft of your grace, or remote from your purifying power. Spread the story of your mercy through the simple witness of my obedience, my Lord and my God. Amen.

Understanding the Name

The Greek word *Kyrios* (KU-ree-os) is used in the New Testament to refer to an owner, emperor, king, father, husband, or master. It can also translate three Hebrew names and titles of God: *Yahweh, Adonai,* and *Elohim.* When people addressed Jesus as *Kyrios* or "Lord" in the Gospels, they were often simply showing respect to him as a rabbi or teacher, addressing him as "sir" rather than acknowledging him as God. But after his death and resurrection, the title "Lord" began to be widely used by believers.

Remember the apostle Thomas, who at first doubted accounts of Christ's resurrection? When Jesus appeared to him after his death, Thomas instinctively responded with a confession of faith, saying: "My Lord and my God!" (John 20:28). Over time, the title "Lord" began to take on the characteristics of a name. As such, it clearly identifies Jesus with *Yahweh*, the covenant name of God in the Hebrew Scriptures. Of the 717 passages in which *kyrios* occurs in the New Testament, the majority are found in Luke's Gospel, the Acts of the Apostles, and Paul's writings.

Studying the Name

1. How does God's idea of greatness differ from the usual definition?

2. What do you think it means that every tongue will confess that Jesus Christ is Lord?

3. How have you experienced Jesus being Lord in your life?

PRAYING THE NAME

*To the L*ORD *your God belong the heavens, even the highest heavens, the earth and everything in it. Yet the L*ORD *set his affection on your forefathers and loved them, and he chose you, their descendants, above all the nations, as it is today. Circumcise your hearts, therefore, and do not be stiff-necked any longer. For the L*ORD *your God is God of gods and Lord of lords, the great God, mighty and awesome, who shows no partiality and accepts no bribes.*

DEUTERONOMY 10:14–17

Not everyone who says to me, "Lord, Lord," will enter the kingdom of heaven, but only those who do the will of my Father who is in heaven.

MATTHEW 7:21

Reflect On: Deuteronomy 10:14–17 and Matthew 7:21.
Praise God: Because he is the Lord of heaven and earth.
Offer Thanks: Because Christ has set his affection on you.
Confess: Any tendency to place yourself rather than Jesus at the center of the universe.
Ask God: To make you hungry for a deeper connection with Jesus, the Lord.

What body of water is fifty miles long, ten miles wide, and 1,300 feet deep? With the sun dancing across its waves, it looks refreshing, as though its vast watery depths must be teeming with life. But a year spent fishing in these waters wouldn't yield a single catch because nothing but a few bacteria live beneath the surface. Located at the lowest point on earth, the Salt Sea in southeastern Israel contains the highest concentration of minerals and salt of any body of water in existence, making it unsuitable for sustaining life. No wonder it is also known as the Dead Sea.

Our lives as Christians can sometimes devolve spiritually so that we feel we are living at the lowest point on earth. On the surface everything may look fine, but underneath we feel restless, bored, confused, and afraid. Not only are we not growing spiritually, our spiritual lives seem to be shriveling, growing smaller not larger. Where is the power we once experienced? What happened to the sense of purpose we had? What about the joy and the wonder that comes from a living, vibrant relationship with the Lord?

Though there can be various reasons for feeling this way, surely a primary one has to do with whether we are vitally connected with the source of love and power. Try using a power tool with a faulty plug. Unless the electricity is flowing freely through the wire, the tool will be useless. It's like that in our relationship with Christ. But instead of an electrical cord, his power flows along the lines of our faith and obedience. If we only relate to Jesus as Savior but not as Lord, then there is something fundamentally wrong with our connection to Christ.

Whether your spiritual life seems strong or weak, it's a good idea to ask yourself and God how things are going. Think over the last week. How well did you do at letting Jesus be Lord of all your days? Were you primarily looking out for his interests or for your own? Were your prayers self-centered or focused outward, on the things that are closest to God's heart? Ask Christ to show you where you did well and where you still need to grow.

If you have been reserving any part of your life—a relationship, a habit, a dream, or a concern—because you fear what the Lord may ask of you, tell him you want the grace to relinquish it today. As you seek to do Christ's will in every area of your life, you will find that you are no longer living your faith at the lowest point on earth. No matter what is happening on the surface, your spiritual life will be growing stronger, not weaker, because of your connection with the Lord of lords and King of kings.

Wednesday

PRAYING THE NAME

He [Christ] humbled himself
and became obedient to death—even death on a cross!
Therefore God exalted him to the highest place
and gave him the name that is above every name,
that at the name of Jesus every knee should bow,
in heaven and on earth and under the earth,
and every tongue confess that Jesus Christ is Lord,
to the glory of God the Father.

PHILIPPIANS 2:8–11

Reflect On: Philippians 2:5–11.
Praise God: For Christ's victory on the cross.
Offer Thanks: Because you share in Christ's victory.
Confess: Any tendency to forget what God has done for you.
Ask God: To sharpen your spiritual vision.

My favorite Bible promise is this: "Love Wins." Okay, so it's really a bumper sticker and not a Bible promise. But doesn't the Bible say that Jesus died for us because he loved us? And doesn't it also say that God has exalted him to the highest place of all so that at the name of Jesus every knee should bow and every tongue confess that Jesus Christ is Lord? So, in the end, it does seem that the Bible promises us that "Love Wins."

Here's another little slogan I saw on the marquee of a church the other day: "Heavenly Forecast—Reign Forever." Corny as it sounds, it happens to be true. Jesus has already won the most important battle in history, and now he is on the throne and calling the shots. But if it is true that Jesus is the clear winner in the fight against sin and evil, why does it sometimes seem as though the outcome, at least in our corner of the world, is still in doubt? Because Satan has not yet admitted defeat. Because God wants to bring as many people into his kingdom as he can before wrapping things up. Because Christ wants our faith to be honed and perfected and that can only be accomplished in an environment of conflict and battle.

Have you heard of contrarians, people who buy stocks when everyone else is selling? Though this is not a strategy for the weak-kneed, it can yield enormous returns for those whose vision is clear. I believe that Jesus wants our spiritual vision to be so clear that we can become spiritual contrarians: people who continue to believe when life is at its worst, people who keep faith though everyone around us loses faith, people who continue to obey no matter how high the cost. If the apostle Paul had not had this deep certainty of Jesus' power and authority, of his ability to keep his promises come what may, how could he have endured being whipped, beaten, shipwrecked, stoned, and imprisoned, "in danger from rivers, in danger from bandits, in danger," as he says, "from my own countrymen, in danger from Gentiles; in danger in the city, in danger in the country, in danger at sea; and in danger from false brothers" (2 Corinthians 11:26)? How could he have labored and toiled and gone without sleep and been hungry and thirsty, cold and naked? How could he have endured martyrdom?

Paul was the ultimate contrarian. I wish I were more like him. I want to stop complaining over small things and large, to press on no matter what presses against me, to have so clear a vision of what it means that Jesus is Lord that my natural pessimism is converted into a fierce kind of spiritual optimism.

Join me today in praising the Lord and in repenting for having so little faith. Let us plead with him, begging him to open our eyes through faith so that we will know the full measure of his love and the greatness of his power.

Thursday

PRAYING THE NAME

For you were once darkness, but now you are light in the Lord. Live as children of light (for the fruit of the light consists in all goodness, righteousness and truth) and find out what pleases the Lord.

EPHESIANS 5:8–10

Reflect On: Ephesians 5:8–10.

Praise God: Who gives us the grace to follow his Son.

Offer Thanks: For the ways in which the Lord has already reshaped your life.

Confess: Any tendency to resist the Lord.

Ask God: To make you eager to experience Jesus as Lord.

The apostle Paul uses the characteristic phrase "in the Lord" many times in his letters. He speaks about:

> *Believing* in the Lord
> *Loving* in the Lord
> *Working hard* in the Lord
> *Boasting* in the Lord
> *Being faithful* in the Lord
> *Being strong* in the Lord
> *Hoping* in the Lord
> *Standing firm* in the Lord
> *Rejoicing* in the Lord

Paul even talks about being a *prisoner* in the Lord, and the book of Revelation makes it clear that it is possible to *die* in the Lord. Clearly, the early Christians considered Jesus to be not just their Savior but also their Lord. He was the atmosphere in which they lived, worked, prayed, suffered, and loved. They understood that their happiness depended not on having things their way, but on being completely aligned with

Christ, uniting themselves to his character and purposes regardless of the personal cost. And when Paul spoke about being "in the Lord," he was necessarily implying that it is possible to do things "outside of the Lord."

A friend of mine specializes in renovating old houses. When bidding on a job, Bill always begins by noting any structural defects or problems he discovers in the house. I was startled the first time I heard him refer to such defects as "sins." But the more I thought about it, the more sense it made because unless such problems are fixed, the house can never be restored to pristine condition. Likewise, sin has created an enormous structural problem in the world God made, allowing evil to deform it by threading its way through individuals, families, neighborhoods, institutions, and nations. To say that creation is off-kilter is to be guilty of an understatement.

But Jesus came to remedy this problem and to restore fallen creation. His mission is to break sin's power, and he does this by saving us and then taking our disordered lives and reshaping them into his likeness. But how much like him we become depends on our giving constant consent to his lordship. That's how we learn to do things "in the Lord." We know from Scripture that Christ will continue this work until the end of the world, when every kind of disorder—from petty squabbles to world wars, from thunderstorms to tsunamis, from diabetes to death (the ultimate disorder)—will cease to exist because everything and everyone will be exactly as God intends.

It is vital, then, that we know Jesus not only as Savior but also as Lord because that is the only way we can participate in building up his kingdom. Resisting his lordship, then, is more than a personal tragedy because it not only impedes the way God wants to work *in* us but also the way in which he wants to work *through* us. Our failures to believe and obey can have grave consequences for others.

Take a few moments today to be still in the Lord's presence. Bow your head before him, acclaiming him as *Kyrios*, your Lord forever. Then imagine your life in perfect alignment with his and let this picture become your prayer. Pray that Jesus will be all in all, working out his plans and extending his kingdom both in you and through you, world without end. Amen.

Friday

PROMISES ASSOCIATED WITH HIS NAME

What do you have in common with Billy Graham, Osama bin Laden, Stevie Wonder, and Indira Gandhi? I can think of only one thing—each of you will someday bow your heads and bend your knees with billions of others in the presence of the Lord. In his hands, all greatness, power, wisdom, and authority will be consolidated. Nothing of his power will remain hidden. Nothing will be held back. And you will see in his eyes either complete acceptance or complete rejection.

Now we see dimly. Then we will see clearly. Let us pray in this time of mercy for those who do not yet perceive Jesus as Lord. And let us pray for ourselves so that we are as ready as we can be for the great day of his coming.

Promises in Scripture

But do not forget this one thing, dear friends: With the Lord a day is like a thousand years, and a thousand years are like a day. The Lord is not slow in keeping his promise, as some understand slowness. He is patient with you, not wanting anyone to perish, but everyone to come to repentance.

But the day of the Lord will come like a thief. The heavens will disappear with a roar; the elements will be destroyed by fire, and the earth and everything in it will be laid bare.

2 PETER 3:8–10

You, then, why do you judge your brother or sister? Or why do you look down on your brother or sister? For we will all stand before God's judgment seat. It is written:

> *" 'As surely as I live,' says the Lord,*
> *'every knee will bow before me;*
>> *every tongue will confess to God.' "*

So then, we will all give an account of ourselves to God.

ROMANS 14:10–12

Continued Prayer and Praise

Follow the Lord. (Mark 10:42–45)

Rejoice in the Lord. (Luke 2:8–14; Philippians 4:4)

Worship the Lord. (Luke 5:4–8)

Believe in the Lord. (John 20:24–29)

Be assured: Jesus is both Lord and Christ. (Acts 2:29–36)

Confess that he is Lord. (Romans 10:9–13)

Live "in the Lord." (Romans 16:12; Ephesians 6:10; Philippians 2:19; 3:1)

Remember that the Lord is building his kingdom. (1 Corinthians 15:20–28)

16

FRIEND

φίλος

PHILOS

The Name

Jesus is not only Lord and Master but the greatest of all friends, who willingly proved his friendship by his death on the cross. By this costly gesture he has won the friendship of millions of men and women from every tongue and tribe and nation. When you pray to Jesus your Friend, you are praying to the One who loved you before you were loveable and who links you together with his many friends throughout the world.

Key Scripture

Greater love has no one than this: to lay down one's life for one's friends.

JOHN 15:13

Monday

HIS NAME REVEALED

As the Father has loved me, so have I loved you. Now remain in my love. If you keep my commands, you will remain in my love, just as I have kept my Father's commands and remain in his love. I have told you this so that my joy may be in you and that your joy may be complete. My command is this: Love each other as I have loved you. Greater love has no one than this: to lay down one's life for one's friends. You are my friends if you do what I command. I no longer call you servants, because servants do not know their master's business. Instead, I have called you friends, for everything that I learned from my Father I have made known to you. You did not choose me, but I chose you and appointed you so that you might go and bear fruit—fruit that will last—and so that whatever you ask in my name the Father will give you.

JOHN 15:9–16

You see, at just the right time, when we were still powerless, Christ died for the ungodly. Very rarely will anyone die for a righteous person, though for a good person someone might possibly dare to die. But God demonstrates his own love for us in this: While we were still sinners, Christ died for us.

Since we have now been justified by his blood, how much more shall we be saved from God's wrath through him! For if, when we were God's enemies, we were reconciled to him through the death of his Son, how much more, having been reconciled, shall we be saved through his life! Not only is this so, but we also boast in God through our Lord Jesus Christ, through whom we have now received reconciliation.

ROMANS 5:6–11

Jesus, you valued my friendship more than you valued your life. How can I begin to understand that kind of love? Help me to be among those you count as faithful friends, living in a way not that repays your friendship, because that is impossible, but in a way that reflects my gratitude. Thank you, my Friend. Amen.

Understanding the Name

The Greek word *philos* (FEE-los) means "friend" or "relative." Occurring twenty-eight times in the New Testament, it is also used to describe the close relationship that exists among believers, related to each other by virtue of their faith in Jesus. This word is related to *phileo*, the most general term for "to love" in the New Testament, and to the word *philema*, which means "a kiss." In fact, the early Christians used to greet each other with a holy kiss, signifying their close relationship.

John's Gospel indicates that Jesus not only called his disciples his friends but defined his own relationship with them by what was to be the greatest of all acts of friendship, in which he would lay down his life for them. Unlike most men of his day, Jesus had both male and female friends. Luke addressed his Gospel to someone named *Theophilus*, a proper name meaning "friend of God." The designation "friends" has survived as another name for those who belong to the religious group known as Quakers.

Studying the Name

1. Explain in your own words how Jesus defines friendship in the passage from John 15:9–16.

2. Describe the best friendship you have ever had. How does it compare with the way you have experienced Jesus' friendship?

3. How can you deepen your friendship with Christ?

4. If Jesus died for us while we were still his enemies, as Romans 5:6–11 tells us, how should we regard our own enemies?

Tuesday

PRAYING THE NAME

One who has unreliable friends soon comes to ruin,
but there is a friend who sticks closer than a brother.

PROVERBS 18:24

Early in the morning, Jesus stood on the shore, but the disciples did not
realize that it was Jesus.

He called out to them, "Friends, haven't you any fish?"

"No," they answered.

He said, "Throw your net on the right side of the boat and you will find
some." When they did, they were unable to haul the net in because of the
large number of fish.

Then the disciple whom Jesus loved said to Peter, "It is the Lord!"

JOHN 21:4–7

Reflect On: Proverbs 18:24 and John 21:4–7.

Praise God: For being the greatest Friend you have.

Offer Thanks: For the ways you have experienced Christ's friendship
in your life.

Confess: Any tendency to think of God's friendship as fickle.

Ask God: To deepen your confidence in his friendship.

It is hardly surprising, in an industry built on relationships, that greeting cards are rife with sentimental quotations extolling the virtues of friendship. My personal favorites, I confess, run in the opposite direction. Here are a few of those least likely to be inducted into the greeting card hall of fame:

"One who looks for a friend without faults will have none."
(Hasidic saying)

"Friends are God's way of apologizing to us for our families."
(Anonymous)

"If this is how you treat your friends, no wonder you have so few
of them." (Teresa of Avila)

You may have heard this last one. But did you know that this quip
was directed not at a human companion but at the Lord himself? It
was the quick retort of Teresa of Avila, a sixteenth-century nun, who
uttered it right after being dumped in the mud when her cart over-
turned during a journey she had undertaken for the Lord. I nearly
laughed out loud when I heard it, appreciating both her spunk and her
ability to capture the frustration we all feel when life doesn't go our
way, especially when we are doing our best to serve God.

Her words made me wonder about my own response. How do I act
when life seems nothing but an uphill climb? The more I considered
this question, the more I began to recognize a pattern of insecurity
in my relationship with Christ. When bad things happen, I tend to
blame both the Lord and myself, wondering what I've done to make
him angry. Here's my line of reasoning:

1. I realize that Jesus has the power to prevent bad things from
   happening.
2. So why doesn't he do a better job of protecting me?
3. If life is difficult, maybe it's because he doesn't really love me.
4. How could he love me when I do the things I do?
5. No doubt I am getting exactly what I deserve.

This kind of thinking, reasonable as it may seem in light of God's
power and my obvious defects and failings, is distorted because it
directly contradicts Scripture. Furthermore, it makes the Lord seem
as though he has an irritable temperament, as though he is someone I
need to tiptoe around lest I offend him. But that is so far from the Jesus
revealed in the New Testament, so far from the One who proved his
friendship not merely with words but by allowing himself to be tortured
and put to death in my place. Is that the kind of friend who's going to
turn away from me when I fail to do things perfectly?

Whether you are inclined to blame God or yourself for life's difficulties, join me today in praying for the grace to get one thing straight. It's what Teresa of Avila seemed to know despite her circumstances. The Lord of the universe is also our Friend. Let us rise each morning and go to bed each evening thanking and praising our great Friend, affirming the love he has already shown in such a marvelous way.

Wednesday

PRAYING THE NAME

Wounds from a friend can be trusted,
but an enemy multiplies kisses.

PROVERBS 27:6

Now a man named Lazarus was sick. He was from Bethany, the village of Mary and her sister Martha. This Mary, whose brother Lazarus now lay sick, was the same one who poured perfume on the Lord and wiped his feet with her hair. So the sisters sent word to Jesus, "Lord, the one you love is sick."

When he heard this, Jesus said, "This sickness will not end in death. No, it is for God's glory so that God's Son may be glorified through it." Jesus loved Martha and her sister and Lazarus. Yet when he heard that Lazarus was sick, he stayed where he was two more days.

JOHN 11:1–6

Reflect On: John 11:1–44.
Praise God: For revealing himself not only as Master but also as Friend.
Offer Thanks: Because Christ has set his affection on you.
Confess: Your need for greater confidence that Jesus remains your Friend despite the circumstances.
Ask God: To help you keep faith even when his friendship seems in doubt.

The man lay on his bed, his face shining with sweat. He fell in and out of dreams. He was standing at the edge of a great fire. The whole mountain was burning. Then two stone tablets came crashing down the cliff, heading his way. He covered his head, about to be crushed. The scene shifted. Now he lay on his back in the middle of a road in some God-forsaken place, unable to move, barely able to breathe. A stranger bent over him, lifted his head, and pressed a flask to his lips. But nothing came out. The sick man choked back his disappointment, his head falling onto the bed. Sitting next to him, clutching his hand, his sister Mary made calming noises, trying to hush away his fears, her own hand trembling as it pressed a cold rag against his forehead.

Where was their great friend, she wondered, the one who had healed so many people in Palestine? Surely he would come. But it had been two days since she and Martha had sent an urgent message to Jesus about their brother, Lazarus. And he had not even bothered to reply; he sent no one to explain his absence.

It isn't hard to imagine Mary and Martha wrestling with all that was *not* happening in response to their plea for help. They had counted on Jesus' friendship to save their brother. But he had let them down — or so it seemed.

Sometimes it's like that in our own lives. Jesus seems to fail the test of friendship. He isn't there when we need him. He doesn't answer our prayers. We feel confused and disappointed as our children step into roads of their own making and are run over, as our spouses stray, as our churches split. We feel abandoned. At such times I wonder if we relate to God more as an enemy than a friend. He asks such hard things of us. Surely he can't literally mean that we take up our cross and follow him. He can't mean that we turn our cheeks for yet another blow. He can't mean that the only way to life is through death.

But what if he does? How do we respond? How do we embrace the friendship of a man who, when his own friend lay dying, deliberately waited two days to be certain that his friend would in fact die? We do the only thing we can do. We hold on, we endure, we keep praying. And we remember how the story ends for Lazarus — and presumably for us. And in the midst of our journey of faith we begin to realize that we are not just making friends with a man but with God, with someone whose thoughts are not our thoughts and whose ways are not our ways.

Aristotle once remarked that a friend is a single soul in two bodies, meaning that friendship is based on a unity of mind and heart between two people. If this is so, it is we and not God who must change before the two can become one. And this truth is at the root of our discomfort. Because Jesus is both our greatest friend and our worst enemy—he hates our sins but loves our souls. Fortunately his love is the ultimate tool he uses to overcome our sins, for "greater love has no one than this: to lay down one's life for one's friends" (John 15:13).

Today as you think of Jesus, let his greater love shape your response to every disappointment and to every fearful thought. Let it transform you as it transformed Mary and Martha and Lazarus and every single person who, for the last two thousand years, has been invited to call God "Friend."

Thursday

PRAYING THE NAME

The Son of Man came eating and drinking, and they say, "Here is a glutton and a drunkard, a friend of tax collectors and 'sinners.' "

MATTHEW 11:19

Don't you know that friendship with the world is hatred toward God? Anyone who chooses to be a friend of the world becomes an enemy of God. Or do you think Scripture says without reason that the spirit he caused to live in us envies intensely? But he gives us more grace. That is why Scripture says:

"God opposes the proud
but gives grace to the humble."

Submit yourselves, then, to God. Resist the devil, and he will flee from you. Come near to God and he will come near to you. Wash your hands, you sinners, and purify your hearts, you double-minded. Grieve, mourn and wail. Change your laughter to mourning and your joy to gloom. Humble yourselves before the Lord, and he will lift you up.

JAMES 4:4–10

Reflect On: James 4:4–10.
Praise God: For drawing near to us.
Offer Thanks: For the ways God has humbled you, making you more open to his grace.
Confess: Any patterns of pride in your life.
Ask God: Ask God to show you areas in your life that require greater humility.

⌒

Between the ages of six and fourteen I attended eight different schools. Each time I dreaded the transition, bracing myself for the job of crossing a divide that seemed too wide for a shy girl to bridge. Over and over, making new friends, finding my place, trying to get comfortable in my uncomfortable skin—I hated the whole thing.

A couple of years ago I read *My First White Friend*, the compelling story of African-American writer Patricia Raybon's struggles to stop hating white people. At the core of her book is an experience she had in junior high. Excluded by the all-white student body, her sense of alienation was at least partially healed when one of the white students befriended her. My own transitions seemed easy by comparison. The passage below is from a letter she wrote but never sent to Kerry Monroe, the girl who crossed the playground to become her first white friend:

> "You were blonde and, truthfully, pretty. And always so *happy*.
>
> "And up close your dazzling brightness—and that perky, bubbly effervescence: like a white champagne that wouldn't go flat—was otherworldly.
>
> "TV didn't prepare me for my first white friend.
>
> "TV primed me, in fact, to hate anybody who looked anything like you....
>
> "But you were saving me. And I watched you, talking to me and laughing matter-of-factly on that playground, and I could have knelt down on the ground and held you tight, and let the gratitude wash over me, even while I wanted not to need your human kindness.
>
> "At fourteen, I couldn't admit I needed it.
>
> "Even now, I'm supposed to dismiss your little niceness. I can even hear in my head, as I did then, the memory of the practiced put-downs:
>
> "White girls—they so *phony*. . . .
>
> "But, Kerry, here's the thing:
>
> "After all these years, I have to say it. *Thank you*.
>
> "Thank you, Kerry Monroe.
>
> "This thing you did was a full thing. A God thing, maybe."

"A God thing, maybe"—a Christ thing, certainly. Like Kerry Monroe crossing that playground to make friends with Patricia Raybon, Jesus took the first step toward us, basing his offer of friendship not on a set of shared interests or on mutual admiration—the usual basis for friendship—but solely on his love.

But there's a catch: None of us will ever be attractive enough, good enough, or successful enough to warrant his friendship. Paradoxically, it is only by exposing the brokenness inside us that we can be admitted to this friendship. Because Jesus is only and always a friend of sinners, of people who are broken enough to know their need.

As you seek to deepen your friendship with Christ, ask for the grace to expose your brokenness to him. Let Jesus probe you and wash you and reveal to you any ways in which you may be compromising your relationship with him by making friends with this world. Then stick close to him by cultivating the virtue of humility, letting him decide when and how to lift you up.

Friday

PROMISES ASSOCIATED WITH HIS NAME

Absolute Friends is the title of a novel by spymaster John Le Carré. It chronicles the relationship of two friends who become spies during the Cold War and beyond. Unfortunately for both men, their absolute friendship leads to their mutual destruction. And so it is with some relationships, though usually on a less dramatic scale.

I know a father, for instance, who is very worried about a friendship his twelve-year-old son has recently forged, aware as he is that two rebellious adolescents usually hurtle downhill faster than one. This father knows that friendships are rarely neutral and that they usually take us somewhere, either up or down. Even the best friendship can take a downward turn at times because it is forged by two imperfect people. But what happens when the equation changes, when one side of the friendship consists of someone who is absolutely perfect? Doesn't it have the potential, depending on our willingness, to always take us upward? Thank Christ today for being the only Friend capable of loving you always. Let his friendship bring joy to your heart.

Promises in Scripture

> A friend loves at all times,
>> and a brother is born for a time of adversity.
>>>> PROVERBS 17:17

> Perfume and incense bring joy to the heart,
>> and the pleasantness of a friend
>> springs from their heartfelt advice.
>>>> PROVERBS 27:9

Continued Prayer and Praise

Recall that God speaks to his friends. (Exodus 33:7–11)

Pray for Christ to watch over you. (Job 29:2–6)

Consider that a cord of three strands is not easily broken.
(Ecclesiastes 4:9–12)

Remember that it is possible to betray Christ's friendship. (Matthew
26:47–51)

Consider how Jesus befriends sinners. (Luke 5:17–20)

Recognize Christ as your Friend. (John 21:4–7)

Act like Christ's friend. (James 2:20–24)

17

ALPHA AND OMEGA

ἄλφα καὶ Ὦ

ALPHA KAI OMEGA

The Name

In the last book of the Bible, Jesus reveals himself as "the Alpha and the Omega, the First and the Last, the Beginning and the End." Present at the world's beginning, Jesus will also be present at its end, when he and his work are finally and fully revealed. When you pray to Christ as the Alpha and the Omega, you are praying to the One who is, who was, and who is to come. He is our all-sufficient Lord, who will not fail to complete the good work he has begun in us.

Key Scripture

"I am the Alpha and the Omega, the First and the Last, the Beginning and the End."

REVELATION 22:13

HIS NAME REVEALED

Listen to me, O Jacob,
 Israel, whom I have called:
I am he;
 I am the first and I am the last.

ISAIAH 48:12

He who was seated on the throne said, "I am making everything new!" Then he said, "Write this down, for these words are trustworthy and true."

He said to me: "It is done. I am the Alpha and the Omega, the Beginning and the End."

REVELATION 21:5–6

"Behold, I am coming soon! My reward is with me, and I will give to everyone according to what he has done. I am the Alpha and the Omega, the First and the Last, the Beginning and the End."

REVELATION 22:12–13

Lord, you are Alpha and Omega, Beginning and End, First and Last. You are the source of all life and the fulfillment of all desire. You made the world from nothing and then remade it through your love. Help me to be so rooted in you that I never lose heart. May every beginning and every ending in my life be something that glorifies you.

Understanding the Name

The title "Alpha and Omega" occurs only three times in the Bible, and all three are in the book of Revelation. Because *Alpha* and *Omega* are the first and last letters in the Greek alphabet, Revelation 22:13 could be paraphrased: "I am the A and the Z, the First and the Last, the Beginning and the End." These verses in Revelation probably allude to passages in Isaiah in which God identifies himself as being both the first and the last (Isaiah 44:6; 48:12).

Studying the Name

1. Can you imagine a human being claiming to be the A to Z? Why or why not?

2. How do you think this title relates to Christ's divinity?

3. Try to relate this title, Alpha and Omega, to Jesus' role in both creation and in world history. What do you think it means?

4. What would it mean to say that Jesus is first and last in your own life?

Tuesday

PRAYING THE NAME

This is what the LORD says —
> Israel's King and Redeemer, the LORD Almighty:
I am the first and I am the last;
> apart from me there is no God.

ISAIAH 44:6

Look, he is coming with the clouds,
> and every eye will see him,
even those who pierced him;
> and all the peoples of the earth will mourn because of him.
> > So shall it be! Amen.

"I am the Alpha and the Omega," says the Lord God, "who is, and who was, and who is to come, the Almighty."

REVELATION 1:7–8

Reflect On: Isaiah 44:6 and Revelation 1:7–8.
Praise God: For speaking to us.
Offer Thanks: For the way Jesus communicates God's love.
Confess: Your need for Jesus to be your Alpha and Omega, your
                 beginning and your end.
Ask God: To give you ears to hear and eyes to see.

The longer I live, the more I am impressed with the importance of stories. I think stories are like air — it's impossible to live without them. I'm not saying we would die without novels, plays, or movies, though the quality of our lives would certainly diminish. What I am saying is that you cannot live without an overarching story that explains the world and your place in it. Muslims, Jews, Hindus, Mormons, Buddhists, and Christians — we all have stories that shape our lives.

Even atheists have a storyline that shapes their response to the world. It's that for them there is no ultimate story, no higher power, no absolute truth, and no afterlife. To be true to that story, the atheist must either despair or simply face the facts bravely, determined to live without the comforts of religion.

But what does this talk of stories have to do with the title "Alpha and Omega"? These two letters are, of course, the first and last letters of the Greek alphabet. In fact the word "alphabet" is formed from the first two letters of the Greek language — *alpha* and *beta*. When Jesus calls himself the Alpha and the Omega, he is implying not just these two letters but all the letters in between. And letters, of course, are the basic building blocks for words. So it seems entirely fitting to say that Jesus, who is the Word of God, is also the Alpha and the Omega. He is the One who perfectly communicates, through his words and the story of his life, who God is and who we are. He tells us what has happened to break the world and what is necessary to fix it. He shows us that love is not merely one of God's attributes but that God *is* love. And then he tells us how we are to live in light of this overarching story.

The Canadian preacher A. B. Simpson spoke of Jesus as the key to interpreting the entire Bible:

> Jesus, in the story of creation, already planning the new creation; Jesus supreme above the ruins of the fall; Jesus in the ark, the rainbow and the dove; Jesus in the sacrifice on Mount Moriah, the ladder of Jacob, and the story of Joseph; Jesus in the Paschal lamb, the desert manna.... The face of Jesus can be traced like water lines in fine paper back of every page, for He is the Alpha and the Omega: the first and the last of this Holy Book.

As the Alpha and the Omega Jesus has eloquently communicated the story of salvation to anyone who has ears to hear and eyes to see. As Warren Wiersbe puts it:

> If you want to understand God, you have to know Jesus Christ. I have met people who say, "Well, I get so much truth about God

from walking in the woods." You can learn some things about God by walking in the woods, but you cannot get the full revelation you have in Christ. Some say, "I love to sit and look at a beautiful sunset; it tells me so much about God." Well, it can; but you will learn much more of God's revelation through His Son, Jesus Christ. God has spoken in Jesus Christ, and this is His last word. Jesus Christ is God's last word, and if you want to know about God, you have to come to Jesus Christ. Jesus Christ is Alpha and Omega; His ministry is the ministry of revelation—He reveals God to us.

If Jesus is the Alpha and the Omega, the beginning and the end of the world's painful but hopeful story, it is vital that we not only listen but that we respond, letting Christ weave our own small stories into the greatest story ever told. This week, spend some time thinking about the story of your life thus far. Take everything you remember, both the good and the bad, and give it to Jesus. Tell him you want to surrender your life in an even deeper way so that he alone will be the Alpha and the Omega, the beginning and the end of the story of your life.

Wednesday

PRAYING THE NAME

He is the image of the invisible God, the firstborn over all creation. For by him all things were created: things in heaven and on earth, visible and invisible, whether thrones or powers or rulers or authorities; all things were created by him and for him. He is before all things, and in him all things hold together. And he is the head of the body, the church; he is the beginning and the firstborn from among the dead, so that in everything he might have the supremacy. For God was pleased to have all his fullness dwell in him, and through him to reconcile to himself all things, whether things on earth or things in heaven, by making peace through his blood, shed on the cross.

COLOSSIANS 1:15–20

Reflect On: Colossians 1:15–20 and Revelation 21:1–7.
Praise God: For his all sufficiency.
Offer Thanks: That Christ did not cling to equality with God but emptied himself in order to save us.
Confess: Your tendency to rely on yourself rather than God.
Ask God: To help you face the emptiness inside.

The word "abundance" made a bit of a comeback a few years ago when a feel-good book entitled *Simple Abundance* scaled the best seller lists. This book of daily readings tapped into the sense many of us have that our lives are long on stress and short on serenity. Though we may live in the midst of affluence, many of us sense that something vital is lacking. We long for a greater sense of purpose and a deeper sense of fulfillment.

But how does our need for fulfillment connect with Jesus as the Alpha and the Omega? Herbert Lockyer, British pastor and author, once described Jesus as "A and Z, and all in between—the Center and Circumference of all things." I like that description because it echoes the statement in Colossians that God was pleased to have all his fullness dwell in Jesus. Christ is indeed the source of all beauty and the end of all yearning. He is truth, peace, healing, comfort, purity, power, and love. He is the beginning of the world and the end of the world, and it is literally true that we have no good apart from him. To say that God's fullness dwells in Jesus is to say that though Christ is human, there is no part of him that is not divine. Deity fills him. As one theologian puts it, "From him as the bearer of the divine fullness … vital powers flow into the church, so that he may be said to fill it."

But if "vital powers" are to flow into us by virtue of our belonging to Christ, why is it that we often feel so lacking in power? Perhaps it is because we are so busy trying to fill ourselves with things incapable of satisfying. You can't, after all, fill a bucket with fine-cut diamonds if it is already packed to the brim with potting soil. Perhaps too we fail to grasp an obvious fact: that God's power flows down and not up. In other words, receiving everything that Christ has for us requires a willingness to tolerate our emptiness for a while. It requires admitting our inability to satisfy our deepest needs, all the while believing that Christ will. And this faith, joined with humility and obedience, will act as a powerful force, a kind of spiritual gravity to attract God's gifts and his blessings.

In 1 Corinthians, Paul talks about God's ultimate aim. He says there will come a time when, through the work of Christ, God will finally be *all in all.* Everywhere you look — God. Everyone you look at — God within. That is God's plan for you, for the church, and for this world. He wants to fill us with himself, the richest of all blessings.

Pray for the grace to admit your need, to empty yourself of all that opposes God's presence. Repent especially of the self-reliance that keeps you from trusting him. Then pray for the wisdom, peace, and power to serve him in a way that will fulfill his purpose for your life.

Thursday

PRAYING THE NAME

Let us fix our eyes on Jesus, the author and perfecter of our faith.

HEBREWS 12:2

Jesus Christ is the same yesterday and today and forever.

HEBREWS 13:8

I turned around to see the voice that was speaking to me. And when I turned I saw seven golden lampstands, and among the lampstands was someone "like a son of man," dressed in a robe reaching down to his feet and with a golden sash around his chest. . . .

When I saw him, I fell at his feet as though dead. Then he placed his right hand on me and said: "Do not be afraid. I am the First and the Last. I am the Living One; I was dead, and behold I am alive for ever and ever! And I hold the keys of death and Hades."

REVELATION 1:12–13, 17–18

Reflect On: Hebrews 12:2; 13:8 and Revelation 1:12–13, 17–18.
Praise God: Because he has no beginning and no end.
Offer Thanks: Because Jesus is the same yesterday, today, and forever.
Confess: Any fear that drives your life.
Ask God: To reveal the fault lines in your life.

ᐧ

September 11, the Asian tsunami, and Hurricane Katrina—natural and unnatural disasters that have dramatically exposed the fault lines within governments, societies, and nature itself. Day after day we have watched the unfolding drama of disasters that most of us could never have imagined—the latest in New Orleans, a city described as one of the most romantic, historic, and musical cities in the world.

Overnight Hurricane Katrina turned this city, known as the Big Easy, into the hardest place on earth to live. With unintended irony, one New Orleans website still advises would-be visitors: "One thing you should remember to do before coming to New Orleans: forget everything you know."

Today that advice seems apt. Forget the graceful antebellum mansions, the rich cuisine, the annual Mardi Gras festival, and the sweet sound of New Orleans jazz floating across the French Quarter. Remember, instead, the hunger, the bedlam, and the human misery that New Orleans' poorest and weakest residents suffered as they waited for someone, anyone, to save them after the levees broke. Remember the shame and horror we all felt as we watched their despair.

The same website goes on to describe the city's legendary appeal:

> This is New Orleans. Queen City of the South. An exotic temptress. Steamy, sultry and sensual. For three centuries sunken lazily in the bend of a mighty river near the edge of a continent. Suitors come from near and far—drawn by her beauty, intrigued by her sounds and smells, beguiled by her grace, enchanted by her spirit.
>
> This is New Orleans. Feel free to fall in love. Sin at will. There's always time for guilt tomorrow, or the next day.

No doubt the vast majority of the city's residents have lived more virtuous lives than this copywriter's version of New Orleans might indicate. But how telling that the city's seductive charm, famous for more than two hundred years, vanished in an instant.

I live in a solid Midwestern city, a city that, though pleasant, could hardly be described as seductive. But recent events have caused me to wonder what fault lines lie hidden within it. Couldn't everything I love and cherish in Grand Rapids, Michigan, be swept away in an instant, just as it was in New Orleans? What would happen if my city's infrastructure suddenly collapsed? If there weren't enough food, water, and shelter to go around? What kind of people would we prove to be? How would we treat our poor? Our sick and elderly? Would middle-class values and middle-class dreams survive such a catastrophe?

This is a question I'm asking these days, not just about my city but about myself. Where are my fault lines? How would I act under the kind of pressure that was brought to bear on the citizens of New Orleans?

What am I basing my life on? I wish I could tell you my confidence has grown as I try to imagine myself confronting similar conditions. But truly it is hard to be anything but frightened by such thoughts. When worse comes to worst, I know it will only be God's mercy that will sustain me and those I love.

Today I pray that you and I will learn before it is too late how to fix our eyes on Christ, who is God forever. He is the One who is, who was, and who will be—the One who banishes our fear because he holds the past, present, and future in his all-powerful hands. Neither New Orleans nor Grand Rapids nor any other city in the world will last forever. But Jesus will.

May he be the beginning and the end of everything we believe, everything we strive for, everthing we trust in. May he be first in our families, first in our relationships, first in our businesses, and first in all the days that lie ahead for us. Then, no matter what happens, we will be given the grace to stand, knowing that our lives are hidden in the hands of the only One able to save us both now and forever. Amen.

PROMISES ASSOCIATED WITH HIS NAME

On October 29, 1941, Winston Churchill delivered a speech, at Harrow, a prestigious boarding school in northwest London, in which he uttered these now famous words: "Never give in. Never give in. Never, never, never, never — in nothing, great or small, large or petty — never give in, except to convictions of honor and good sense. Never yield to force. Never yield to the apparently overwhelming might of the enemy." The speech was given against the dark backdrop of World War II. Churchill's spirit of defiance helped to bolster the faith of a nation under siege.

This kind of never-give-up attitude should characterize our lives as Christians, because Jesus himself never gave up. His last words on the cross were not about surrendering in the face of overwhelming opposition but about finishing — "It is finished!" he cried. This determination to finish what he had begun is still true of Christ, who is Alpha and Omega, the Lord of both beginnings and endings.

What good works has he begun in your life, in your marriage, in your children, in the church? All these may at one time or another come under siege, but if you hold fast to Christ through perseverance, you will not be overcome.

Promises in Scripture

I thank my God every time I remember you. In all my prayers for all of you, I always pray with joy because of your partnership in the gospel from the first day until now, being confident of this, that he who began a good work in you will carry it on to completion until the day of Christ Jesus.

PHILIPPIANS 1:3–6

These are the words of him who is the First and the Last, who died and came to life again. I know your afflictions and your poverty—yet you are rich! . . . Do not be afraid of what you are about to suffer. I tell you, the devil will put some of you in prison to test you, and you will suffer persecution for ten days. Be faithful, even to the point of death, and I will give you the crown of life.

He who has an ear, let him hear what the Spirit says to the churches. He who overcomes will not be hurt at all by the second death.

REVELATION 2:8–11

Continued Prayer and Praise

Praise the Lord from beginning to end. (Psalm 113:1–3)

Remember Daniel's vision of the Ancient of Days. (Daniel 7:9–13)

Consider how Jesus, the Alpha and Omega, preexisted creation. (John 1:1–3; 8:54–58)

Rejoice because Jesus is the Beginning and he is the End. (Revelation 21:1–7)

18

JESUS THE SAVIOR

יְשׁוּעַ Ἰησοῦς σωτήρ
YESHUA, IESOUS SOTER

The Name

Just as *Yahweh* is God's personal name revealed in the Old Testament, Jesus is the personal name of the One we call Redeemer, Lord, and Christ. His name is intimately linked to the God of the Hebrew Scriptures because it means "*Yahweh* is salvation." Indeed, Jesus is *Yahweh* come to earth. If you have ever pictured God as a distant, wrathful Being, you will have to reconsider that portrait in light of Jesus Christ, who is God bending toward us, God becoming one of us, God reaching out in mercy, God humbling himself, God nailed to a cross, God rising up from the grave to show us the way home. Jesus, name above all names, beautiful Savior, glorious Lord!

Key Scripture

Joseph son of David, do not be afraid to take Mary home as your wife, because what is conceived in her is from the Holy Spirit. She will give birth to a son, and you are to give him the name Jesus, because he will save his people from their sins.

MATTHEW 1:20–21

HIS NAME REVEALED

This is how the birth of Jesus Christ came about: His mother Mary was pledged to be married to Joseph, but before they came together, she was found to be with child through the Holy Spirit. Because Joseph her husband was a righteous man and did not want to expose her to public disgrace, he had in mind to divorce her quietly.

But after he had considered this, an angel of the Lord appeared to him in a dream and said, "Joseph son of David, do not be afraid to take Mary home as your wife, because what is conceived in her is from the Holy Spirit. She will give birth to a son, and you are to give him the name Jesus, because he will save his people from their sins."

All this took place to fulfill what the Lord had said through the prophet: "The virgin will be with child and will give birth to a son, and they will call him Immanuel"—which means, "God with us."

When Joseph woke up, he did what the angel of the Lord had commanded him and took Mary home as his wife. But he had no union with her until she gave birth to a son. And he gave him the name Jesus.

MATTHEW 1:18–25

Yeshua, my Savior. You are God forever. Thank you for saving me from all my sins. You reached down from on high to rescue me. Help me to live with the continual awareness of my need for your saving grace, now and always. Amen.

Understanding the Name

Luke's Gospel tells us that the infant Christ was given the name "Jesus" at the time of his circumcision, a name given him by the angel Gabriel, who appeared to his mother Mary (Luke 1:31; 2:21).

"Jesus" was a common name in first-century Palestine, and it has been found on various grave markers and tombs in and around Jerusalem. The full name of Barabbas, the insurrectionist Pilate released instead of Jesus, was probably Jesus Barabbas. To distinguish him from others of the same name, Jesus is sometimes referred to in the Gospels as Jesus of Nazareth, Jesus the son of Joseph, or Jesus the Nazarene. Later on, particularly in Acts and the New Testament letters, he is referred to as "Jesus Christ," as though Christ is his surname. By the second century the name "Jesus" had become so closely associated with Jesus of Nazareth that it nearly disappeared as a name given to either Christians or Jews.

The name "Jesus" (in English) or "*Iesous*" (in Greek) is the equivalent of the Hebrew "*Yeshua*," itself a contraction of the Hebrew name "*Yehoshua*," translated "Joshua" in English Bibles. The name Joshua is the oldest name containing *Yahweh*, the covenant name of God, a name so sacred it was considered too holy to pronounce. Both "Jesus" and "Joshua" mean "*Yahweh* is help" or "*Yahweh* is salvation." *Yeshua* is also related to the word *yeshu'ah*, which means "salvation."

"*Soter*" is the Greek word translated "Savior." Its Hebrew equivalent is *Moshia*. In Greek, "Jesus the Savior" is rendered *Iesous Soter* (yay-SOUS so-TAIR). Through the centuries, the church has affirmed the belief of the earliest followers of Jesus that "salvation is found in no one else, for there is no other name given under heaven by which we must be saved" (Acts 4:12).

Studying the Name

1. What comes to mind when you hear the name "Jesus"?

2. Though "Jesus" was a common name in first-century Palestine, God sent an angel to announce the name to Joseph. Comment on the significance of this.

3. Why do you think Jesus' name is linked to the name of *Yahweh*, the covenant name of God in the Hebrew Scriptures?

4. Describe what salvation means to you.

Tuesday

PRAYING THE NAME

Now the tax collectors and "sinners" were all gathering around to hear him. But the Pharisees and the teachers of the law muttered, "This man welcomes sinners and eats with them."

Then Jesus told them this parable: "Suppose one of you has a hundred sheep and loses one of them. Does he not leave the ninety-nine in the open country and go after the lost sheep until he finds it? And when he finds it, he joyfully puts it on his shoulders and goes home. Then he calls his friends and neighbors together and says, 'Rejoice with me; I have found my lost sheep.' I tell you that in the same way there will be more rejoicing in heaven over one sinner who repents than over ninety-nine righteous persons who do not need to repent."

LUKE 15:1–7

But Zacchaeus stood up and said to the Lord, "Look, Lord! Here and now I give half of my possessions to the poor, and if I have cheated anybody out of anything, I will pay back four times the amount."

Jesus said to him, "Today salvation has come to this house, because this man, too, is a son of Abraham. For the Son of Man came to seek and to save what was lost."

LUKE 19:8–9

Reflect On: Luke 15:1–7 and 19:8–9.
Praise God: Who is the Seeker of the lost.
Offer Thanks: Because God has pursued you.
Confess: Any complacency toward those who are lost.
Ask God: To align your heart with his purposes.

Rick Warren's *The Purpose Driven Life* stunned the publishing world by selling twenty-three million copies in just three years. The book's subtitle, "What on Earth Am I Here For?" poses a question most of us ask ourselves at least once a lifetime. But the most purpose-driven person in history may not have needed to pose the question at all because his purpose was announced before his birth.

Presumably Joseph, Mary's anxious husband-to-be, knew that *Yeshua* meant "Yahweh is salvation," but the angel in his dream was careful to spell it out for him: "You are to give him [the baby in Mary's womb] the name *Yeshua*, because he will save his people from their sins" (Matthew 1:21). From the beginning the single purpose of Jesus' life was to seek out sinners and then to save them. He was God hunting souls, not to hurt them but to help them — and that is still his purpose.

I wonder how many of us really believe this. Do we have the slightest idea of how driven Christ is to dwell with the least attractive among us, with people who not only look bad but are bad? And if he has this drive to dwell with the worst and the lowest, doesn't that say something about his commitment to being with us when we are at our worst?

Theologian and writer Robert Farrar Capon has an interesting take on the parable Jesus told to disgruntled scribes and Pharisees about the shepherd who leaves ninety-nine *found* sheep in order to search for one *lost* sheep. The religious leaders had been grumbling about Jesus. How could a man with friends like tax collectors and sinners presume to teach them anything? It was against the backdrop of their self-righteousness that Jesus told them the parable, asking how they would respond if they owned a hundred sheep and one got lost.

Capon begins by pointing out that most shepherds wouldn't think of leaving ninety-nine sheep to go in search of one lost sheep because to do so would be to leave the rest of the flock vulnerable to predators. Instead, as Capon writes,

> You cut your losses, forget about the lost sheep, and go on with the ninety-nine.... In this parable, Jesus never goes back to the ninety-nine sheep. The ninety-nine sheep are a set-up. Jesus has divided the flock into one sheep and ninety-nine sheep.... I think the real meaning of the one and the ninety-nine is that the one lost sheep is the whole human race as it really is. And the ninety-nine "found" sheep who never get lost are the whole human race as we think we are.

No wonder Jesus liked to hang out around sinners. There are no other kinds of people to associate with. But as the parable implies, Jesus can do little for the strong and the self-righteous who don't even know they are lost. It's the poor, the weak, the addicted, the troubled, and the fractured people — those who have an inkling of how off course their lives have become who are often the most responsive to grace. This principle applies even after our conversion. Jesus seeks to bless the people who admit their need, not the ones who act as though they know it all and have it all. Blessed are the poor in spirit, the meek, those who hunger and thirst. Blessed are the empty, not the full.

Pray today for the grace to know how much you still need Jesus. Ask him for the grace to see beyond your wants to the things you really need — more compassion and less harsh judgment, more generosity and less fear, more patience and less irritability, more faith and less doubt. Pray that Jesus will enable you to move beyond the kind of selfish praying we all do so that you can pray in a way that reflects his heart, letting whatever moves him move you. Then pray for the privilege of joining him as he seeks out and saves those who are lost.

Wednesday

PRAYING THE NAME

Therefore God exalted him to the highest place
and gave him the name that is above every name,
that at the name of Jesus every knee should bow,
in heaven and on earth and under the earth,
and every tongue confess that Jesus Christ is Lord,
to the glory of God the Father.

PHILIPPIANS 2:9–11

Once when we were going to the place of prayer, we were met by a slave girl who had a spirit by which she predicted the future. She earned a great deal of money for her owners by fortune-telling. This girl followed Paul and the rest of us, shouting, "These men are servants of the Most High God, who are telling you the way to be saved." She kept this up for many days. Finally Paul became so troubled that he turned around and said to the spirit, "In the name of Jesus Christ I command you to come out of her!" At that moment the spirit left her.

ACTS 16:16–18

Reflect On: Philippians 2:9–11 and Acts 16:16–18.
Praise God: For manifesting his power and authority through Jesus, his Son.
Offer Thanks: For the surpassing power of Jesus Christ.
Confess: Any occasions on which you have taken the Lord's name in vain.
Ask God: To lift up the name of his Son in your life.

‿

There's power in the name of Jesus, even wonder-working power. But the name "Jesus" is not some kind of magical incantation. Invoking it is not like rubbing a lamp to conjure a genie. No, the power of the name of Jesus is released when people earnestly cry out to him and when they live in submission to him.

I've heard many stories that drive this home. One was told by a woman in my church. While walking to her car in a deserted garage one night, a thug accosted her, knife in hand. Though she was terrified, this woman managed to command her would-be mugger, carjacker, rapist, murderer, or whatever he was: "Get away from me in the name of Jesus!" To her astonishment, though they were alone in the garage, the man backed up as though someone had just threatened him with a knife. Then he turned and fled.

Then there's the story of E. P. Scott, a missionary to India. One day Scott decided to visit a mountain tribe who had never heard of Jesus. But as he approached the mountain, a band of angry tribesmen surrounded him with spears pointed straight at his chest. On impulse, the missionary took out the violin he was carrying, closed his eyes, and began playing and singing a hymn in their native language. When Scott finally found the courage to open his eyes, he was amazed to see that his attackers had dropped their spears and that several of them had tears in their eyes. Scott spent the rest of his life preaching and serving the people of that tribe, many of whom became believers. What was the hymn he sang? "All Praise the Power of Jesus' Name!"

Jim Cymbala, pastor of the Brooklyn Tabernacle, tells a more recent story about a homeless heroin addict named Danny Velasco. Though a friend by the name of Wanda had shared the gospel with him, Danny had dismissed it as so much nonsense. After three years on the street he had contracted Hepatitis A, B, and C, and his 108-pound body was covered with sores. Passersby could hear him talking to the swarm of voices that screamed in his head. This is what happened when Danny landed in a hospital in the Bronx, seemingly on his deathbed:

> When I woke up, I found myself in a bed, covered in my own vomit. Suddenly all the voices in my head started screaming, creating total chaos within me. I was so disoriented, I wanted to die! But I couldn't jump out a window because they were barred.
>
> Then, in the midst of all my pain, something or someone whispered words I had heard before: *The day you call on the Lord, he will set you free.* All the other voices tried to drown it out, but they

couldn't! I don't know if it was an angel or the Holy Spirit, but the words came through clearly: "The day you call on the Lord, he will set you free." In absolute desperation I screamed from my bed, "Jesus help me! O God, help me with everything! You're my only hope, so please help, Jesus!" I didn't understand anything about prayer, so I even used "personal references" as I cried out: "Jesus, Wanda said that when I called on your name, you would deliver me. So help me now, O God."

At that moment Almighty God swept over me and around me. I knew he was real because all the voices in my head suddenly stopped their hellish screaming and the ball of fear that had been weighing on me lifted. I knew everything had changed even though nothing outwardly had—I was still lying in my vomit in a hospital bed in the Bronx. But I was a million miles from where I had been before I said that prayer.

Eleven years later, Danny is alive and well, a million miles from the hopeless addict he had been before he cried out to Jesus. The demons that plagued him could not withstand the power of the name of Jesus. His story affirms the words of another popular hymn, reminding us that "at the name of Jesus, every knee shall bow, every tongue confess him, King of glory now!"

Thursday

PRAYING THE NAME

[The angel said to the shepherds,] "Today in the town of David a Savior has been born to you; he is the Messiah, the Lord. This will be a sign to you: You will find a baby wrapped in cloths and lying in a manger."

Suddenly a great company of the heavenly host appeared with the angel, praising God and saying,

> *"Glory to God in the highest heaven,,*
> *and on earth peace to those on whom his favor rests."*

LUKE 2:11 – 14

With this in mind, we constantly pray for you, that our God may count you worthy of his calling, and that by his power he may fulfill every good purpose of yours and every act prompted by your faith. We pray this so that the name of our Lord Jesus may be glorified in you, and you in him, according to the grace of our God and the Lord Jesus Christ.

2 THESSALONIANS 1:11 – 12

Reflect On: Luke 2:11 – 14 and 2 Thessalonians 1:11 – 12.
Praise God: For the greatness of his glory.
Offer Thanks: Because God has created you to be his image bearer.
Confess: Any tendency to be more concerned for your glory than for God's.
Ask God: To fulfill his primary purpose for your life.

∞

My daughters love things that sparkle — stars that glow in the dark, rainbow stickers, pink glittery wands. Through the years I have had to fend off many a request for gaudy red shoes "just like the ones Dorothy wore in Oz." I trace these attractions not so much to feminine stereotypes as to a basic human yearning. Boys display their own form of this yearning when they wear superhero capes and brandish plastic swords. But what is this yearning? It's a longing for something beautiful and shining and powerful, for something beyond ourselves that we can make a part of ourselves. It's a yearning for glory.

But what does this yearning have to do with Jesus as Savior? To begin with, it is important to realize that Jesus' saving work has both negative and positive dimensions. First, we are saved *from* something — Jesus rescues us from God's wrath directed at our sins. Second, we are saved *for* something — Jesus saves us so that we can fulfill the primary purpose for which God made us. Think for a moment of a time when you sat by the edge of the ocean or by a lake, transfixed by the beauty of the waves as sunlight danced across them. That's a picture of how we are meant to reflect God's glory to the world. We are to shine with his presence, power, and love.

Scripture is full of this notion. The book of Daniel tells of a time when those who belong to God "will shine like the brightness of the heavens ... like the stars for ever and ever" (Daniel 12:3). St. Paul assures the Roman Christians: "I consider that our present sufferings are not worth comparing with the glory that will be revealed in us" (Romans 8:18). Additional passages speak of "the Lord of glory," "Christ in you, the hope of glory," and "the crown of glory that will never fade away."

This craving for glory seems to be imbedded in our spiritual DNA. It is something God has hardwired into our souls. But sin has so distorted the human genome that our search for glory is often misguided. We look for it in flimsy, temporal things, such as success, money, relationships, personal charm, and beauty — none of which can ultimately satisfy. No matter how many sparkling red shoes we own or how many superhero capes we don, we find they are never enough.

Carol Cymbala, director of the Brooklyn Tabernacle Choir, gives us a glimpse of what it means to seek true glory.

> The Brooklyn Tabernacle Choir doesn't perform. We haven't provided backup to musical superstars or sung at national political conventions, even though we've been asked to more than once. Our call, our greatest joy, is to worship God, and to lead other Christians to experience him in worship. We also want to sing the message of the gospel to those who don't know Christ. So week

after week, we open our hearts to him eagerly waiting, painfully aware that if God doesn't come to meet us, we will never accomplish our purpose.

We are not naïve about the dangers that come with apparent success, because we know that self-aggrandizement displeases God. And God won't bless us if we're out to please ourselves. I tell the choir, "God has allowed us to win four Grammys. But there are better choirs out there. The only reason he's blessed us is so he can use us to reach more people. So just remember who you are, and I'll remember who I am. Apart from God we're nothing."

Carol means what she says. She understands that worldly glory is like tinsel compared to God's glory. Today as you worship *Yeshua*, the Lord of glory, give in to your appetite for glory by praying the refrain from Graham Kendrick's well-known song:

> *Shine, Jesus, shine!*
> *Fill this land with the Father's glory.*
> *Blaze, Spirit, blaze!*
> *Set our hearts on fire.*
> *Flow, river, flow!*
> *Flood the nations with grace and mercy.*
> *Send forth your word,*
> *Lord, and let there be light.*

Friday

PROMISES ASSOCIATED WITH HIS NAME

The hurricane that devastated New Orleans in the fall of 2005 left us with images we will never forget. Day after day, we saw people perched on rooftops, desperately waiting for someone to rescue them. Many of them must have wondered if their world was about to end. Everywhere they looked—death, destruction, danger. The scenes were pitiful, heartrending, frightening.

This is a powerful picture of what life would be like were it not for Jesus, who is himself the greatest of all the promises in the Bible. Even his name is a promise—*Yahweh is salvation.* He is rescue, help, deliverance. Remember this in your times of trial. Call on his name. Trust in his name. Live in his name. Let the name "Jesus" be the first prayer you pray in the morning and the last prayer you say at night. Jesus, the only name in which there is salvation.

Promises in Scripture

Peter replied, "Repent and be baptized, every one of you, in the name of Jesus Christ for the forgiveness of your sins. And you will receive the gift of the Holy Spirit. The promise is for you and your children and for all who are far off—for all whom the Lord our God will call."

ACTS 2:38–39

Jesus did many other miraculous signs in the presence of his disciples, which are not recorded in this book. But these are written that you may believe that Jesus is the Christ, the Son of God, and that by believing you may have life in his name.

JOHN 20:30–31

Continued Prayer and Praise

Believe in the power of Jesus' name. (Matthew 12:15 – 21; John 3:16; Acts 3:1 – 10; 4:1 – 12; Romans 5:9 – 11)

Rejoice when you are found worthy to suffer for the sake of the name. (Acts 5:40 – 42; 21:10 – 14)

Do everything in the name of the Lord Jesus. (Colossians 3:15 – 17)

Trust in Jesus for salvation. (Titus 3:3 – 8)

19

BRIDEGROOM, HUSBAND

νυμφίος, ἀνήρ
NYMPHIOS, ANER

The Name

God is not content to be known merely as Creator, Lord, or even Father. Incredibly he reveals himself also as Bridegroom or Husband. The Hebrew Scriptures contain numerous allusions to *Yahweh* as Israel's divine Husband, and the New Testament presents Christ as the church's Bridegroom. He is the Holy One who did not cling to his divinity but left his Father's house to dwell among us, calling us to become one with him in the most intimate way possible. To all of us, male and female, Christ offers himself as our provider and protector, the one who has forever pledged himself in faithfulness and love.

Key Scripture

Blessed are those who are invited to the wedding supper of the Lamb!

REVELATION 19:9

Monday

HIS NAME REVEALED

"For your Maker is your husband—
    the LORD Almighty is his name—
the Holy One of Israel is your Redeemer;
    he is called the God of all the earth.
The LORD will call you back
    as if you were a wife deserted and distressed in spirit—
a wife who married young,
    only to be rejected," says your God.
"For a brief moment I abandoned you,
    but with deep compassion I will bring you back."

ISAIAH 54:5–7

Then I heard what sounded like a great multitude, like the roar of rushing waters and like loud peals of thunder, shouting:

"Hallelujah!
    For our Lord God Almighty reigns.
Let us rejoice and be glad
    and give him glory!
For the wedding of the Lamb has come,
    and his bride has made herself ready.
Fine linen, bright and clean,
    was given her to wear."

(Fine linen stands for the righteous acts of the saints.)

Then the angel said to me, "Write: 'Blessed are those who are invited to the wedding supper of the Lamb!'" And he added, "These are the true words of God."

REVELATION 19:6–9

Lord, you left your Father's house to come to earth and claim me as your own. Thank you for showing me what love is by the way you lived your life. Preserve me from both worldliness and weariness as I await your coming. I pray that on that great and terrible day, I, along with all your people, will be ready, eagerly awaiting your return as our Savior and our Bridegroom.

Understanding the Name

Marriage in Israel was generally considered sacred, the only acceptable state of life for men and women. Despite polygynous practices, whereby a man could marry more than one wife, monogamy was the accepted pattern throughout most of biblical history, especially after the patriarchal period.

Most marriages were arranged by parents. The minimum age for girls was twelve and for boys was thirteen. The period of engagement or betrothal usually lasted a year and was considered so binding that a man who had intimate relations with a virgin betrothed to another man would be stoned. For the year following the marriage, the husband was exempt from military service. This practice prevented the bride from becoming a widow in her first year of marriage and it also allowed the man to devote himself more fully to his wife at the start of their marriage.

Though the marriage ceremony itself was brief, the celebration surrounding it could be elaborate, consisting of seven and sometimes fourteen days of feasting and celebrating. During the festivities, dating from the time of Solomon, both bride and groom were crowned as king and queen and their virtues were extolled in song and poetry.

The Hebrew Scriptures did not hesitate to describe the relationship between God and his people in the most intimate of terms: Yahweh was husband and Israel was his not-so-faithful wife. By referring to himself as the bridegroom, Jesus was clearly linking himself with Yahweh. New Testament writers presented the church as the bride of Christ. *Nymphios* (num-FEE-os) is the Greek word for "bridegroom" or "young husband" while *aner* (an-AIR) can be translated "man" or "husband."

When the disciples of John the Baptist asked Jesus why his disciples did not fast, Jesus replied that it was not possible for the guests of the bridegroom to mourn as long as he was with them (Matthew 9:14–15). John the Baptist used similar imagery when he referred to himself as the "friend who attends the bridegroom" or the best man (John 3:29).

Studying the Name

1. What does the passage from Isaiah reveal about God's character?
2. What does it reveal about the nature of his relationship with his chosen people?
3. How does the passage from Revelation compare and contrast with the passage from Isaiah?
4. What do you think it means that Jesus is the Bridegroom?

Tuesday

PRAYING THE NAME

Then I heard what sounded like a great multitude, like the roar of rushing waters and like loud peals of thunder, shouting:

> "Hallelujah!
>> For our Lord God Almighty reigns.
> Let us rejoice and be glad
>> and give him glory!
> For the wedding of the Lamb has come,
>> and his bride has made herself ready.
> Fine linen, bright and clean,
>> was given her to wear."

(Fine linen stands for the righteous acts of the saints.)

Then the angel said to me, "Write: 'Blessed are those who are invited to the wedding supper of the Lamb!'" And he added, "These are the true words of God."

REVELATION 19:6–9

Reflect On: Revelation 19:6–9.
Praise God: Whose love endures forever.
Offer Thanks: For Christ's intimate love.
Confess: Any distrust of God or his ways.
Ask God: To help you perceive his faithfulness.

I sometimes wonder why I am so easily frustrated, so quick to complain. My computer breaks down, my call is routed to the wrong person, my car won't start. Admittedly these are petty annoyances. But they feel so constant, like a stone in my shoe that I can't shake out. I tell myself my outsized response to such things is not merely a symptom of immaturity but a sign that I may be suffering from a hidden condition. I call it *paradisus absconditus*, otherwise known as the "paradise lost syndrome." You won't find it listed in a medical dictionary, but that doesn't mean it doesn't exist.

Let me explain. You may have heard of something called "phantom limb syndrome," a condition in which a person feels sensation in an amputated limb. Maybe paradise lost syndrome works in a similar way. But rather than experiencing sensation in a body part we no longer possess, we experience sensation about a state of being we no longer possess. My theory is this—that whether or not we know it, each of us has some kind of primeval memory of paradise. We have an instinct that tells us we belong there, and when that instinct is thwarted, as it always is, we feel frustrated, cheated, and disappointed. Everyday life contradicts our secret or not-so-secret belief that we were meant to live as the fairy tales tell us—happily every after. And happily ever after often involves our longing for the perfect relationship, one guaranteed to make us happy.

Our instinct for paradise will serve us well if it leads to the realization that our true happiness lies neither in perfect circumstances nor in finding the perfect relationship here on earth. Instead, it lies in restoring the most important relationship we will ever have, one fractured in Eden and one whose brokenness has spread to every other relationship in our lives.

Over and over, the Hebrew Scriptures present Israel's relationship with God in the most intimate terms possible. He is not just Maker and Lord but also Israel's Husband. But it also describes this as a troubled marriage because even though God is a perfect Lover, his people are not. Instead, they are broken, infected by sin, unable to trust, seduced by other gods. But still the Lord persists in loving them. Intent on restoring the relationship, he sends prophets to call them back and troubles to bring them home. But nothing works for long. So in a final act of mercy he sends his own Son.

This is why the Bible is best understood, neither as a book of rules nor as a compendium of wisdom, but as a love story, prolonged and painful but one that ends on a tremendous note of joy with the greatest of all celebrations: the wedding feast of the Lamb. This is also why the New Testament reveals Jesus as the Bridegroom whom the church awaits with longing. He is the promise we hope for, the purpose for which we were made. He is the One who is able to deal with our brokenness, to heal our sin, and to woo us back to himself through his powerful, self-sacrificing love. He is the paradise we seek.

Today as you suffer life's small indignities, don't allow them to become a source of continual frustration; instead, let them remind you of your longing for something more. Ask the Lord to help you turn your frustrations into occasions for praise as you express your desire to take part one day in the greatest of all celebrations, the wedding feast of the Lamb and his bride, the church.

Wednesday

PRAYING THE NAME

Now we see but a poor reflection as in a mirror; then we shall see face to face. Now I know in part; then I shall know fully, even as I am fully known.

1 CORINTHIANS 13:12

Then I saw "a new heaven and a new earth," for the first heaven and the first earth had passed away, and there was no longer any sea. I saw the Holy City, the new Jerusalem, coming down out of heaven from God, prepared as a bride beautifully dressed for her husband. And I heard a loud voice from the throne saying, "Look! God's dwelling place is now among the people, and he will dwell with them. They will be his people, and God himself will be with them and be their God."

REVELATION 21:1–3

Reflect On: Revelation 21:1–3, 9–27.

Praise God: For revealing his intentions for us.

Offer Thanks: For all the ways God has protected and provided for you, as a loving husband would.

Confess: Your need to experience God's love more consistently in your life.

Ask God: To help you prepare for the day of his coming.

⁀ↄ

You have probably heard about Plato's allegory of the cave and shadows. Here's how it works. Plato pictured a cave in which prisoners were chained together in a line. Unable to turn their heads, they could only see the cave wall directly in front of them. Behind them in the cave a fire burned and between them and the fire stood puppeteers supported by a parapet. Though the prisoners could see shadows of puppets cavorting across the wall in front of them, they could see neither the puppets nor their puppeteers. Hence they mistook the shadows for the real thing. By creating this allegory, Plato was helping us to understand how limited our perceptions are. Seeing the shape or the shadow of something, we mistake it for the thing itself.

I think we can apply Plato's cave story to one of our most cherished institutions — that of marriage itself. What if marriage in its ideal form is meant to be a shadow or an image of an even more intimate relationship for which all of us — single and married — are destined? What if it is meant to be not only the basic structure of human society but the structure of heaven itself, in which God will one day be perfectly and intimately united with his people?

Dan Brown's *The Da Vinci Code* advances the canard that Jesus and Mary Magdalene were lovers. But there is no evidence in the Gospels or in any of the ancient texts that this was so. And despite the fact that it would have been unusual for a man of his age to remain unmarried, there is no evidence that Jesus ever married. What if Jesus refrained from marriage to make the point that he is not just one woman's spouse but that he is every believer's intended?

Gary Thomas, the author of *Sacred Marriage*, debunks the popular notion that the primary purpose of human marriage is to provide two people with fulfilling companionship. "More than seeing marriage as a mutual comfort, we must see it as a word picture of the most important news humans have ever received — that there is a divine relationship between God and his people." He paints marriage not as an end in itself but as a staging ground for eternity, a spiritual discipline designed to lead married couples into greater holiness and intimacy with Christ.

The good news for single people and for couples is that Jesus is the One who ultimately fulfills our need for intimacy. He is the One who draws us out of our isolation and loneliness by uniting us to himself and to those who belong to him. We bear fruit to the degree that we are united to him.

But even if you are among those fortunate enough to lay claim to a good marriage or a strong church, you will at times feel lonely. When this happens, resist the temptation to either ignore the feeling or chase it away. Instead, let yourself feel empty and needy for a while. And

then pray into your loneliness this song of faith, written by Charles
Wesley:

> *Jesus, lover of my soul, let me to thy bosom fly,*
> *While the nearer waters roll, while the tempest still is high.*
> *Hide me, O my Savior, hide, till the storm of life is past;*
> *Safe into the haven guide; O receive my soul at last.*
>
> *Other refuge have I none, hangs my helpless soul on thee;*
> *Leave, ah! leave me not alone, still support and comfort me.*
> *All my trust on thee is stayed, all my help from thee I bring;*
> *Cover my defenseless head with the shadow of thy wing.*
>
> *Plenteous grace with thee is found, grace to cover all my sin;*
> *Let the healing streams abound; make and keep me pure within.*
> *Thou of life the fountain art, freely let me take of thee;*
> *Spring thou up within my heart; rise to all eternity.*

Thursday

PRAYING THE NAME

At that time the kingdom of heaven will be like ten virgins who took their lamps and went out to meet the bridegroom. Five of them were foolish and five were wise. The foolish ones took their lamps but did not take any oil with them. The wise, however, took oil in jars along with their lamps. The bridegroom was a long time in coming. . . . While they were on their way to buy the oil, the bridegroom arrived. The virgins who were ready went in with him to the wedding banquet. And the door was shut.

Later the others also came. "Sir! Sir!" they said. "Open the door for us!" But he replied, "I tell you the truth, I don't know you."

Therefore keep watch, because you do not know the day or the hour.

MATTHEW 25:1–5, 10–13

Reflect On: Matthew 25:1–13.

Praise God: Who calls us into his kingdom.

Offer Thanks: That God has invited you to the wedding feast of the Lamb.

Confess: Any complacency about Christ's return.

Ask God: To reveal areas of your life that require better preparation.

Take a few moments to imagine that you are about to be married. Yours is not a conventional twentieth-century wedding. No, the preparations for your wedding are much more elaborate because you are Jewish woman living in Palestine at the time of Jesus. You and your fiancé have already taken the first step, called the *kiddushin*, or betrothal. Once the marriage covenant is agreed on and the bride price paid, your engagement is so binding that your relationship with your fiancé can now be dissolved only by death or divorce. If another man were to accost you, he would be stoned to death. But despite the strong bond you have formed with your prospective husband, you and he are still living separately, both within your parents' homes. It will be another twelve months until the two of you can live together as husband and wife.

You will use the remaining months to prepare yourself for the responsibilities of marriage, making sure that your trousseau is complete. Meanwhile, your fiancé will be working hard to prepare a place for the two of you to live in, not somewhere out in the suburbs but in a house right next to his father's or even a room within his father's house. Once the preparations are complete, he will come for you at night, accompanied by a procession of friends and musicians. You will be wearing the family jewels, clothed in a white linen dress that has been stitched with fine gold thread. While you eagerly await your groom, your friends will wait with you. But sadly, some of them will miss the feast because they are ill prepared to celebrate it. Regardless, your bridegroom will take you home to celebrate the wedding feast with songs, music, and dancing.

This is the picture the New Testament paints concerning the spiritual time frame in which we are living. Just as the Jewish bridegroom comes for his bride after paying the bride price and completing a lengthy period of engagement, Jesus will come for his bride, the church. He will take us home to his Father's house to live with him forever. Right now we are living in a period analogous to the betrothal period. As members of the church, we need to get ready for the Bridegroom's coming. But how do we prepare, especially when we don't know exactly when he will come?

Though Jesus' second coming will be a time of great rejoicing for the faithful, Scripture also portrays it as a time when sudden disaster will overtake the world. But how can we possibly prepare for such a cataclysmic event as the end of the world? The only way we can is to live as though Jesus' coming is imminent, as though he may come today, tomorrow, or next week. Just as disaster-preparedness experts advise us to focus on natural basics like food, water, and medicine when preparing for a natural disaster, our readiness plan should involve focusing on the spiritual basics. Here is a quick list of items for your spiritual preparedness kit along with some Scripture passages for reference:

1. Repent daily (Matthew 3:2).

2. Get caught serving (Matthew 25:14–30).

3. Be quick to forgive (Matthew 18:23–32).

4. Never let the sun go down on your anger (Ephesians 4:25–27).

5. Pray always (1 Thessalonians 5:17).

6. Give thanks in all circumstances (1 Thessalonians 5:18).

7. Be generous to the poor (Luke 12:33–34).

8. Remember, no matter what, that God is faithful (1 Corinthians 10:12–13).

9. Link your life with other believers (1 Corinthians 12:12–27).

If you want to be like the wise virgins in the story from Matthew's Gospel, make certain you are at least practicing these basics of the faith. Doing so will help you deal with whatever personal disasters or challenges you may face, regardless of whether Jesus returns now or a thousand years from now. Once you have taken inventory of these basic spiritual practices, consider putting together your own spiritual readiness kit with faith practices that will help you effectively prepare for the coming of the most desirable of all bridegrooms, our Lord and Savior Jesus Christ.

Friday

PROMISES ASSOCIATED WITH HIS NAME

Think of the most troubled marriage you know of. Living in such a marriage must be miserable, nearly intolerable. Maybe that's how God felt about his relationship with his people, who had repeatedly responded to him like an unfaithful wife intent on pursuing affairs with other men. But rather than suing for divorce, God made the most gracious gesture imaginable. He came himself, in the person of Jesus Christ, to call his people back. Just like a Jewish groom, Jesus left his Father's house to come and pay the bride price for his beloved. But instead of paying in so many coins, Jesus secured the marriage covenant with his own blood.

Some of us are so familiar with the gospel that we are dulled to the shocking evidence it contains—that God loves us as a bridegroom who is passionately in love with his bride. Let us pray today for the grace to understand the lengths to which God has already gone to unite us to himself. And let us heed the voice of Jesus who tells us not to let our hearts be troubled as we wait for him, but to take heart because he is preparing a place for us—not on the margins or outskirts of heaven, but right inside his Father's house.

Promises in Scripture

> As a young man marries a maiden,
>   so will your sons marry you;
> as a bridegroom rejoices over his bride,
>   so will your God rejoice over you.
>
> ISAIAH 62:5

> I will betroth you to me forever;
>   I will betroth you in righteousness and justice,
>   in love and compassion.
> I will betroth you in faithfulness,
>   and you will acknowledge the LORD.
>
> HOSEA 2:19–20

Do not let your hearts be troubled. Trust in God; trust also in me. In my Father's house are many rooms; if it were not so, I would have told you. I am going there to prepare a place for you. And if I go and prepare a place for you, I will come back and take you to be with me that you also may be where I am.

JOHN 14:1–3

Continued Prayer and Praise

Read this extended poem as an image of God's love for his people. (Song of Songs)

Delight in the Lord for he delights in you. (Isaiah 61:10–62:5)

Remember that God is a husband who is always faithful. (Jeremiah 3:14–17, 20)

Consider God's mercy toward his bride. (Hosea 2:13–3:1)

Be ready for the coming wedding feast. (Matthew 22:1–14)

Consider the freedom you have because you belong to Christ. (Romans 7:1–6)

Understand the kind of husband Jesus is. (Ephesians 5:15–32)

Picture what God has for you. (Revelation 22:1–17)

20

SON OF DAVID

υἱὸς Δαυίδ

Huios Dauid

The Name

David was Israel's greatest king, a man whom the Bible describes as having the very heart of God. So it may not be surprising that the New Testament both begins and ends with references to Jesus as the Son or Offspring of David. He is the One who fulfilled the promise of a coming King so beloved by God that his throne will endure forever.

Like David, Jesus was born in Bethlehem (the city of David). And like David, who established his kingdom by overcoming Israel's enemies and uniting God's people, Jesus would establish his kingdom by defeating the principalities and powers, making a way for us to become part of it as we confess our faith in him. When you pray to Jesus as the Son of David, you are praying to the long-awaited King, human by virtue of his descent from David and divine by virtue of being God's only Son.

Key Scripture

The Lord God will give him the throne of his father David, and he will reign over the house of Jacob forever; his kingdom will never end.

LUKE 1:32–33

Monday

HIS NAME REVEALED

"Now then, tell my servant David, 'This is what the LORD Almighty says: I took you from the pasture and from following the flock, to be ruler over my people Israel. I have been with you wherever you have gone, and I have cut off all your enemies from before you. Now I will make your name like the names of the greatest men of the earth. And I will provide a place for my people Israel and will plant them so that they can have a home of their own and no longer be disturbed. Wicked people will not oppress them anymore, as they did at the beginning and have done ever since the time I appointed leaders over my people Israel. I will also subdue all your enemies.

"'I declare to you that the LORD will build a house for you: When your days are over and you go to be with your fathers, I will raise up your offspring to succeed you, one of your own sons, and I will establish his kingdom. He is the one who will build a house for me, and I will establish his throne forever. I will be his father, and he will be my son. I will never take my love away from him, as I took it away from your predecessor. I will set him over my house and my kingdom forever; his throne will be established forever.'"

1 CHRONICLES 17:7–14

In the sixth month, God sent the angel Gabriel to Nazareth, a town in Galilee, to a virgin pledged to be married to a man named Joseph, a descendant of David. The virgin's name was Mary. The angel went to her and said, "Greetings, you who are highly favored! The Lord is with you."

Mary was greatly troubled at his words and wondered what kind of greeting this might be. But the angel said to her, "Do not be afraid, Mary, you have found favor with God. You will be with child and give birth to a son, and you are to give him the name Jesus. He will be great and will be called the Son of the Most High. The Lord God will give him the throne of his father David, and he will reign over the house of Jacob forever; his kingdom will never end."

LUKE 1:26–33

Jesus, Son of David, take up your throne! Drive out your enemies and be our protector. Then rule with your wisdom and grace. Scatter the proud and raise up the lowly. Establish your kingdom now and forever. Amen.

Understanding the Name

The New Testament tells a story that cannot be adequately understood without reference to the Old Testament. Though composed of many books written at different times by different authors, much of the Bible is a continuing narrative that tells the story of salvation in ever-deepening detail. One of the ways it does this is by encapsulating the story or part of the story in the life of a particular person in the Bible whose shadow is then cast forward across the remaining pages of the Bible.

David is certainly one of these characters for in many ways his life prefigures the life of Christ. Like Christ, David conquered against incredible odds. Like Christ, he was beloved of God. And like Christ, he was a warrior king who defeated God's enemies. David began as a shepherd boy signifying Jesus' coming role as the Good Shepherd who would lay down his life for his sheep.

The Gospels refer to Jesus as the "Son of David" or *Huios Dauid* (hui-OS da-WEED) fifteen times, nine of these in the Gospel of Matthew. Many of the Jews at the time of Jesus believed that the Messiah would be a direct descendant of the great King David, whom God described "as a man after my own heart." More than once in the Gospels people in need of healing cried out to Jesus as the "Son of David," thus confessing their faith in him as the Messiah. The New Testament also refers to Jesus as the "Root and Offspring of David," the "descendant" or "seed" of David, and the one who holds the "key of David." Along with acknowledging Jesus as the rightful heir to David's throne, the title "Son of David" also locates Jesus within a human genealogy, that of Abraham and David.

Studying the Name

1. Do you think the prophecy recounted in 1 Chronicles was fulfilled in the life of David's son Solomon? Why or why not? (See 1 Kings 10:26–11:13.)

2. Compare the lives of Jesus and David. What similarities do you see? What differences?

3. Consider how different life might be if you lived under a completely corrupt or incompetent government. Now think of how different life might be if you lived in a country that was perfectly governed, ruled by a leader who was all-powerful, all-wise, and all-loving. Describe the differences.

Tuesday

PRAYING THE NAME

The LORD says to my Lord:
"Sit at my right hand
until I make your enemies
a footstool for your feet."

PSALM 110:1

While Jesus was teaching in the temple courts, he asked, "How is it that the teachers of the law say that the Christ is the son of David? David himself, speaking by the Holy Spirit, declared:

" 'The Lord said to my Lord:
"Sit at my right hand
until I put your enemies
under your feet." '

"David himself calls him 'Lord.' How then can he be his son?"
The large crowd listened to him with delight.

MARK 12:35–37

Reflect On: Psalm 110:1 and Mark 12:35–37.
Praise God: Who reigns over every earthly power.
Offer Thanks: For Christ's rule in your life and in the world.
Confess: The sins you feel most powerless against.
Ask God: To rule over any and every area of your life.

Every time I watch a presidential debate, I am struck by how much we expect of a would-be president. We want to know what each candidate plans to do to resolve global warming, terrorism, racism, poverty, educational deficiencies, energy shortages, the national debt, environmental problems — you name it. I recall one town hall debate in which a man in a wheelchair approached the platform to ask the candidates what they planned to do to help him with his particular disability. In every case, the candidates answered confidently, assuring their listeners that they were up to the challenge of resolving all these problems, even the one posed by the man in the wheelchair. It seemed to me that the audience had conspired with the candidates to inflate the presidency into an impossible job. I thought of Dorothy and the Wizard of Oz, who turned out to be not a real wizard but merely a mild-mannered man performing tricks behind a curtain.

Perhaps this kind of political inflation is rooted in a deeply held desire for a leader so powerful and wise that he or she is able to solve our intractable problems. In Israel's case, this desire expressed itself in the longing for a Messiah, a descendant of the great King David, who would drive out Israel's persistent enemies and restore the nation to its former glory. When people cried out to Jesus as the "Son of David," they were expressing their faith that he was this long-promised Messiah.

But what the people didn't understand was that they needed not just another David but someone far greater. They dreamed of a military leader who would drive out their Roman overlords, not realizing they needed a Savior who would drive out their sins. They longed for political power to restore the kingdom of Israel to its former glory, never reflecting on the fact that Israel, even at its peak, had never been more than a very small nation, which had flourished as a united nation for only about a hundred and twenty years — equivalent to something like a millisecond in the scope of world history.

Nor did the people of Jesus' day understand that David's Son would exceed David in all things. He would inaugurate a kingdom that extended throughout the world and one in which every trace of sickness and death would eventually be driven out, a kingdom in which the lion and the lamb, the poor and the rich, the great and the small would lie down together perfectly and forever at peace.

Today as you read the headlines or watch the nightly news, remember that it is important to pray for our nation and our political leaders. We should regularly ask God for wise and humble leadership, for men and women who hunger for justice and who are eager to pursue peace.

But remember too that we need more than good leadership. We need our sins forgiven, our relationships healed, our sicknesses overcome, our selfishness defeated. We need Jesus, the only King who is able to drive out our worst enemies and bring us together from every tribe and tongue and nation into a kingdom that will endure forever.

Wednesday

PRAYING THE NAME

As Jesus went on from there, two blind men followed him, calling out, "Have mercy on us, Son of David!"

When he had gone indoors, the blind men came to him, and he asked them, "Do you believe that I am able to do this?"

"Yes, Lord," they replied.

Then he touched their eyes and said, "According to your faith will it be done to you"; and their sight was restored.

MATTHEW 9:27–30

Reflect On:	Matthew 9:27–30.
Praise God:	Whose power is unlimited.
Offer Thanks:	That Christ has called you into his kingdom.
Confess:	Any unbelief in Jesus' power and desire to help you.
Ask God:	To strengthen your faith in the Son of David.

You've probably heard of the term "gerrymandering," named after Massachusetts governor Elbridge Gerry, who in 1812 redrew an electoral district in order to enhance his party's political power. As it happened, the district was redrawn in the shape of a salamander—hence the name. One of the most dramatic examples of this tactic took place a while ago in Texas where Democrats accused Republicans of gerrymandering the congressional map. Fifty-one Democratic congressmen holed up in a hotel in Oklahoma, across the border from Texas, in order to avoid debating and voting on a Republican-led bill that they said would turn the Lone Star State into a Republican monopoly.

At least from a distance, this struggle seemed comical, with one renegade congresswoman being forcibly escorted back to the state capitol in Austin, while the remaining "filthy fifty," as they were dubbed, eluded capture. Power grabs and land grabs, even in democratic countries, are commonplace. But this is not how Jesus, the Son of David, goes about extending and strengthening his kingdom.

More than once the Gospels link the title "Son of David" to the healing miracles of Jesus. In one instance, two blind men call out to Jesus as the Son of David. In another, it's the blind Bartimaeus, and in still another, it's a Canaanite woman who begs Jesus as the "Son of David" to cure her demon-possessed daughter. In each case these people confess two things: both their need and their faith. By addressing Jesus as the "Son of David" they are expressing their faith that he is the Messiah who can provide the healing or deliverance they desire. And none of them is disappointed because Jesus confirms their faith by doing as they ask. Because they believe in him, they both experience and display evidence of the new kingdom that is coming.

How can we experience the power of the "Son of David" at work in our own lives? Like the two blind men we need to cry out to Jesus, expressing both our faith in him and our desire to experience his healing, delivering power. As we do, we must seek first his kingdom and not our own. One way to do this is to follow the advice of A. B. Simpson, who said: "You can take Christ as the King of your life by giving Him your difficulties and adversaries to overcome, and permitting Him to subdue all His enemies and yours and reign as Lord of all. Everything that comes up in your life is but another opportunity of giving him a larger and richer crown."

Simpson's words made me wonder about my own difficulties. What things in my life did Christ want to subdue? As I prayed I began to think about the deep-seated, persistent anxiety I often experience with regard to my children. Lately these worries have felt like a constant pressure, making me irritable and impatient toward them. I began by asking the Lord's forgiveness for all my anxious efforts to control my children, asking him to reshape this area of my life with his wisdom, peace, and power. It's a prayer I am still praying, expressing my faith in Jesus and asking him to extend his reign and rule over my family as a way of extending his kingdom in and through us.

What difficulties do you face? What would happen if you asked for the grace to see *every* difficulty as an opportunity, as Simpson says, for giving Jesus, the Son of David, a larger and richer crown, extending his rule in, over, and around you? Start today by asking Jesus to be the King over your loneliness, your sorrow, your hurts, and your weaknesses. Let God's Spirit uncover areas in your life that are not yet fully under Christ's rule. Expose each one to him in prayer, expressing your faith that he is indeed the "Son of David," the Lord who is able to heal and deliver you, the King who wants to extend the boundaries of his kingdom by virtue of what he is doing in you.

Thursday

PRAYING THE NAME

Remember Jesus Christ, raised from the dead, descended from David. This is my gospel, for which I am suffering even to the point of being chained like a criminal. But God's word is not chained. Therefore I endure everything for the sake of the elect, that they too may obtain the salvation that is in Christ Jesus, with eternal glory.

2 TIMOTHY 2:8–10

Reflect On: 2 Timothy 2:8–10.
Praise God: For opening your eyes and ears to his mercy.
Offer Thanks: Because Christ wants to spread his kingdom through you.
Confess: Any reluctance to share your faith with others.
Ask God: To give you opportunities to tell others about how Christ has loved you.

Successful publishers understand how crucial it is to distinguish between "needs" and "felt needs." If a commercial publisher were to form its list simply by asking what people *need* to read rather than what people *want* to read, it wouldn't stay in business for long. Perhaps that's why Christian publishers rarely introduce new books on the topic of missions and evangelism. They know that most readers don't feel the need for such books even though it might be good if they did. And when I say most readers, I am including myself. In fact I confess to having a slight aversion to the word "evangelism" because it reminds me of something I should be doing but would rather not. But why do I find evangelism so difficult?

Jeffrey John, Dean of St. Alban's Cathedral in England, helped me answer that question when he wrote:

Before we can hear the Word of God, we need God himself to open our ears to do so. Our natural state is not one of readiness to hear his message; rather, it is the opposite.... The Prophets were in anguish over the people's spiritual deafness. Jesus wept for Jerusalem.... It is still the case that a Christian priest or minister, or any Christian who attempts to share the gospel, is likely to hit the same barrier and share something of the same agony, the agony of God desperately trying to get through to his estranged children. However we understand the doctrine of the Fall, a large part of its meaning is that we are born spiritually autistic—instinctively self-centred and self-enclosed. In our natural state it is hard for God to break through to us, and for us to break through to him.

No wonder I find it difficult to share my faith! Only grace can forge an opening for the gospel, leaving people free to resist that grace if they choose. But while I, like most people, dislike encountering resistance, I realize that my aversion to evangelism goes far deeper. My biggest problem is not that I hate conflict but that I lack love. Because if I loved people more, I would share more of God's anguish for the lost. Without love's propelling force, I have neither the energy nor the courage to share my faith, despite the fact that I, like all believers, am called to spread the good news of the kingdom.

I want God to change my heart, to help me break out of my own self-centeredness so that I can experience two things—more anguish and more love for his estranged children. Pray with me today to the One who is called the "Son of David," remembering that God described David as "a man after my own heart." Ask Jesus to give you his heart for those who are still far from him. Think especially of the men, women, and children in your own circle of influence. Ask God to break through their blindness and their deafness so that they can begin to perceive his goodness and his love.

Friday

PROMISES ASSOCIATED WITH HIS NAME

What comes to mind when you think of a promise—a rainbow, a ring, a stump? A stump! That is precisely the image Isaiah used when he spoke of the promised Messiah. He was saying that God would fulfill his promise to David despite impossible odds. The New Testament reveals that God kept that promise when, hundreds of years after David's dynasty had fallen, Jesus was born in Bethlehem.

But how does this ancient prophecy apply now, in a world in which the strong still dominate the weak and the poor often have no voice? This word from Isaiah, it would seem, still awaits its completion. Even though the King has been revealed, his power is still veiled and his kingdom often grows in ways that are hidden and obscure. As believers and members of the kingdom we are called to wait in faith, seeking to advance the kingdom until Christ comes again, this time fully revealing his power, his justice, and his majesty. On that day perfect judgment will bring forth perfect peace and all God's people will worship the King, who is called Wonderful Counselor, Mighty God, Prince of Peace.

Promises in Scripture

> A shoot will come up from the stump of Jesse [David's father];
> > from his roots a Branch will bear fruit.
> The Spirit of the LORD will rest on him—
> > the Spirit of wisdom and of understanding,
> > the Spirit of counsel and of power,
> > the Spirit of knowledge and of the fear of the LORD—
> and he will delight in the fear of the LORD.
> He will not judge by what he sees with his eyes,
> > or decide by what he hears with his ears;
> but with righteousness he will judge the needy,
> > with justice he will give decisions for the poor of the earth.

ISAIAH 11:1–4

For to us a child is born,
  to us a son is given,
  and the government will be on his shoulders.
And he will be called
  Wonderful Counselor, Mighty God,
  Everlasting Father, Prince of Peace.
Of the increase of his government and peace
  there will be no end.
He will reign on David's throne
  and over his kingdom,
establishing and upholding it
  with justice and righteousness
  from that time on and forever.
The zeal of the LORD Almighty
  will accomplish this.

ISAIAH 9:6–7

Continued Prayer and Praise

Worship the King. (Matthew 1:1–2:12)

Understand that Jesus is great David's greater son. (Acts 13:21–39)

Consider the key of David. (Revelation 3:7–10)

Remember the Root of David. (Revelation 5:1–5; 22:16)

21

PRIEST, PROPHET

ἱερεύς, προφήτης

HIEREUS, PROPHETES

The Names

Jesus is both Priest—the One who faithfully bears us into God's presence by virtue of his self-sacrifice—and Prophet—the One who perfectly communicates God's Word to us. We are called to listen to him, to trust in his work, and to take our places as part of a kingdom of priests who in Christ Jesus offer ourselves on behalf of others. As you pray to Jesus as both Priest and Prophet, ask him to help you understand the deep meaning of these titles so that you can live out their truths in your life.

Key Scriptures

Therefore, since we have a great high priest who has gone through the heavens, Jesus the Son of God, let us hold firmly to the faith we profess.

HEBREWS 4:14

In the past God spoke to our forefathers through the prophets at many times and in various ways, but in these last days he has spoken to us by his Son.

HEBREWS 1:1

Monday

HIS NAMES REVEALED

Therefore, since we have a great high priest who has gone through the heavens, Jesus the Son of God, let us hold firmly to the faith we profess. For we do not have a high priest who is unable to sympathize with our weaknesses, but we have one who has been tempted in every way, just as we are—yet was without sin. Let us then approach the throne of grace with confidence, so that we may receive mercy and find grace to help us in our time of need.

HEBREWS 4:14–16

The LORD your God will raise up for you a prophet like me [Moses] from among your own brothers. You must listen to him. For this is what you asked of the LORD your God at Horeb on the day of the assembly when you said, "Let us not hear the voice of the LORD our God nor see this great fire anymore, or we will die."

The LORD said to me: "What they say is good. I will raise up for them a prophet like you from among their brothers; I will put my words in his mouth, and he will tell them everything I command him."

DEUTERONOMY 18:15–18

In the past God spoke to our forefathers through the prophets at many times and in various ways, but in these last days he has spoken to us by his Son, whom he appointed heir of all things, and through whom he made the universe. The Son is the radiance of God's glory and the exact representation of his being, sustaining all things by his powerful word.

HEBREWS 1:1–3

Thank you, Lord, for understanding what it means to be weak and tempted, and thank you also for never giving in to temptation. You are the only one able to bring me to the Father so that my sins can be forgiven. Through your life and through your death you have told me who God is and what his plans are for me. Now I pray that you will help me to imitate you, so that others might know you as both Priest and Prophet. Amen.

Understanding the Names

Prophet, priest, and king—these were the three major offices in Israel, titles also ascribed to Jesus. While the king governed as God's representative on earth, the priest's role was to represent the people to God by offering sacrifices, prayers, and praise on their behalf. Unlike kings and priests, which were normally hereditary offices held only by males, prophets had to be commissioned by God, and they could be either male or female.

The role of the priest was to bring the people before God. Moses' brother, Aaron, was the first Jewish priest. Thereafter priests were drawn from among his descendants, and they were given charge of worship, which eventually became centralized in the Jerusalem temple. Unlike worship in many churches today, Jewish worship primarily consisted not in singing songs and listening to sermons but in offering sacrifices as prescribed by the Mosaic law. The priest's role was to offer sacrifices for his own sins and for the sins of the people. The animals killed in the temple served as a continual reminder to both priests and people that the penalty for sin is death.

The priesthood consisted of three groups: the high priest, ordinary priests, and Levites. The Levites occupied the lowest rung of the ladder, taking care of the temple service. The priests, who alone could offer sacrifice, were next. At the pinnacle stood the high priest, the only one authorized to enter the Most Holy Place on the Day of Atonement. On his ephod (a garment attached to the breastpiece) were stones that bore the names of the twelve tribes of Israel, a physical reminder that the high priest was bearing the people into God's presence.

The New Testament identifies Jesus as a priest according to the order of Melchizedek (Melchizedek, a priest who was a contemporary of Abraham, predated the Levites). This was a way of indicating that his priesthood was both different and superior to that of the Levitical priesthood. Though most priests in Jerusalem at the time of Jesus rejected him, the book of Hebrews, emphasizing Jesus' role as High Priest, may have been aimed primarily at priests who became believers after the resurrection. The Greek word for "priest" is *hierus* (hee-uh-REUS).

While the primary role of the priest was to speak to God on behalf of the people, the prophet's primary responsibility was to speak to the people on behalf of God. The great prophets of the Hebrew Scriptures included Moses, Isaiah, Jeremiah, Elijah, and Elisha. While prophets sometimes predicted future events, more often they called people to faithfulness.

Jesus acknowledged that his cousin, John, was a prophet—and more than a prophet because he prophesied most clearly about the Messiah. Though the common people acclaimed Jesus as a prophet and though he seemed comfortable with this title, most of the priests rejected this title for Jesus. In a Jewish context, Jesus' baptism in the Jordan, when the Spirit descended on him, would have been understood as a time of commissioning by God as a prophet. But unlike the prophets who preceded him, Jesus would be the one Prophet who not only perfectly revealed God's Word but who perfectly revealed God himself.

The New Testament identifies several people besides John the Baptist as prophets or as people who prophesied at one time or another. These included John's father, Zechariah; Anna; Simeon; Elizabeth; the high priest Caiphas; Agabus; and Barnabas. The New Testament also indicates that there were prophets in the early church and that prophecy was considered one of the spiritual gifts. The Greek word *prophetes* (pro-PHAY-tays) is found 144 times in the New Testament, which in proportion to its length, contains as many references to prophets and prophecies as do the Hebrew Scriptures.

Studying the Name

1. Why do you think it is important that Jesus, as High Priest, is able to sympathize with our weaknesses?

2. What about Jesus made him capable of sympathizing with us?

3. Why do you think Jesus was more effective than the priests of the Old Testament?

4. What do you think it means to say that "the Son is the radiance of God's glory"?

5. How has Jesus as Prophet revealed God to you?

Tuesday

PRAYING THE NAME

Therefore, since we have a great high priest who has gone through the heavens, Jesus the Son of God, let us hold firmly to the faith we profess. For we do not have a high priest who is unable to sympathize with our weaknesses, but we have one who has been tempted in every way, just as we are—yet was without sin. Let us then approach the throne of grace with confidence, so that we may receive mercy and find grace to help us in our time of need.

HEBREWS 4:14–16

Reflect On: Leviticus 16 and Hebrews 4:14–16.

Praise God: For sending us a High Priest who can sympathize with our weaknesses.

Offer Thanks: For the forgiveness you have been granted.

Confess: Any tendency to believe that you alone can pay for your sins.

Ask God: To help you approach him with confidence because of Jesus.

∽

Remember those Russian nesting dolls? When you open the first one, you discover another just like it nesting inside. As you open each successive doll, you find a smaller one until finally you reach the last and smallest doll of all—a miniature of all the others. I think the Bible often operates like this, only in reverse. You start with the nugget of something, a truth or a promise or a character, and then as the Bible progresses you get larger, more explicit versions of them until all the figures and types and shadows finally converge, coming into focus in the life of one particular man, in the life of Jesus.

Take the Day of Atonement, for instance. Every year for thousands of years, the Jewish people have celebrated this day as the holiest day of the year. But maybe it's misleading to say they "celebrate" it, for the Day of Atonement (Yom Kippur) is a time of fasting, of soul searching, of asking God's forgiveness for wrongs seen and unseen. During Jesus' lifetime and for hundreds of years before that, the high priest would bow his head and walk reverently into the holiest place on earth — the place in the temple where God's presence was thought to dwell. He would enter not as a proud man but as a sinner on behalf of sinners. There he would confess his sins and the sins of all the people, sacrificing animals in order to make things right with God.

But the forgiveness obtained on that day was only partial, and the ceremony had to be repeated year after year. Why? Because the only acceptable payment for sin is death, and animals cannot possibly pay the price for human sin. But if the high priest's offering was mere pocket change in comparison to the size of the debt, why did God insist that the ceremony be repeated over and over?

Last year, my daughter's third grade class spent several weeks immersed in what her teacher called a "mini-economy course." Each child was hired for a particular job, something simple like managing a mini-store in the classroom or recording average daily temperatures as an assistant weather person. Wages were paid in the form of play money, which could then be used to make purchases at the mini-store. But first each child had to set aside enough money to cover basic expenses like food, clothing, shelter, and health care. I felt a twinge of envy when Katie smugly informed me that her health care cost only five dollars a month! But I knew my daughter was learning a little about how real life works.

I think God works in similar ways. He begins by giving his people mini-lessons about how the universe works, showing them that sin exacts a price, that it produces death. And once the people understand this, he makes it clear that they can never pay off the debt their sins have incurred. Then he repeats the lesson year after year to help them understand their predicament.

But not wanting to frustrate them forever, God sent the only High Priest capable of wiping out the debt completely. He sent Jesus, who began by immersing himself in our life and by sharing our sorrows, our hopes, our happiness, our weakness, our temptations. He shared everything but our guilt so that he could represent us, bearing us in his heart without also bearing sin of his own into the presence of God. Instead of placing an animal on the altar like so much play money, Jesus climbed onto it himself, offering the most precious currency of all — his life.

The next time you sin (for most of us that will be today), ask Christ to forgive you. Then picture yourself before your great High Priest. Imagine him not as a scolding, disapproving high priest, but as he is — the One who bears you tenderly in his heart, carrying you straight to the Father who forgives you.

Wednesday

PRAYING THE NAME

When Christ came as high priest of the good things that are already here, he went through the greater and more perfect tabernacle that is not man-made, that is to say, not a part of this creation. He did not enter by means of the blood of goats and calves; but he entered the Most Holy Place once for all by his own blood, having obtained eternal redemption. The blood of goats and bulls and the ashes of a heifer sprinkled on those who are ceremonially unclean sanctify them so that they are outwardly clean. How much more, then, will the blood of Christ, who through the eternal Spirit offered himself unblemished to God, cleanse our consciences from acts that lead to death, so that we may serve the living God!

HEBREWS 9:11 – 14

Reflect On: Hebrews 8:7 – 12; 9:11 – 14.

Praise God: For giving us a High Priest able to deal decisively with our sins.

Offer Thanks: For the way Christ has cleansed your conscience.

Confess: Any tendency to reject the forgiveness that Jesus offers.

Ask God: To help you begin and end each day with the assurance of his forgiveness.

It has been said that the longest distance in the world is the eighteen inches between the head and the heart. That's the distance that belief has to travel before it becomes part of us. We may know something intellectually but not know it emotionally, in a way that shapes our expectations and behaviors. Maybe that's why so many people have trouble with forgiveness. Some of us refuse to accept it until we've punished ourselves for a while, wallowing in guilt or forging the grim determination to do better even and especially if it kills us.

New Orleans in the summer of 1853 was a frightening place to live. Tar-filled barrels were blazing in the streets. Cannons boomed every twenty minutes in an effort to disperse the putrid winds that were thought to cause disease. People covered their mouths with vinegar-soaked cloths and put garlic in their shoes. But these desperate measures did nothing to stop eight thousand people from dying in a yellow fever epidemic. It would be nearly fifty years before researchers would discover that yellow fever is not caused by pestilent air but by biting mosquitoes, and another thirty years before a vaccine would be developed.

From the comfortable perspective of the twenty-first century, setting off cannons to prevent yellow fever seems just shy of ridiculous. But these measures, which must have seemed reasonable at the time, were no further off the mark than our own pathetic efforts to deal with sin our way. Like New Orleans' booming cannons, constant self-recrimination only adds to our suffering. Sooner than later, our grief over sin should give way to the sense that God still loves us, that he is still merciful, still kind, still forgiving. To fail to receive forgiveness is not a sign of humility but of unbelief. And unbelief is a frightening place to live because it multiplies dangers by acting as a barrier to grace, impeding God's plan for our lives.

Jesus is the great High Priest, whose perfect self-offering has won for us complete forgiveness. In a seventeenth-century graveyard in Manhattan stands a gravestone startling in its simplicity. It contains no name or other distinguishing mark, but only a single word—a benediction that captures what it means for us to belong to Christ. That word is "Forgiven." Let us ask the Holy Spirit today to engrave this powerful word not only in our minds but on our hearts so that we can be set free to serve the living God with greater faith and power.

Thursday

PRAYING THE NAME

But you are a chosen people, a royal priesthood, a holy nation, a people belonging to God, that you may declare the praises of him who called you out of darkness into his wonderful light. Once you were not a people, but now you are the people of God; once you had not received mercy, but now you have received mercy.

1 PETER 2:9–10

Follow the way of love and eagerly desire spiritual gifts, especially the gift of prophecy. For those who speak in a tongue do not speak to other people but to God. Indeed, no one understands them; they utter mysteries by the Spirit. But those who prophesy speak to people for their strengthening, encouragement and comfort.

1 CORINTHIANS 14:1–3

Reflect On: 1 Peter 2:9–10; 1 Corinthians 14:1–3.
Praise God: For giving you the privilege of becoming an intercessor.
Offer Thanks: Because Jesus has called you into service in his kingdom.
Confess: Any selfishness that impedes your prayers.
Ask God: To increase the power of your prayers and to give you a desire for the gift of prophecy.

As Christians we know that our primary purpose in life is to imitate Christ. The goal is to become as much like Jesus as possible, expressing his heart to others. But did you know that becoming a "little Christ" also involves taking on certain of his roles? When it comes to Jesus' role as Priest and Prophet, the New Testament makes it clear that believers belong to "a royal priesthood" and that we are all to desire the gift of prophecy.

I don't know about you, but I find it hard to imagine myself presiding over a burnt offering or thunderously declaiming the Word of the Lord to anyone. But, of course, this is not how Christians are to express these roles. To put it simply, we are to be like priests in that we bear the people to God and like prophets in that we bear God's Word to the people. Jesus, of course, was the greatest of all prophets because he was the only one able to represent God perfectly, without distortions. But we too should desire to communicate God in our words and through our deeds.

But what about being priests? What exactly does that mean? One of the most important ways that a priest represented people before God was to intercede for them, carrying them in prayer to God. As believers in Christ we have a great advantage over Old Testament priests because our High Priest has entered not an earthly temple but heaven itself, the holiest place in the universe, where he continually intercedes for us. Our own prayers are meant not to be uttered in isolation but to be spoken in him and through him. I like how Michael Ramsey defines intercession:

> To intercede is to bear others on the heart in God's presence.... Intercession thus becomes not the bombardment of God with requests so much as the bringing of our desires within the stream of God's own compassion.... The compassion of God flows ceaselessly toward the world, but it seems to wait upon the cooperation of human wills. This cooperation is partly by God's creatures doing the things which God desires to be done, and partly by prayers which are also channels of God's compassion.

Real intercession, then, does not consist in presenting God with a laundry list of demands or requests. Instead it involves spending time in God's presence, seeking his will, being guided by his Spirit as we offer up prayers on behalf of others. As Evelyn Underhill put it:

> Each time you take a human soul with you into your prayer, you accept from God a piece of spiritual work with all its implications and with all its cost—a cost which may mean for you spiritual exhaustion and darkness, and may even include vicarious suffering, the Cross. In offering yourselves on such levels of prayer for

the sake of others, you are offering to take your part in the mysterious activities of the spiritual world; to share the saving work of Christ.... Real intercession is not merely a petition but a piece of work, involving costly self surrender to God for the work he wants done on other souls.

Ask Christ to increase your desire to be like him, to speak his Word with a pure heart, and to reflect his love by becoming an intercessor, taking others into your heart so that you can carry them into God's presence through prayer.

Friday

PROMISES ASSOCIATED WITH HIS NAME

Jesus as Prophet is both the Messenger and the Message, communicating God's plan and God's heart in ways that would have startled the greatest of the Old Testament prophets. That God would pare himself to the size of a human being and then walk in a world he had created, teaching people his ways and then dying to pay the debt they owed him — this was beyond the wildest of dreams, the greatest of hopes.

And yet it happened. That's why our hope in Christ will never be disappointed no matter how difficult life in this world may become. The whole point of Christ's coming was not to make us happy for a few years on this earth but to bring us to heaven, where mansions are even now being built, where tears will certainly cease, and where the dead will rise up and live forever.

Promises in Scripture

Let not your heart be troubled; you believe in God, believe also in Me. In My Father's house are many mansions; if it were not so, I would have told you. I go to prepare a place for you. And if I go and prepare a place for you, I will come again and receive you to Myself; that where I am, there you may be also.

JOHN 14:1–3, NKJV

If God is for us, who can be against us? He who did not spare his own Son, but gave him up for us all — how will he not also, along with him, graciously give us all things? Who will bring any charge against those whom God has chosen? It is God who justifies. Who is he that condemns? Christ Jesus, who died — more than that, who was raised to life — is at the right hand of God and is also interceding for us.

ROMANS 8:31–34

Now there have been many of those priests, since death prevented them from continuing in office; but because Jesus lives forever, he has a permanent priesthood. Therefore he is able to save completely those who come to God through him, because he always lives to intercede for them.

HEBREWS 7:23–25

Continued Prayer and Praise

Consider that there is one mediator between God and human beings. (1 Timothy 2:5)

Understand what it meant for Jesus to be High Priest. (Hebrews 2:14–18; 5:4–6; 7:26–9:15)

Remember your priestly call. (1 Peter 2:4–5; Revelation 1:4–6; 5:10)

Draw near to God with confidence. (Hebrews 10:19–25)

Listen to Jesus' high priestly prayer. (John 17)

Remember that the common people thought Jesus was a prophet. (Luke 24:17–24; John 6:12–15; 7:37–52)

Consider that Jesus, like all prophets, will be rejected by some. (Matthew 13:54–58; Luke 13:31–34)

Listen to him. (Matthew 17:1–5; John 3:31–36; 16:12–15; Acts 3:17–22; Hebrews 3:7–14)

Remember God's promise to pour out his Spirit. (Acts 2:14–18)

22

SON OF GOD, SON OF MAN

υἱὸς τοῦ θεοῦ, υἱὸς τοῦ ἀνθρώπου

HUIOS TOU THEOU,
HUIOS TOU ANTHROPOU

The Name

Like the Father, Jesus is God. He always was, always is, and always will be. But unlike the Father, Jesus is also a human being. Though charged with blasphemy and crucified for claiming to be one with the Father, Jesus' resurrection validates his claim to be God's Son in a unique way. When we confess our belief that Jesus is the Son of God, we share in the love the Father has for the Son, becoming adopted children of God.

Though Jesus was the Son of God, he was also the Son of Man, a title that emphasizes both his lowliness and his eventual dominion. Near the end of his life, when the high priest asked him whether he was the Son of God, Jesus no longer avoided the title but said that he would one day "see the Son of Man sitting at the right hand of the Mighty One and coming on the clouds of heaven" (Matthew 26:64). When you pray to Jesus as Son of God and Son of Man, you are praying to the One who is your Brother and your Lord.

Key Scripture

"But what about you?" he asked. "Who do you say I am?"

Simon Peter answered, "You are the Messiah, the Son of the living God."

Jesus replied, "Blessed are you, Simon son of Jonah, for this was not revealed to you by flesh and blood, but by my Father in heaven."

MATTHEW 16:15–17

Monday

HIS NAME REVEALED

In my vision at night I looked, and there before me was one like a son of man, coming with the clouds of heaven. He approached the Ancient of Days and was led into his presence. He was given authority, glory and sovereign power; all nations and peoples of every language worshiped him. His dominion is an everlasting dominion that will not pass away, and his kingdom is one that will never be destroyed.

Daniel 7:13–14

When Jesus came to the region of Caesarea Philippi, he asked his disciples, "Who do people say the Son of Man is?"

They replied, "Some say John the Baptist; others say Elijah; and still others, Jeremiah or one of the prophets."

"But what about you?" he asked. "Who do you say I am?"

Simon Peter answered, "You are the Messiah, the Son of the living God."

Jesus replied, "Blessed are you, Simon son of Jonah, for this was not revealed to you by flesh and blood, but by my Father in heaven. And I tell you that you are Peter, and on this rock I will build my church, and the gates of death will not overcome it. I will give you the keys of the kingdom of heaven; whatever you bind on earth will be bound in heaven, and whatever you loose on earth will be loosed in heaven." Then he ordered his disciples not to tell anyone that he was the Messiah.

From that time on Jesus began to explain to his disciples that he must go to Jerusalem and suffer many things at the hands of the elders, the chief priests and the teachers of the law, and that he must be killed and on the third day be raised to life.

Matthew 16:13–21

Lord, Jesus, open my eyes to the mystery of who you are — God's only Son who became a man that we might be reconciled to the Father. Open my ears to hear your voice and my heart to do your will. Shape me in your likeness by the power of your Spirit as I grow in greater maturity as a child of the living God.

Understanding the Name

Though the phrase "sons of God" was occasionally used in the Hebrew Scriptures, the Greek phrase "Son of God," *Huios tou Theou* (hui-OS tou the-OU) belongs to Jesus in a unique way. Jesus himself indicates that he and the Father are one. He is the only man who could bear the title without dishonoring the Father.

But Jesus is God's Son not in the sense that most Westerners think of sonship, as though the Father preexisted him. Instead, Jesus is God's Son in the sense that he shares his nature and represents his intentions. He is fully divine and therefore perfectly capable of representing the Father on earth. Twice in the Gospels — at Jesus' baptism and at the transfiguration — a voice from heaven announced: "This is my Son whom I love." During Jesus' earthly ministry, even the demons recognized Christ as the "Son of God." However, it was this politically charged title that led to Jesus' death, which may be why he avoided it until the end of his life. Recognizing this as a primary title of Christ, the early church baptized those who confessed Jesus Christ as the Son of God. These early believers understood, as we do, that our relationship with Christ enables us to become adopted children of the Father.

Though Jesus was the Son of God, his favorite title for himself was the "Son of Man," *Huios tou Anthropou* (hui-OS tou an-THROW-pou). It's a somewhat enigmatic title. But certainly a primary meaning of it is that Jesus is the perfect Human Being. He shows us through his life on earth what men and women were intended by God to be before we fell prey to sin. But the title also has messianic connotations and is closely connected with Jesus' second coming.

Together the titles Son of Man and Son of God express the incredible mystery of the incarnation — that the second person of the Trinity came down from heaven to become one of us so that we could be one with him. When Jesus rose from the dead, he ascended into heaven, not just as God but also as a man. C. S. Lewis remarked on this truth, saying: "I seldom meet any strong or exultant sense of the continued, never-to-be-abandoned, Humanity of Christ in glory, in eternity. We stress the Humanity too exclusively at Christmas, and the Deity too exclusively after the Resurrection; almost as if Christ once became a man and then presently reverted to being simply God. We think of the Resurrection and Ascension (rightly) as great acts of God; less often as the triumph of Man."

Studying the Name

1. How did Jesus fulfill Daniel's vision of "one like a son of man"?

2. What do you think it means to say that Jesus is the Son of God?

3. Why do you think Jesus cautioned his disciples against telling anyone that he was the Messiah?

4. Describe your image of the ideal father. How does this compare with your image of who God is?

5. Describe your image of the ideal son or daughter. How does this compare with your image of yourself in relationship to God?

6. How does Jesus as the ideal Human Being reflect your understanding of God's purpose for all human beings?

Tuesday

PRAYING THE NAME

When Jesus came to the region of Caesarea Philippi, he asked his disciples, "Who do people say the Son of Man is?"

They replied, "Some say John the Baptist; others say Elijah; and still others, Jeremiah or one of the prophets."

"But what about you?" he asked. "Who do you say I am?"

Simon Peter answered, "You are the Messiah, the Son of the living God."

MATTHEW 16:13–16

Reflect On: Matthew 16:13–16.

Praise God: Who is Infinite Mystery.

Offer Thanks: For Jesus who is both Son of God and Son of Man.

Confess: Your limited understanding.

Ask God: To give you deeper insights into his nature.

I have a sneaking suspicion that many of us who believe in the doctrine of the Trinity still tend to relate to Jesus and the Father as though they are two separate deities. Last year I tried to shore up my theological understanding by purchasing a couple of hefty tomes on the Trinity. Perhaps I am naïve, but I expected it to be a thrilling experience. After all I was hunting God, intent on knowing him better. What could be more exciting?

But sadly my search produced more yawns than insight. After wading through page after page of theological lingo, I still didn't get it—how could there be three Persons in one God? I was reduced to thinking about all the simplistic metaphors that have been devised to help children approach this awesome mystery—water as liquid, steam, and ice; a clover with three leaves; a chord with three notes; an egg with shell, white, and yolk; sunlight refracted into a rainbow of colors.

I have the same problem when it comes to understanding the mystery of how Jesus can be both Son of God and Son of Man. How can these two natures coexist? Not meaning to be irreverent, I think of my favorite salad dressing, a calorie-rich balsamic vinaigrette. But this isn't a workable analogy because the oil in the dressing always separates from the vinegar, settling on top like a thick yellow ribbon. Maybe, I think, it is more like a vial of clear water into which brightly colored dye is poured. The water is still water but every bit of it is imbued with the color of the dye. But this seems like such a feeble way of imagining a muscular theological truth. In the end, I simply give up. I cannot fathom how Jesus can be both human and divine though I believe he is.

Toward the end of his life, one of the twentieth century's most famous theologians had the humility to remark about himself that "the angels are laughing at old Karl Barth for trying to grasp God." All of us need this kind of humility when it comes to understanding the mystery of who God is.

George Washington Carver, a former slave who became a scientist, is famous for his many discoveries, including hundreds of uses for the peanut. He once charmingly remarked, "When I was young, I said to God, 'God, tell me the mystery of the universe.' But God answered, 'That knowledge is for me alone.' So I said, 'God, tell me the mystery of the peanut.' Then God said, 'Well, George, that's more nearly your size.'"

So God is mystery, unfathomable and profound. Yet he reveals as much of himself as we can take in, that he is powerful, loving, good, and forgiving, and that in the Person of Jesus he has taken up our infirmities and carried our sorrows in order to save us. When it comes to penetrating the mystery of Christ, love is a better tool even than intellectual curiosity. To quote George Washington Carver again: "Anything will give up its secrets if you love it enough. Not only have I found that when I talk to the little flower or to the little peanut they will give up their secrets but I have found that when I silently commune with people they give up their secrets also — if you love them enough." Today, may we love Christ enough to entice him to reveal more of who he is and how he cares for us.

Wednesday

PRAYING THE NAME

In the same way the chief priests, the teachers of the law and the elders mocked him. "He saved others," they said, "but he can't save himself! He's the King of Israel! Let him come down now from the cross, and we will believe in him. He trusts in God. Let God rescue him now if he wants him, for he said, 'I am the Son of God. . . .'"

And when Jesus had cried out again in a loud voice, he gave up his spirit.

At that moment the curtain of the temple was torn in two from top to bottom. The earth shook and the rocks split. The tombs broke open and the bodies of many holy people who had died were raised to life. They came out of the tombs, and after Jesus' resurrection they went into the holy city and appeared to many people.

When the centurion and those with him who were guarding Jesus saw the earthquake and all that had happened, they were terrified, and exclaimed, "Surely he was the Son of God!"

MATTHEW 27:41–43, 50–54

> *The eternal God is your refuge,*
> *and underneath are the everlasting arms.*
>
> DEUTERONOMY 33:27

Reflect On   Matthew 27:41–54 and Deuteronomy 33:27.
Praise God: For sending his beloved Son.
Offer Thanks: Because God considers you his child.
Confess: Your faith in Jesus as the Son of God.
Ask God: To deepen your sense of being his son or his daughter.

Have you ever played a game in which you let yourself fall backward into someone else's arms? It's difficult not to hedge your bets, not to sneak a look around to see whether the other person stands ready to catch you. Now imagine a more difficult challenge. This time you stand with your back toward an open grave and your task is to fall backwards into it. Your friend has assured you he will be there to catch you as you fall. The success of this venture depends on two things: your trust and your friend's ability to keep his promise.

I imagine that Jesus' death must have been something like that. Though he was God, he had to fall back helplessly into a human grave, trusting that the Father who loved him would raise him up. To do this, Jesus had to have been absolutely secure in his identity as God's Son.

In fact, Jesus never called God by any other name than Father, except once, when quoting directly from a psalm. Over and over, it was always "Father":

Didn't you know I had to be in my *Father's* house?
Father, protect them by the power of your name.
Father, I want those you have given me to be with me where I am.
Abba, Father, everything is possible for you.
Father, forgive them, for they do not know what they are doing.
Father, into your hands I commit my spirit.

Jesus was crucified for one thing—for claiming to be God's Son. So it is interesting to note that when the earth shook at the moment of his death—the exact moment when the Son, falling into the grave, had need of his *Abba's* all-powerful arms to raise him up—the centurion and those with him guarding Jesus exclaimed in terror: "Surely he was the Son of God!" (Matthew 27:54).

Abba, a word derived from baby language to describe Almighty God! A word that would have sounded shocking to pious Jews! This is how Jesus expressed his relationship with *Yahweh*—as my Daddy, my Dear Father. It is the way he wants all of his followers to think of God. Listen to what Paul says to the Galatian Christians: "Because you are sons, God sent the Spirit of his Son into our hearts, the Spirit who calls out, 'Abba, Father'" (Galatians 4:6).

Your *Father* knows what you need before you ask him.
This, then, is how you should pray: "Our *Father* in heaven,
    hallowed be your name."
How much more will your *Father* in heaven give good gifts to
    those who ask him!
If you forgive others when they sin against you, your heavenly
    Father will also forgive you.
It is your *Father's* good pleasure to give you the kingdom.

Because of what Jesus our Brother has done for us, we too have
become children of God. As his sons and daughters, we can be absolutely confident that underneath our deepest griefs will always be the
everlasting, ever-loving arms of God our heavenly Father.

Thursday

PRAYING THE NAME

How great is the love the Father has lavished on us, that we should be called children of God! And that is what we are! The reason the world does not know us is that it did not know him. Dear friends, now we are children of God, and what we will be has not yet been made known. But we know that when he appears, we shall be like him, for we shall see him as he is. . . .

This is how God showed his love among us: He sent his one and only Son into the world that we might live through him. This is love: not that we loved God, but that he loved us and sent his Son as an atoning sacrifice for our sins. Dear friends, since God so loved us, we also ought to love one another. No one has ever seen God; but if we love one another, God lives in us and his love is made complete in us.

1 JOHN 3:1–4; 4:9–12

Reflect On: 1 John 3:1–4; 4:9–12.

Praise God: For calling us to become his children through faith in his Son.

Offer Thanks: Because God loved you before you ever thought of loving him.

Confess: Any failures to love others as Christ has loved you.

Ask God: To shape you into the image of his Son.

∽

I am a news junkie. I love listening to the radio, reading the paper, and watching news channels on TV. But a steady diet of it does nothing to stoke my optimism. Often it steals my peace. To curb my appetite for it, I've relegated our television set to a room in the basement that I call the TV pit. The room is so small, unattractive, and uncomfortable that I rarely spend time there. But even without watching TV, it's hard to avoid headlines that break your heart and make you wonder about the future.

Last week's news focused on cleanup efforts in the city of New Orleans in the wake of Hurricane Katrina. The one word that kept surfacing was "debris." Over and over, people talked not about cleaning up their houses, restoring their furniture, or repairing their automobiles, but only about getting rid of all the "debris," because in many cases that's all that was left. Every beautiful and useful thing acquired over the course of a lifetime had been suddenly transformed into a whole lot of debris. Tragically, even the bodies that floated in the flooded streets immediately following the hurricane looked like nothing but toxic debris.

I couldn't help looking around at the things I love in my own home, like the down-filled sofa I bought from a friend, the rows of books (some of them autographed by their authors) that fill my bookshelves, or the splash of white calla lilies that brighten a corner of the living room. All of these and more would sooner or later be reduced to rubbish. And though it crossed my mind, I didn't have the nerve to look in the mirror and speculate about what would someday happen to the face that looked back at me.

I have felt in this year of disasters—from tsunamis to hurricanes to earthquakes—that surely God must be speaking, reminding us urgently of truths we daily forget. That material goods aren't as important as we think they are. That life can change in an instant. That none of us will live forever. That now is the time to seek him.

But what does it mean to seek Jesus, whose favorite title for himself was the Son of Man? One of the things it means is to seek to be like him, because Jesus shows us humanity as it is ultimately meant to be. As the Son of Man Jesus is the ideal Human Being. While on earth Jesus lived with an unbroken connection to the Father. Because we are united to him through the Holy Spirit, we can enjoy this same intimate connection to our Father in heaven.

It sounds good in theory, but what does it mean in practical terms? What does it mean when you have yelled at your kids for the umpteenth time, as I did this morning? Or when you are party to a messy divorce? Or when you are struggling with an addiction? Or when you have just lost your job? What does it mean when you are weary, frustrated, and confused? It means that you take whatever mess you are in and bring it to straight to Jesus, desperately praying for his mercy. It means you open your soul to his healing, cleansing grace. It means that you count on him because you cannot count on yourself.

Join me today in yielding to God's Spirit, who is at work to rehabilitate the image of Christ within us. Remember that your soul is the only indestructible thing about you. Everything else is fragile, temporary, passing. Then pray for the first five people you meet today, that God will open their eyes to what really matters in this world.

PROMISES ASSOCIATED WITH HIS NAME

Few things are as hard in this world as growing up without a family. What must it be like to live without the sense that you are deeply connected to other human beings who will stand by you no matter what? I remember waiting for a flight to arrive at Detroit Metro Airport a few years ago. Several families were also waiting at the gate. They seemed tense, expectant. It didn't take long to realize just who they were waiting for. Six little black-haired babies were carried off the plane, lovingly cradled in the arms of a stranger who had watched over them during their long journey from South Korea to America. Now each infant was tenderly transferred into the arms of a waiting parent. The families were jubilant—the mothers teary-eyed, the children jumping up and down for a closer look at their new brother or sister, the fathers grinning broadly.

The scene I was privileged to witness is an image of the rejoicing that goes on in heaven whenever one of us crosses over from darkness to light, placing our faith in Jesus as God's Son. Today as you consider what Christ has done for you, imagine the rejoicing that went on in heaven when God changed your status from that of a spiritual orphan to a beloved son or daughter, no longer a slave but an heir to all of his promises.

Promises in Scripture

> *"I will be a Father to you,*
> *and you will be my sons and daughters,*
> *says the Lord Almighty."*
> 2 CORINTHIANS 6:18

But when the time had fully come, God sent his Son, born of a woman, born under law, to redeem those under law, that we might receive the full rights of sons. Because you are sons, God sent the Spirit of his Son into our hearts, the Spirit who calls out, "Abba, Father." So you are no longer a slave, but a son; and since you are a son, God has made you also an heir.

GALATIANS 4:4–7

And we know that in all things God works for the good of those who love him, who have been called according to his purpose. For those God foreknew he also predestined to be conformed to the likeness of his Son, that he might be the firstborn among many brothers. And those he predestined, he also called; those he called, he also justified; those he justified, he also glorified.

ROMANS 8:28–30

For the Son of Man is going to come in his Father's glory with his angels, and then he will reward each person according to what he has done.

MATTHEW 16:27

Continued Prayer and Praise

Consider why Jesus was killed. (Matthew 26:63–66; John 10:22–33)

Listen to God's Son. (Mark 9:2–7; Hebrews 1:1–5)

Understand that Jesus came to suffer and serve. (Matthew 12:38–42; 16:24–26; 20:20–28)

Eagerly await the coming of the Son of Man. (Matthew 25:31–33; 26:64)

Remember why God sent his Son. (John 3:16–17)

Trust in the promises of God's Son. (John 14:12–14; Ephesians 1:3–6)

Act like a child of God. (Romans 8:14–17; Philippians 2:14–15; Hebrews 12:4–11)

Remember that the Son of Man is reigning in heaven. (Daniel 7:13–14, Revelation 1:12–18)

23

GOOD SHEPHERD

ποιμὴν καλός
POIMEN KALOS

The Name

One of the most tender images of Jesus is one he supplied when referring to himself as the Good Shepherd. This name reminds us both of our own vulnerability and Jesus' watchful, protecting care. It evokes a sense of belonging, intimacy, and trust, revealing the Good Shepherd as the One who lays down his life for his sheep. When you pray to the Good Shepherd, you are admitting your need for his care and your confidence in his ability to watch over and protect you.

Key Scripture

I am the good shepherd. The good shepherd lays down his life for the sheep.

JOHN 10:11

Monday

HIS NAME REVEALED

"Very truly I tell you Pharisees, anyone who does not enter the sheep pen by the gate, but climbs in by some other way, is a thief and a robber. The one who enters by the gate is the shepherd of his sheep. The gatekeeper opens the gate for him, and the sheep listen to his voice. He calls his own sheep by name and leads them out. When he has brought out all his own, he goes on ahead of them, and his sheep follow him because they know his voice. But they will never follow a stranger; in fact, they will run away from him because they do not recognize a stranger's voice." Jesus used this figure of speech, but the Pharisees did not understand what he was telling them.

Therefore Jesus said again, "Very truly I tell you, I am the gate for the sheep. All who have come before me were thieves and robbers, but the sheep have not listened to them. I am the gate; whoever enters through me will be saved. They will come in and go out, and find pasture. The thief comes only to steal and kill and destroy; I have come that they may have life, and have it to the full.

"I am the good shepherd. The good shepherd lays down his life for the sheep. The hired hand is not the shepherd and does not own the sheep. So when he sees the wolf coming, he abandons the sheep and runs away. Then the wolf attacks the flock and scatters it. The man runs away because he is a hired hand and cares nothing for the sheep.

"I am the good shepherd; I know my sheep and my sheep know me—just as the Father knows me and I know the Father—and I lay down my life for the sheep. I have other sheep that are not of this sheep pen. I must bring them also. They too will listen to my voice, and there shall be one flock and one shepherd. The reason my Father loves me is that I lay down my life—only to take it up again. No one takes it from me, but I lay it down of my own accord. I have authority to lay it down and authority to take it up again. This command I received from my Father."

JOHN 10:1–18

Lord, I belong to you and no one else. Thank you for watching over and protecting me as a shepherd cares for his sheep. Help me to listen for your voice, confident that even if I walk through the valley of the shadow of death, you will be there with your rod and your staff to comfort me.

Understanding the Name

Scripture uses various metaphors to describe God's people — a temple, a body, a bride, a garden, a vineyard, or a flock of sheep. Shepherding, in fact, was an important occupation in ancient Palestine, practiced by such biblical notables as Abel, Abraham, Isaac, Jacob, Moses, and David. The role of the shepherd was to provide three things for the flock in his care: food, protection, and guidance.

Just as God's people are sometimes described in Scripture as a faithless bride, they are also pictured as a scattered flock. At such times, their leaders are portrayed as false shepherds who care little for the well-being of the flock entrusted to them. Without a shepherd to watch over them, the sheep scatter, becoming easy prey for wild animals and thieves.

Out of love for his wayward people, God promises to become their Shepherd. The book of Isaiah paints one of the most poignant images of God in the Hebrew Scriptures:

> *He tends his flock like a shepherd:*
> *He gathers the lambs in his arms*
> *and carries them close to his heart;*
> *he gently leads those that have young.*
>
> ISAIAH 40:11

Jesus shows us the lengths to which he as the Good Shepherd, or *Poimen Kalos* (poi-MAIN ka-LOS), will go in order to protect his sheep. Unlike those who merely work for pay, Jesus will never abandon his sheep. Instead, he will defend them with his own life. After his resurrection, Jesus exhorted Peter to follow his example by feeding his sheep. Leaders of the early church were referred to as "pastor," another translation of the Greek word *poimen*.

Studying the Name

1. Why do you think Jesus describes his relationship to his people as Shepherd and sheep?

2. This passage from John contains both frightening and comforting images. It is frightening to think that thieves, robbers, and wolves want to prey on the sheep, but comforting to know that Jesus will go to any lengths to protect them. How do these images express spiritual realities?

3. The phrase "good shepherd" implies that there are also bad shepherds. How is it possible to tell the difference?

4. Describe an experience in which you recognized the voice of Jesus in your own life.

5. Describe ways in which Jesus has watched over and protected you as your Shepherd.

Tuesday

PRAYING THE NAME

What do you think? If a man owns a hundred sheep, and one of them wanders away, will he not leave the ninety-nine on the hills and go to look for the one that wandered off? And if he finds it, I tell you the truth, he is happier about that one sheep than about the ninety-nine that did not wander off. In the same way your Father in heaven is not willing that any of these little ones should be lost.

MATTHEW 18:12–14

For the Son of Man came to seek and to save what was lost.

LUKE 19:10

Reflect On: Matthew 18:12–14 and Luke 19:10
Praise God: For telling us stories that reveal his love.
Offer Thanks: For God's persistence.
Confess: Any despair you feel over a lost relationship.
Ask God: To draw the lost to himself.

Last year I read a novel about a fourteen-year-old girl who died suddenly in tragic circumstances. I wasn't prepared for the storm of grief that Alice Sebold's *The Lovely Bones* unleashed in me. Odd as it sounds, the story is told from the murdered girl's vantage point in the afterlife. In fact, the narrative is so compelling that it brought back memories of the sudden death of my sixteen-year-old sister in very different circumstances. I could feel the long-buried ache of missing her, as though she had been killed yesterday. I wondered how different life would have been had she lived. How many nieces and nephews would I have had? How many cousins would my children have had? How would our already close family have become even closer, our celebrations richer?

Most of us know what it is like to miss someone so much that it literally hurts to think about their absence. Jack Roeda comments on this sense of loss, but from a different vantage point:

> In Genesis 3 we find that after Adam and Eve sinned against God, they hid from God. And we're told, "But the LORD God called ... 'Where are you?'" (3:9). Most of the time I've heard anger in that question. God is calling them on the carpet. But perhaps it expresses sadness as well: "Where are you? I miss you." The whole Bible—and Jesus' coming, in particular—is the story of God seeking us, making peace so that he'll not have to miss us again.

Several years ago a close friend was going through a rough time. I was fairly certain she was a closet alcoholic. Her constant need for alcohol had transformed her from a kind, gentle, caring person to a self-absorbed, emotionally unstable woman whose frequent outbursts alienated family and friends. As I prayed for her, I felt God easing my worry and directing my prayers toward the parable of the lost sheep. I began to understand that I wasn't the only one who felt the ache of missing her. Eventually God brought her through her time of difficulty in a very gentle way. I remember feeling so much joy watching the transformation that came with a deeper understanding of God's love.

Perhaps you are missing someone right now—a son, a daughter, a parent, a friend, or a spouse. Maybe that person is still alive but living in a way that estranges them from others and from God. If that is so, you can use your own sense of loss to energize your prayers, confident that Someone else is also missing them—Someone who came into this world with only one thing in mind: to seek out and save what is lost.

 *Wednesday*

PRAYING THE NAME

> The LORD *is my shepherd, I shall not be in want. . . .*
> *Even though I walk*
>   *through the valley of the shadow of death,*
> *I will fear no evil,*
>   *for you are with me;*
> *your rod and your staff,*
>   *they comfort me.*
>
> PSALM 23:1, 4

My sheep listen to my voice; I know them, and they follow me. I give them eternal life, and they shall never perish; no one can snatch them out of my hand. My Father, who has given them to me, is greater than all; no one can snatch them out of my Father's hand.

JOHN 10:27–29

Reflect On: Psalm 23 and John 10:27–29.

Praise God: Because he watches over you.

Offer Thanks: For your pastor and for other pastors who have helped you in the past.

Confess: Your need for a Shepherd to watch over you.

Ask God: To encourage and strengthen your pastor.

It happened last Sunday. I was sitting in church at the start of the sermon and sinking fast, feeling overwhelmed by life and thinking thoughts I shouldn't have. *God, why won't you help me? Can't you hear me? Am I such a rat* [an inner voice quickly assured me I was]*?* And then, *Please help me! I'm desperate. I need you!*

That's how inelegant and faithless my prayers can be. It had been a trying weekend, topping off a difficult week, capping off a challenging month. Circumstances related to one of my children had conspired to make me feel like a cat that was constantly being stroked backwards —a slow and steady torture.

But then came the answer. It was almost a physical sensation. I could feel myself rising up, leaving despair behind. Grace was reaching me through the words of the sermon. The reading that day was from Paul's letter to the Philippians: "Finally, brothers and sisters," Paul counseled, "whatever is true, whatever is noble, whatever is right, whatever is pure, whatever is lovely, whatever is admirable — if anything is excellent or praiseworthy—think about such things" (Philippians 4:8). And then a quote from Martin Luther: "Temptations, of course, cannot be avoided, but because we cannot prevent the birds from flying over our heads, there is no need that we should let them nest in our hair."

The sermon was wise, and it went straight to the heart of what was bothering me—the faithless, doubting, complaining thoughts that were flying around my head like sparrows looking for a place to nest. But it was more than that. It was the way the words were delivered—with the love of Christ, as though Jesus were speaking directly to me through my pastor—which, of course, he was.

I couldn't help but reflect on how right this seemed, because the word "pastor" is another word for "herdsman" or "shepherd." Pastor was the title given to leaders in the early church who were called to be shepherds after the example of the Good Shepherd. Certainly my pastor had done that for me that day. I had heard Christ's voice speaking through him.

Later I reflected on Psalm 23, which talks about fearing no evil, about being comforted by the fact that the shepherd stands near with his rod and his staff in hand. The rod the psalmist speaks of was a club that the shepherd used to ward off attacks from wild animals. As I thought back to my experience in church that day, I pictured Jesus standing next to me, club in hand, beating down all the faithless thoughts that tempted and discouraged me. I thought too of another image, one that made me smile. It's an arcade game in which you get to use a big hammer to pound down plastic gophers that pop up willy nilly. It's a great stress reliever!

What is causing you stress right now? What temptations are you facing? As you pray today, imagine yourself in the presence of Jesus, your Good Shepherd, who stands ready with his club in hand, able to ward off the enemy and keep you safe.

PRAYING THE NAME

Open for me the gates of righteousness;
I will enter and give thanks to the LORD.
This is the gate of the LORD
through which the righteous may enter.

PSALM 118:19–20

Therefore Jesus said again, "Very truly I tell you, I am the gate for the sheep. All who ever came before me were thieves and robbers, but the sheep have not listened to them. I am the gate; whoever enters through me will be saved. They will come in and go out, and find pasture. The thief comes only to steal and kill and destroy; I have come that they may have life, and have it to the full."

JOHN 10:7–10

Reflect On: John 10:7–10.
Praise God: For calling us into his kingdom.
Offer Thanks: For the way that Jesus has watched over you.
Confess: Any failure to listen to the voice of the Good
                 Shepherd.
Ask God: To stand guard over your mind and your heart.

Whenever I read this familiar passage from the Gospel of John, I think of a neighbor of mine who once invited a homeless man to spend the night. When it came time to settle down for the evening, my kind-hearted neighbor became uneasy, wondering if the man sleeping in the downstairs guest room was as harmless as he seemed. To ease his fears, this father of five young children did the only thing he could think of. Instead of sleeping in his own bed that night, he slept in the hallway at the top of the stairs, determined to guard his sleeping family.

But what does this story have to do with Jesus, who calls himself the gate of the sheep? When we think of a gate, most of us imagine a pivoting gate attached to a wooden corral or fence. But Jesus was talking about a different kind of gate.

In Palestine, shepherds often slept, not in a house, but out in the open where there was good grazing for their sheep. At the end of each day, the shepherd would stand inside a low, circular sheep pen. As he called to his flock, each sheep would enter through an opening about six feet wide. Only when the last animal was safely inside the pen would the shepherd close the gate. He did this not by shutting a physical gate but by lying down in the opening with his staff and his rod beside him. During the night, the shepherd's body became the living gate through which no intruder could enter.

That's the image Christ wants us to have regarding the way he watches over us. By his sacrifice on the cross, Jesus restores our relationship with God. Through him we enter into eternal life. So we are Christ's sheep, purchased by the Good Shepherd with his own blood. And we are called by his voice to enter his kingdom.

But in this world, sheep are still among the most vulnerable of creatures. Scripture tells us that the devil is on the prowl, like a roaring lion looking for someone to devour. Just as ordinary sheep often lack the intelligence to protect themselves, we often lack the spiritual intelligence to know what is best for us. Fortunately, the Good Shepherd is still vigilant, still watchful, still ready and able to protect his sheep. One of the ways he does this is by giving us his Spirit to guide us.

In his letter to the Romans, Paul says that "those who live according to the sinful nature have their minds set on what that nature desires; but those who live in accordance with the Spirit have their minds set on what the Spirit desires" (Romans 8:5). Your mind, in fact, is the gateway to the future because it shapes your will and emotions. Think a thought long enough and it will surely lead you somewhere. Without the enabling grace of the Holy Spirit, the human mind often cannot distinguish the right path.

Spend time today thanking the Good Shepherd for watching over and protecting you. Then ask him to show you any thought patterns that are at work to lead you away from him. As you pray, you may discover habitual thoughts—anxious, greedy, lustful, complaining, or envious thoughts—that tend to dominate your mind. Bring whatever you find before the Good Shepherd in prayer, telling him that you no longer want these patterns to dominate your mind and heart. Then imagine him as the living gate, standing guard over your mind, protecting you from anything or anyone who wants to enter without his permission. Ask for the grace to listen for his voice so that you may lie down in peace, confident of his watchful, loving care.

Friday

PROMISES ASSOCIATED WITH HIS NAME

I have a friend whose young daughter is a gifted sleeper, a trait that makes it difficult for her to stay dry at night. My friend has tried all the obvious things, including pajama alarms that shriek in the middle of the night, waking everyone but her daughter. Finally, my friend decided to try a different tactic. "What fabulous reward," she asked, "would help you stay dry for thirty nights in a row?"

"Baby Annabell!" was her daughter's quick reply. She wanted the doll who can burp, yawn, and make little baby snoring noises. But best of all, she told her mother, "Baby Annabell knows how to cry real tears."

Unlike my friend's daughter, I find myself motivated by the thought of an opposite reward—a promise to end all tears. It's the promise Jesus makes to his harassed and helpless sheep—to you and to me. He tells us that a day will come when weeping will end. When sorrow will vanish. When fear will disappear. Even now, while we live in this wounded world, we can be comforted by the knowledge that the Lord himself has promised to gather the lambs in his arms and carry them close to his heart.

Promises in Scripture

> *See, the Sovereign LORD comes with power,*
> *and his arm rules for him.*
> *See, his reward is with him,*
> *and his recompense accompanies him.*
> *He tends his flock like a shepherd:*
> *He gathers the lambs in his arms*
> *and carries them close to his heart;*
> *he gently leads those that have young.*
>
> ISAIAH 40:10–11

I will make a covenant of peace with them and rid the land of wild beasts so that they may live in the desert and sleep in the forests in safety. I will bless them and the places surrounding my hill. I will send down showers in season; there will be showers of blessing. The trees of the field will yield their fruit and the ground will yield its crops; the people will be secure in their land. They will know that I am the LORD, when I break the bars of their yoke and rescue them from the hands of those who enslaved them. They will no longer be plundered by the nations, nor will wild animals devour them. They will live in safety, and no one will make them afraid. I will provide for them a land renowned for its crops, and they will no longer be victims of famine in the land or bear the scorn of the nations. Then they will know that I, the LORD their God, am with them and that they, the house of Israel, are my people, declares the Sovereign LORD. You my sheep, the sheep of my pasture, are people, and I am your God, declares the Sovereign LORD.

EZEKIEL 34:25–31

*For the Lamb at the center of the throne
   will be their shepherd;
he will lead them to springs of living water.
   And God will wipe away every tear from their eyes.*

REVELATION 7:17

Continued Prayer and Praise

Take heart; the Lord is your shepherd. (Ezekiel 34:1–24; Matthew 9:36; 1 Peter 2:24–25)

Remember that the Lord will judge the nations, separating the sheep from the goats. (Matthew 25:31–33)

Consider what it means to pastor God's people. (John 21:15–19; 1 Peter 5:1–4)

24

SERVANT, SERVANT OF GOD, MAN OF SORROWS

אֶבֶד , παῖς τοῦ θεοῦ
אִישׁ מַכְאֹבוֹת

EBED, PAIS TOU THEOU, ISH MAKOBOTH

The Name

Like most of us, Jesus' disciples were sometimes caught up with a sense of their own self-importance, at times even arguing with each other about which of them was greatest. Jesus startled them by reversing the natural order in which it is the weak who serve the strong. He assured them, instead, that he came not in order to control and dominate but in order to serve.

Though prophets, judges, and kings were called servants of God in the Bible, Jesus is the greatest of all God's servants, the Man of Sorrows who laid down his life in obedience to his Father. He is the Servant who through his suffering has saved us. When you pray to Jesus as Servant or as the Man of Sorrows, you are praying to the Lord who has loved you in the most passionate way possible, allowing himself to be nailed to a cross in order that you might have life and have it to the full.

Key Scripture

He was despised and rejected, a man of sorrows, acquainted with bitterest grief.

ISAIAH 53:3, NLT

The Son of Man did not come to be served, but to serve.

MATTHEW 20:28

Monday

HIS NAME REVEALED

See, my servant will prosper; he will be highly exalted....

My servant grew up in the LORD's presence like a tender green shoot, sprouting from a root in dry and sterile ground. There was nothing beautiful or majestic about his appearance, nothing to attract us to him. He was despised and rejected—a man of sorrows, acquainted with bitterest grief. We turned our backs on him and looked the other way when he went by. He was despised, and we did not care.

Yet it was our weaknesses he carried; it was our sorrows that weighed him down. And we thought his troubles were a punishment from God for his own sins! But he was wounded and crushed for our sins. He was beaten that we might have peace. He was whipped, and we were healed!

ISAIAH 52:13; 53:2–5, NLT

Whoever wants to become great among you must be your servant, and whoever wants to be first must be your slave—just as the Son of Man did not come to be served, but to serve, and to give his life as a ransom for many.

MATTHEW 20:26–28

Lord, I was like a bruised reed you would not break, a smoldering wick you would not put out. Instead you allowed yourself to be pierced for my transgressions, crushed for my iniquities. You were despised and rejected, a man of sorrows and familiar with suffering. The punishment that brought me peace was placed on you. My Lord and my God, I worship you.

Understanding the Name

After God led the Israelites out of their slavery in Egypt, he did not treat them as slaves but as his own people, his sons and daughters. Though slavery was practiced in Israel, the Law forbade the forcible enslavement of freeborn individuals. To kidnap or sell such a person was to incur the death penalty. However, people could sell themselves in order to pay off their debts. Even so, Hebrew slaves were to be released after a certain number of years because no child of God was meant to live in perpetual bondage.

Though the Israelites were not considered God's slaves, they were considered his servants, freely putting his interests before their own, confident of his care and protection. To be God's servant involved living with an attitude of dependence and obedience. Scripture speaks of Moses, Joshua, Hannah, David, Isaiah, Mary the mother of Jesus, and many others as God's servants because they lived a life of faithful obedience.

The Servant Songs in Isaiah (42:1–4; 49:1–7; 50:4–9; 52:13–53:12) all speak of a mysterious Servant who would bring justice to the nations. Through his suffering this Man of Sorrows (ISH mak-uh-BOTH) would redeem many. The Jews may have understood this as a reference to Israel while early Christians understood these passages as messianic prophecies pointing to the suffering, death, and resurrection of Jesus Christ. By becoming one of us, Jesus suffered both with and for us. He was the Servant (E-bed) par excellence, the Servant of God (PAIS tou the-OU), who not only obeyed God but obeyed to the point of death.

As his people, we are to follow his example, remembering his words that "the greatest among you will be your servant." Jesus' words make particular sense in light of the fact that in ancient times, a servant's status was directly related to the status of his master. To be a servant of the King of kings, then, is the greatest of privileges. It is no surprise to discover that the word "minister," derived from a Latin word, and the word "deacon, derived from a Greek word, both mean "servant."

Studying the Name

1. How does the passage from Isaiah fit or fail to fit with your image of Jesus?

2. When you think of Jesus' suffering, how does it make you feel about him, about yourself, about others?

3. Describe an experience in which someone served you? How did it affect you?

4. Describe experiences in which you have been able to serve someone else with the love of Christ.

Tuesday

PRAYING THE NAME

See, my servant will prosper; he will be highly exalted. . . .

My servant grew up in the LORD'S presence like a tender green shoot, sprouting from a root in dry and sterile ground. There was nothing beautiful or majestic about his appearance, nothing to attract us to him. He was despised and rejected—a man of sorrows, acquainted with bitterest grief. We turned our backs on him and looked the other way when he went by. He was despised, and we did not care.

Yet it was our weaknesses he carried; it was our sorrows that weighed him down. And we thought his troubles were a punishment from God for his own sins! But he was wounded and crushed for our sins. He was beaten that we might have peace. He was whipped, and we were healed!

ISAIAH 52:13; 53:2–5, NLT

Reflect On: Isaiah 52:13–53:12.
Praise God: For raising up his Son, Jesus.
Offer Thanks: For Christ's long-suffering love.
Confess: Any pride that keeps you from receiving the
               forgiveness Jesus offers.
Ask God: To help you look into the face of Christ on the cross.

◠

I will never forget the profound silence that characterized the crowd as we streamed out of the theater after viewing *The Passion of the Christ.* For 126 minutes we had been painfully transfixed by Mel Gibson's graphic depiction of the last twelve hours of the life of Christ. It left us speechless. What words could we summon to defend ourselves? How could we explain the mitigating circumstances that made us not responsible for everything that had happened to Jesus? Words do not exist for such a task, and so we shuffled out in grim silence. It felt as though the wretchedness of the whole human race had been glaringly exposed. Our condition was far worse than I had imagined. How else to explain the magnitude of God's suffering?

John Calvin believed that human beings cannot attain true self-knowledge without first contemplating the face of God. He compared our distorted self-perception to an eye that has only been exposed to the color black. When that eye is exposed to a lighter color, even something with a brownish hue, it may mistake it for white because it doesn't have a clue about what white looks like. In other words, we are misshapen human beings surrounded by other misshapen human beings. Some of us may look good compared to others but we are still deeply flawed compared to God and to the kind of person he means us to become.

Jack Roeda, a pastor and professor of preaching at Calvin Theological Seminary, comments on John's Gospel, saying:

> John wants us to look on the face of Jesus until the conviction becomes rooted in our hearts that we are looking into the human face of the living God. Perhaps this face of God comes most into focus when it wears the crown of thorns. As Nicholas Wolterstorff writes, "It is said of God that no one can behold his face and live. I always thought this meant that no one can see his splendor and live. A friend said perhaps it meant that no one could see his sorrow and live. Or perhaps his sorrow is his splendor."

I think Wolterstorff is right. God's sorrow is his splendor. His goodness, standing as it does in contrast to our sinfulness, enables him to see with absolute clarity how far human beings have fallen. His sorrow is a gauge of his love, because it expresses what he was willing to endure, in the person of his Son, in order to heal our wretchedness. Jesus, the Man of Sorrows, reveals the splendor of God's face to us.

Dorothy Ranaghan writes about the difficulty of facing God when we know we have done wrong:

> Averting the eyes because I am not worthy to look upon the face of God and live is one kind of response. But to run away internally or, worse, to cease praying for a period of time because I only want to see the Lord smiling at me is self-centered. The only

corrective is to look upon the bloody, agonized face of Christ crucified and accept in those eyes of pain neither disgust nor approval,
but only salvation and love beyond comprehension.

Jesus came to show us God's face. At times it is a face consumed by
sorrow. Pray today for the grace to gaze on Jesus, seeing not only what
he has suffered but why. Then praise him for his salvation and his love
beyond comprehension.

 Wednesday

PRAYING THE NAME

Now before the festival of the Passover, Jesus knew that his hour had come to depart from this world and go to the Father. Having loved his own who were in the world, he loved them to the end. . . . During supper Jesus, knowing that the Father had given all things into his hands, and that he had come from God and was going to God, got up from the table, took off his outer robe, and tied a towel around himself. Then he poured water into a basin and began to wash the disciples' feet and to wipe them with the towel that was tied around him.

JOHN 13:1–5, NRSV

Reflect On: John 13:1–5.
Praise God: For loving us to the end through his Son, Jesus Christ.
Offer Thanks: Because Jesus has cleansed you from the defiling power of sin.
Confess: Your unworthiness.
Ask God: To help you receive the gift of salvation with gladness.

Imagine that you are living in first-century Palestine. Though you are in the prime of life, you know that you will die within the next twenty-four hours. In fact, you have known this for some time. Despite your efforts to prepare your friends, they seem thickheaded, unable to grasp the situation. You know that your death will shatter them. They will flee from shadows that will overtake you, terrified lest they also be overtaken. In the hours and days that follow, each will be tempted to despair, thinking that your promises were nothing more than well-intentioned dreams.

Now, before it happens, you long to comfort them, assuring them that everything will be all right, but they aren't listening. Instead they are distracted by trivialities, arguing which of them is greatest. And they are doing this in the middle of the Passover feast, the last meal you will share with them prior to your death.

Something else is in your mind too, a kind of confidence that seems strange in light of your knowledge of coming events. You know both who you are and where you are going. You also know you are precisely where you should be in God's timetable. You are determined to move forward, knowing that nothing can happen without your consent. But before you walk headlong into darkness, you decide to make one more attempt to communicate with your slow-witted disciples. You choose to do this not with words they are too deaf to hear but by acting out a parable. So you get up from the table and remove your outer clothing. Wrapping a towel around your waist, you pour water into a basin. Then you stoop down and start wiping the grime from your friends' feet. It's what a slave would do. By now the bickering has stopped. Each man looks at you with bewildered eyes. You are certain that each of your friends will remember this moment for the rest of their lives.

John's Gospel tells us not only that Jesus loved his disciples but that he loved them to the end. What he did for them the night before his death illustrates the extent of his love. But the meaning of that acted-out parable eluded them at first. Later, in excited conversations, they would have begun to understand what Jesus was trying to tell them.

The night before he died, Jesus removed his outer garments. Wasn't he showing them a picture of what was about to happen, when the next day he would be stripped of his clothing before being nailed to a cross? And what about the water he had poured into the basin in order to cleanse them? Hadn't he also poured out his blood for them on the cross? Surely Jesus had acted the part of a slave by washing their feet. Wasn't he also executed as a slave? Crucifixion, they knew, was a punishment so cruel it was reserved for subjugated peoples and slaves. In the midst of his disciples' reflections, one of them would have recalled Jesus' words shortly before the Passover feast: "I lay down my life for the sheep.... No one takes it from me but I lay it down of my own accord" (John 10:15, 18).

Jesus gave his life—not grudgingly, but gladly. He stripped himself of power so that a deeper power could be at work reversing the deadly effects of our sin. Today, when you think of Jesus as the Suffering Servant, think not so much of what you have done to cause his suffering but of what he has done to cause you joy. Dwell not on your own unworthiness but on his worthiness. Think about his willing sacrifice, his determination, and his love. Just as Jesus loved his disciples to the end, he will love you to the end. Praise him for saving you and changing you through his great, long-suffering love.

Thursday

PRAYING THE NAME

When he had finished washing their feet, he put on his clothes and returned to his place. "Do you understand what I have done for you?" he asked them. "You call me 'Teacher' and 'Lord,' and rightly so, for that is what I am. Now that I, your Lord and Teacher, have washed your feet, you also should wash one another's feet. I have set you an example that you should do as I have done for you. I tell you the truth, no servant is greater than his master, nor is a messenger greater than the one who sent him. Now that you know these things, you will be blessed if you do them."

JOHN 13:12–17

Reflect On: John 13:12–17.
Praise God: For sending his Son to show us how to live.
Offer Thanks: For the humble, practical ways others have served you.
Confess: Your sorrow at the opportunities you have missed to serve others.
Ask God: To give you the heart of a servant.

Do you ever question your purpose in life? As a zealous young Christian I used to wonder what I could do to make the most impact. What single thing, what career or ministry, would enable me to make the greatest contribution to the kingdom of God? That question, full of youthful ambition, recycled itself in my mind off and on for many years. Finally an answer occurred to me that took me completely by surprise. It was simple, unspectacular, but true. It didn't involve giving up all my worldly possessions. Nor did it mean moving to the inner city to help the poor, good as that might be. In fact, it required no drastic change in terms of what I was already doing.

I began to realize that the secret to fulfilling God's purpose for my life resided not so much in *what* I did as in *how* I did it. It didn't matter whether God gave me a large role or a tiny one; I could still have impact if I could learn to do one thing—to love people in whatever circumstance I found myself. Why? Because love lasts. Because love never fails. Because love does not envy, and it never boasts. It is neither proud nor rude. Love is not easily angered, and it keeps no record of wrongs. Love always protects, always trusts, always hopes. Love never gives up. God is love. Love, in fact, is the hardest, most powerful thing in the world. Whether driving a child to school, leading a church, cleaning a bathroom, heading up a multinational corporation, or washing feet, love is the secret to making a lasting impact.

To be truthful, I would have found it easier to move to a Third World country to live among the poor than to try and make God's love present within my family, my neighborhood, and my church. Even now, after years of knowing the Lord, I am aware of the meagerness of my efforts, of how tainted they are by selfishness. Speaking of how difficult it can be at times to love others, Mother Teresa once remarked, "I have found the paradox that if I love until it hurts, then there is no hurt but only more love." This remarkable woman knew the power of loving in simple, practical ways:

> Some of my sisters work in Australia. On a reservation, among the Aborigines, there was an elderly man. I can assure you that you have never seen a situation as difficult as that poor old man's. He was completely ignored by everyone. His home was disordered and dirty.
>
> I told him, "Please, let me clean your house, wash your clothes, and make your bed." He answered, "I'm okay like this. Let it be."
>
> I said again, "You will be still better if you allow me to do it."
>
> He finally agreed. So I was able to clean his house and wash his clothes. I discovered a beautiful lamp, covered with dust. Only God knows how many years had passed since he last lit it.
>
> I said to him, "Don't you light your lamp? Don't you ever use it?"
>
> He answered, "No. No one comes to see me. I have no need to light it. Who would I light it for?"
>
> I asked, "Would you light it every night if the sisters came?"
>
> He replied, "Of course."

From that day on the sisters committed themselves to visiting him every evening. We cleaned the lamp, and the sisters would light it every evening.

Two years passed. I had completely forgotten that man. He sent this message: "Tell my friend that the light she lit in my life continues to shine still."

I thought it was a very small thing. We often neglect small things.

Ask for the grace today to be mindful of the things that seem too small to capture your attention. Ask God to help you slow down and recognize the opportunities he is giving you right now to make a lasting impact in this world through the power of his love.

Friday

PROMISES ASSOCIATED WITH HIS NAME

One of the most winsome promises Jesus made to his followers was the promise of rest. But when was the last time you felt rested? Like the people Jesus was addressing, we often feel burdened by "laws" we have difficulty keeping. In our case, it may not be laws made by religious leaders but by our culture or by our families. Our children must be perfect, our bodies shapely, our careers impressive. The list of standards that we consciously or unconsciously adopt can be endless.

Of course we can also get bogged down in legalistic forms of religion that produce weariness rather than peace and joy. This is why some of us feel so fatigued despite Jesus' promise that his burden is light. Part of the secret of receiving the rest Jesus speaks of is to be sure that we are wearing the right "yoke." A yoke is an instrument used to harness two animals together so that they can combine their strength to carry a load. Jesus tells us his burden is light not because it is easy but because he is on the other side of the yoke, helping us to serve with his strength. Ask Jesus today to free you, his servant, from burdens he does not want you to carry. Tell him you want to rest in his promises and trust in his strength.

Promises in Scripture

> The LORD redeems his servants;
> no one will be condemned who takes refuge in him.
>
> PSALM 34:22

> Come to me, all you who are weary and burdened, and I will give you rest. Take my yoke upon you and learn from me, for I am gentle and humble in heart, and you will find rest for your souls. For my yoke is easy and my burden is light.
>
> MATTHEW 11:28–30

Then the angel showed me the river of the water of life, as clear as crystal, flowing from the throne of God and of the Lamb down the middle of the great street of the city. On each side of the river stood the tree of life, bearing twelve crops of fruit, yielding its fruit every month. And the leaves of the tree are for the healing of the nations. No longer will there be any curse. The throne of God and of the Lamb will be in the city, and his servants will serve him. They will see his face, and his name will be on their foreheads. There will be no more night. They will not need the light of a lamp or the light of the sun, for the Lord God will give them light. And they will reign for ever and ever.

REVELATION 22:1–5

Continued Prayer and Praise

Remember that Jesus is the Suffering Servant. (Isaiah 42:1–4; 49:1–6; 50:4–9; Matthew 12:9–21; John 17:4–5)

Make your attitude the same as that of Christ Jesus. (1 Corinthians 9:19–23; Philippians 2:3–11; Hebrews 10:5–7)

Be ready when the Master comes. (Matthew 24:42–51)

25

THE REDEEMER

גָּאַל λύτρον
GA'AL, LYTRON

The Name

Without a Redeemer willing and able to pay the high price necessary to liberate us from the power of sin, the story of our lives in this world would be nothing but a story of hopelessness. But because of Christ's redemptive love, we look forward with hope to a day when the world itself will be completely liberated from the power of sin and death. Until then we can express our faith in Christ by echoing the words of Scripture: "I know that my Redeemer lives and that in the end he will stand upon the earth. And ... in my flesh I will see God" (Job 19:25–26).

Key Scripture

For even the Son of Man did not come to be served, but to serve, and to give his life as a ransom for many.

Mark 10:45

HIS NAME REVEALED

> No one can redeem the life of another
> or give to God a sufficient ransom —
> the ransom for a life is costly,
> no payment is ever enough —
> so that someone should live on forever
> and not see decay.
>
> PSALM 49:7–9

Jesus called them together and said … "The Son of Man did not come to be served, but to serve, and to give his life as a ransom for many."

MARK 10:42, 45

> You are worthy to take the scroll
> and to open its seals,
> because you were slain,
> and with your blood you purchased for God
> members of every tribe and language and
> people and nation.
>
> REVELATION 5:9

Lord, you paid for me with the most valuable currency of all. May the investment you have made appreciate to your glory. Help me to live in a way that expresses your redeeming love so that many others may know you as their Lord and Redeemer. Amen.

Understanding the Name

Redemption involves winning back, buying back, or repurchasing something that belongs to you or to someone else. The most dramatic example of this in the Old Testament was the exodus of God's people from Egypt. The former slaves praised Yahweh for acting as their Redeemer (Exodus 15:13). Subsequently, the prophets often linked redemption with freedom from political oppression.

But redemption came into play within Israel itself because first-born males, slaves, and lands, as well as people, objects, and animals consecrated to God, all had to be redeemed by means of some kind of payment. In certain instances, such as when land had been sold to pay a debt (Leviticus 25:25–28) or a person had sold himself into slavery, the person's closest relative, called the "kinsman redeemer," had the right to step in and pay off the debt so the land could be returned or the person could be freed.

God is often called "Redeemer" (*Ga'al*; ga-AL) in the Old Testament. Though the New Testament never directly refers to Jesus as the Redeemer, it makes it clear that he offered himself as a ransom or as redemption (*Lytron*; LU-tron) when he died on the cross. Rather than liberating his people from political oppression as many expected the Messiah to do, Jesus came to free his people from the demonic powers to which they were enslaved because of sin. His blood was the purchase price, offered not to Satan but to the Father as the ultimate expression of his love. By giving his life for them and for us, Jesus didn't make light of our guilt but lifted us, as one commentator has said, "out of disobedience into his own obedience," thereby freeing us from the bondage of sin and remaking us in his image.

Studying the Name

1. If Christ has purchased you with his blood, what are the implications for your sense of self-worth? For your sense of the worth of others?

2. The passage from Revelation indicates that you were purchased *for* God. If that is so, what are the implications for your life?

3. Scripture says that Jesus has purchased members from every tribe and language and people and nations. Is that diversity represented in your denomination or your local church? If not, why not?

PRAYING THE NAME

I know that my Redeemer lives,
  and that in the end he will stand upon the earth.
And after my skin has been destroyed,
  yet in my flesh I will see God.

JOB 19:25–26

Reflect On: Job 19:25–26.
Praise God: For redeeming your life through the blood of his Son.
Offer Thanks: To Jesus Christ who has purchased you for God.
Confess: Any lack of generosity in your life.
Ask God: To help you grow into the likeness of Christ.

Many of us cannot remember a time in which we did not know about Jesus' death on the cross. But some of us may know the story both too well and too little. We have heard it so often that we have been dulled to its drama. With gold crosses that dangle from chains around our necks, we forget that we are wearing a symbol of one of the most painful kinds of death imaginable.

The early Christians had the advantage of being closer to the story. Some of them could still feel the crush of the crowd, could still see the anguish of the man hanging from the cross. The tragic and wonderful events of that story would never be far from their conscious minds. It was so much a part of them that they could not keep quiet. So the first disciples told the story again and again. They told it not just with words but without words, by the way they lived and by the way they died. You could say they became little versions of the Big Story.

It's the same today. People are still telling the story of Jesus, and some of them are telling it by laying down their lives in imitation of Christ. I have a friend who has the privilege of being related to someone who did exactly that. The name of her relative is Maximilian Kolbe, a Polish priest imprisoned in Auschwitz in 1941. Frequently beaten and abused because of his faith, those who knew him say that he never complained about how he was treated but always prayed for his tormenters and encouraged others to do the same. When his fellow prisoners jostled for a place in the bread line, all of them half-starved, he often stood aside so they would have more to eat. When someone asked whether such self-denial made sense when his own survival was at stake, he answered: "Every man has an aim in life. For most men it is to return home to their wives and families, or to their mothers. For my part, I give my life for the good of all men."

In the summer of 1941, a prisoner escaped from his cell block in Auschwitz. As retaliation, the remaining prisoners in the block were lined up and ten of them were sentenced to death. It would be a slow, excruciating death from thirst and starvation. On hearing his name called, one of the condemned men, Franciszek Gajowniczek, cried out in despair, lamenting the fact that he would never see his wife or children again.

At that moment prisoner number 16670 stepped forward, offering himself as a substitute for Gajowniczek. Joining the nine condemned men, Maximilian Kolbe was led off to an underground bunker where he would eventually die. Bruno Borgowiec, an assistant to the janitor and an interpreter in the bunkers, told how Kolbe led the condemned men in prayer and singing day after day. Borgowiec could hear their prayers and singing resounding in the corridors of the bunker, so much so that he had the impression he was in church.

One by one the men died off until only Father Kolbe was left. Impatient to reclaim the cell for new victims, the Nazis decided to kill him by injecting him with carbolic acid. Bruno Borgowiec tells of watching Kolbe, with a prayer on his lips, hold out his arm to the executioner. After excusing himself so he would not have to witness the priest's death, Borgowiec later returned to find Kolbe leaning in a sitting position against the back wall with his eyes open and his head dropping sideways. He described his face as "calm and radiant."

What was it like for Franciszek Gajowniczek, the man whose life was spared? Every year on August 14, the day Kolbe died, he returned to Auschwitz to pay honor to the man who had saved him. A few years after Kolbe's death, he described his feelings about what had happened:

> I could only thank him with my eyes. I was stunned and could hardly grasp what was going on. The immensity of it: I, the condemned, am to live and someone else willingly and voluntarily offers his life for me — a stranger. Is this some dream?
>
> I was put back into my place without having had time to say anything to Maximilian Kolbe. I was saved. And I owe to him the fact that I could tell you all this. The news quickly spread all round the camp. It was the first and the last time that such an incident happened in the whole history of Auschwitz.
>
> For a long time I felt remorse when I thought of Maximilian. By allowing myself to be saved, I had signed his death warrant. But now, on reflection, I understood that a man like him could not have done otherwise.

Gajowniczek lived to be ninety-five, dying in Poland in 1995. Another Auschwitz survivor by the name of Jerzy Bielecki declared that Kolbe's death was "a shock filled with hope, bringing new life and strength.... It was like a powerful shaft of light in the darkness of the camp."

Maximilian Kolbe, with the love of Christ compelling him, faced great evil and rose above it, lifting other men with him. What he did is a picture of what Jesus has done for us. It's a little version of the Big Story. Of course, Jesus' sacrifice was uniquely effective. He alone is the Redeemer who has purchased us with his own blood, lifting us above evil so that we can be united with God forever.

Wednesday

PRAYING THE NAME

We know that the whole creation has been groaning as in the pains of childbirth right up to the present time. Not only so, but we ourselves, who have the firstfruits of the Spirit, groan inwardly as we wait eagerly for our adoption, the redemption of our bodies. For in this hope we were saved. But hope that is seen is no hope at all. Who hopes for what they already have? But if we hope for what we do not yet have, we wait for it patiently.

ROMANS 8:22–25

Reflect On: Romans 8:22–25.
Praise God: For lifting our burdens.
Offer Thanks: For his plan of redemption.
Confess: Any habit of doubting and forgetting God's promises.
Ask God: To give you a deeper awareness of the full redemption that still awaits you.

Technology has changed our world in remarkable ways. One of the ways it has streamlined my life is by giving me a simple way of categorizing people. As I see it, there are only two kinds of people in the world: those who forward emails loaded with advice, jokes, lists, causes, petitions, prayers, stories, and cool graphics and those who, even on pain of threatened consequences, don't.

At least a few of these endlessly forwarded emails are ones that contain long lists of self-defense tips for women. Here's some advice about precautions to take in a parking lot: "Never smell proffered perfume samples because someone may be trying to drug you," or "upon discovering a would-be attacker in the back seat of your car, drive straight into the nearest parked car (assuming no one is in it)—your air bag will inflate protecting you while he will suffer brain damage from being violently thrown around in the back," or "if a van is parked next to you and you are alone, always enter your car on the passenger side lest you be abducted." What a shame that there is any need for such warnings.

The sad fact is that people like Ted Bundy and Jeffrey Dahmer do exist, though the chance of crossing paths with one of them is slim to none. But these are only small-time killers compared to the worst serial killer of all time. You know his name, though it may elude you for a moment. In fact, he is known by various names: Satan, the devil, the adversary, Lucifer, the prince of this world, the evil one, the accuser. Regardless of what you call him, he is cunning and dangerous, intent on destroying as many human souls as possible.

So how do we protect ourselves against such a predator? Scripture tells us that sin is what makes us vulnerable to Satan. If it weren't for sin we could simply laugh him off. If it weren't for sin there would be no such thing as death, because death — the separation of the soul from the body — is solely a byproduct of sin. Fortunately, our Redeemer has come to reverse the curse of sin and death and to free us from the predatory power of evil. It's as though Jesus took on the role of an undercover police officer assigned the task of luring a serial killer out into the open. But Jesus wasn't just posing as a target with other officers standing ready to rescue him. He had to submit to death, to enter into it in order to undo it.

Through his death and resurrection, Jesus has defeated Satan and secured our future. He has bridged the unbridgeable gap between sinful humanity and a holy God, providing a way for us to be united to God forever. But there is a sense in which the work of redemption is not yet complete. We still suffer loss and endure hurts beyond our comprehension. We still die. Even so, Scripture tells us not only that our souls will live forever but that our souls will one day be joined to glorified bodies that will never get sick, never suffer, and never die. Here is how Paul expressed it to the Corinthian Christians:

> Listen, I tell you a mystery: We will not all sleep, but we will all be changed—in a flash, in the twinkling of an eye, at the last trumpet. For the trumpet will sound, the dead will be raised imperishable, and we will be changed. For the perishable must clothe itself with the imper-

ishable, and the mortal with immortality. When the perishable has been clothed with the imperishable, and the mortal with immortality, then the saying that is written will come true: "Death has been swallowed up in victory."

1 CORINTHIANS 15:51–54

Meanwhile, we who were formerly enslaved by sin, in bondage to Satan, may well echo the sentiments of a woman named Mary Reynolds, who was born into slavery in Louisiana. Toward the end of her life, when she was over a hundred years old, still poor but now free, Mary told an interviewer: "I members bout the days of slavery and I don't lieve they ever gwine have slaves no more on this earth. I think Gawd done took that burden offen his black chillum and I'm aimin' to praise him for it to his face in the days of Glory what ain't so far off."

As former slaves, let us rise up and thank Christ for the burdens he has lifted from us, confident that we too will praise him for it to his face in the days of glory, which aren't far off.

Thursday

PRAYING THE NAME

Then I saw a Lamb, looking as if it had been slain, standing in the center before the throne, encircled by the four living creatures and the elders. The Lamb had seven horns and seven eyes, which are the seven spirits of God sent out into all the earth. He went and took the scroll from the right hand of him who sat on the throne. And when he had taken it, the four living creatures and the twenty-four elders fell down before the Lamb. Each one had a harp and they were holding golden bowls full of incense, which are the prayers of God's people. And they sang a new song, saying:

> *"You are worthy to take the scroll*
> *and to open its seals,*
> *because you were slain,*
> *and with your blood you purchased for God*
> *members of every tribe and language and people*
> *and nation."*

REVELATION 5:6–9

Reflect On: Revelation 5:6–9.

Praise God: For his mighty acts of redemption.

Offer Thanks: Because of how highly Christ values you.

Confess: Any tendency to forget what Christ has already done for you.

Ask God: To help you share your faith with others.

☙

In his best-selling book *In His Image*, coauthored with Philip Yancey, the renowned surgeon Paul Brand pointed out that modern people often have difficulty relating to the blood symbolism of the Old and New Testaments. Unlike traditional societies, people in the modern world don't usually butcher their own food nor do they make animal sacrifices or seal contracts through the shedding of blood. Old hymns that speak of "a fountain filled with blood" or being "washed in the blood of the Lamb" or the "wonder-working power in the blood" tend to repulse or mystify rather than to inspire. Most of us prefer that the sticky red substance stays right where it belongs, pumping along inside our veins. How, then, do we make sense of all the New Testament references to blood, such as drinking Jesus' blood, being justified by his blood, being redeemed by his blood, being purchased by his blood, being purified by his blood, being sprinkled with his blood, and making peace through his blood?

Modern medicine has confirmed what ancient people knew instinctively — that life is in the blood. Blood provides our bodies with the oxygen and nutrients we need to survive. Without blood we couldn't keep warm or cool down, couldn't fight off infections, and couldn't rid ourselves of waste products that would otherwise poison us. Little wonder then that Jesus equated his blood with eternal life.

In his book Paul Brand confesses that he never intended to become a physician. But one day he had an experience while enrolled in a training course in tropical medicine that would prepare him to do missionary work in India. It changed his life. A beautiful young woman was suddenly rushed unconscious into the ward where he was working. She had lost a lot of blood in an accident. One of the attending physicians quickly thrust a blood pressure cuff into Paul's hands, but Paul couldn't locate a pulse. Here is his account of what happened:

> She looked like a waxwork Madonna or an alabaster saint in a cathedral. Her lips, too, were pallid.... I felt sure she was dead.
>
> The nurse arrived with a bottle of blood, which she buckled into a high metal stand as the doctor punctured the woman's vein with a large needle.... The staff told me to keep watch over the emptying bottle while they scurried off for more blood.
>
> Nothing in my memory can compare to the excitement of what happened next. Certainly the precise details of that scene remain vividly with me to this day. As I nervously held her wrist while the others were gone, suddenly I could feel the faintest press of a pulse. Or was it my own pulse? I searched again — it was there, barely perceptible but regular, at least. The next bottle of blood arrived and

was quickly connected. A spot of pink appeared on her cheek and spread into a beautiful flush. Her lips darkened pink, then red, and her body quivered in a kind of sighing breath.

Then her eyelids fluttered lightly and at last parted. She squinted at first, as her pupils adjusted to the bright lights of the room, and at last she looked directly at me.... That young woman entered my life for only an hour or so, but the experience left me utterly changed. I had seen a miracle: the creation of Eve when breath entered into and animated her body, the raising of Lazarus.

Like the young woman who was verging on death when Paul Brand first encountered her, some of us have experienced stunning transformations as the result of Jesus' redemptive sacrifice. Through a divine transfusion of his love and mercy, we have literally been transferred from death to life. Thank Christ today for loving you to the point of shedding his blood. Ask him for the grace to share his love by telling others the story of what he has done for you.

PROMISES ASSOCIATED WITH HIS NAME

I don't know about you, but sometimes I find it easy to relate to the people of Israel. Take the passage from Isaiah in which God calls his people by unflattering names. "O worm Jacob, O little Israel," he says (Isaiah 41:14). I felt just like that this morning after dealing poorly with a difficult situation. So wormlike, so little, so unable to rise to the occasion in the way I wanted to. Afterward, I felt defeated and depressed, but not too depressed to pray. I asked God to help me and steady me and cheer me up.

A partial answer to that prayer came in the shape of a man named Harvey whom I had hired to do some work on my home. A gregarious man, Harvey told me all about how God had saved him when he was a drug dealer many years ago. Now, in addition to having his own business, Harvey serves as the pastor of a local church. Before he left, Harvey asked if he could pray with me. Taking hold of my hand, he prayed for encouragement and wisdom and endurance, citing James 1. After he left, I read the whole chapter, and it spoke to me about my circumstances. In this way God was helping me in my littleness and in my wormlike weakness. Today let us ask God for the help he promises to give, remembering that the Holy One of Israel is our Redeemer. He is the God of all the earth.

Promises in Scripture

> "Do not be afraid, O worm Jacob,
>   O little Israel,
> for I myself will help you," declares the LORD,
>   your Redeemer, the Holy One of Israel.

ISAIAH 41:14

For your Maker is your husband—
the LORD Almighty is his name—
the Holy One of Israel is your Redeemer;
he is called the God of all the earth.

ISAIAH 54:5

But God will redeem my life from the grave;
he will surely take me to himself.

PSALM 49:15

There will be signs in the sun, moon and stars. On the earth, nations will be in anguish and perplexity at the roaring and tossing of the sea. People will faint from terror, apprehensive of what is coming on the world, for the heavenly bodies will be shaken. At that time they will see the Son of Man coming in a cloud with power and great glory. When these things begin to take place, stand up and lift up your heads, because your redemption is drawing near.

LUKE 21:25–28

Continued Prayer and Praise

Remember God's faithful, redeeming love. (Exodus 12:12; Deuteronomy 7:8; 2 Samuel 7:22; Psalm 130:7–8; Jeremiah 50:33–34; Luke 1:67–75; Ephesians 1:3–10)

Live as though you have been redeemed. (Romans 12:1–2; Galatians 3:10–14; 4:1–7; Ephesians 4:29; Colossians 1:9–14; Titus 2:11–14; Hebrews 9:11; 1 Peter 1:17–20)

26

I AM

ἐγώ εἰμι

EGO EIMI

The Name

In Jesus we have the richest, most vivid picture of God imaginable. No longer does God seem implacably remote, displeased with the world he has made. Instead, he bends toward us, sharing our weakness and shouldering our burdens. Through the perfect offering of his life he becomes our Way back to the Father. He is the True Vine in which we abide, bearing fruit for God's kingdom. He is the loving God who will never abandon us, but who will be present with us always, leading us to life eternal.

Key Scriptures

Moses said to God, "Suppose I go to the Israelites and say to them, 'The God of your fathers has sent me to you,' and they ask me, 'What is his name?' Then what shall I tell them?"

God said to Moses, "I AM WHO I AM. This is what you are to say to the Israelites: 'I AM has sent me to you.'"

EXODUS 3:13–14

"You are not yet fifty years old," the Jews said to him [Jesus], "and you have seen Abraham!"

"I tell you the truth," Jesus answered, "before Abraham was born, I am!"

JOHN 8:57–58

Monday

HIS NAME REVEALED

Moses said to God, "Suppose I go to the Israelites and say to them, 'The God of your fathers has sent me to you,' and they ask me, 'What is his name?' Then what shall I tell them?"

God said to Moses, "I AM WHO I AM. This is what you are to say to the Israelites: 'I AM has sent me to you.'"

EXODUS 3:13–14

"I am not seeking glory for myself; but there is one who seeks it, and he is the judge. I tell you the truth, if anyone keeps my word, he will never see death."

At this the Jews exclaimed, "Now we know that you are demon-possessed! Abraham died and so did the prophets, yet you say that if anyone keeps your word, he will never taste death. Are you greater than our father Abraham? He died, and so did the prophets. Who do you think you are?"

Jesus replied, "If I glorify myself, my glory means nothing. My Father, whom you claim as your God, is the one who glorifies me. Though you do not know him, I know him. If I said I did not, I would be a liar like you, but I do know him and keep his word. Your father Abraham rejoiced at the thought of seeing my day; he saw it and was glad."

"You are not yet fifty years old," the Jews said to him, "and you have seen Abraham!"

"I tell you the truth," Jesus answered, "before Abraham was born, I am!" At this, they picked up stones to stone him, but Jesus hid himself, slipping away from the temple grounds.

JOHN 8:50–59

Lord, Jesus, you are our great covenant-keeping God, the One who was, who is, and who is to come. You are the Resurrection and the Life, the True Vine, the Way, the great I AM. Help us, O Lord, to abide in you, bearing fruit that will last through the power of your Spirit both now and forever. Amen.

Understanding the Name

When Moses first encountered God in the wilderness, in the figure of a burning bush, he asked God to reveal his name. But the reply he received seemed only to add to the mystery of who God is. Instead of describing himself as the Living God or the Almighty God or the Everlasting God or the Creator God, the Lord instructed Moses, saying, "This is what you are to say to the Israelites: 'I AM has sent me to you.'" In fact, the name "I AM" closely related to the four Hebrew consonants that make up the name *Yahweh*, the covenant name of God in the Old Testament. Though the exact meaning of this name is difficult to know with certainty, the Lord may have been revealing himself not only as the God who has always existed but also as the God who is always present with his people.

When Jesus was being attacked by the religious leaders who failed to recognize him as the Messiah, he shocked them not by claiming to be the Messiah but by identifying himself with Yahweh, saying: "Before Abraham was born, *I am*." Recognizing that Jesus was claiming to be divine, the scandalized religious leaders tried to stone him. In fact, John's Gospel contains several self-descriptions of Jesus introduced by the emphatic expression *Ego Eimi* (e-GO ay-MEE), "I AM."

I AM the bread of life. (6:35)
I AM the light of the world. (8:12)
Before Abraham was born, I AM. (8:58)
I AM the gate for the sheep. (10: 7)
I AM the good shepherd. (10:11)
I AM the resurrection and the life. (11:25)
I AM the way and the truth and the life. (14:6)
I AM the true vine, and my Father is the gardener. (15:1)

Jesus emphatically described himself as the "resurrection and the life," "the way and the truth and the life," and the "true vine." Each of these images has something important to reveal to us about the character and purpose of Jesus Christ.

Studying the Name

1. Some scholars think that by saying "I am who I am" God was saying he would always be present with his people. How have you experienced God's faithful presence in your life?

2. What do you think it means to keep Jesus' word, and why does Jesus link it with never seeing death?

3. Why do you think the religious leaders responded to the "good news" as though it were "bad news"?

Tuesday

PRAYING THE NAME

During the fourth watch of the night Jesus went out to them, walking on the lake. When the disciples saw him walking on the lake, they were terrified. "It's a ghost," they said, and cried out in fear.

But Jesus immediately said to them: "Take courage! It is I. Don't be afraid."

MATTHEW 14:25–27

Jesus, knowing all that was going to happen to him, went out and asked them, "Who is it you want?"

"Jesus of Nazareth," they replied.

"I am he," Jesus said. (And Judas the traitor was standing there with them.) When Jesus said, "I am he," they drew back and fell to the ground.

JOHN 18:4–6

Reflect On: Matthew 14:25–27 and John 18:4–6.
Praise God: For being with his people.
Offer Thanks: For the ways Christ has been present in your life.
Confess: Any fear that God may abandon you in a time of need.
Ask God: To open your eyes to his presence and his power.

Imagine that you are Michaelangelo, the greatest of artists. Unfortunately something has gone terribly wrong with your favorite painting. You try adjusting the colors, creating new scenes, adding layers of paint. But no matter what you do to the canvas, nothing seems to fix it. Instead of trashing the painting you decide on a new approach. Fortunately, in addition to creating works of breathtaking beauty, you have the uncanny ability to enter your works and to walk among the people your artistry has made. You do just that with this painting, intending to restore it from the inside. But the people within the painting, so carefully and lovingly sketched by your hand, seemed to have changed—and not for the better. They are bad-hearted and dim-witted, evidence of the problem you came to fix. They do not recognize you—the genius who shaped them and brought them to life. Instead of expressing their gratitude, they treat you with contempt. The more you reach out to them, the more they reject and despise you.

John's Gospel, in its first chapter, tells us that the world Jesus made was so dim-witted that it did not recognize him when he entered it. The most momentous thing to have occurred since the world's begin-ning—God becoming a human being—and hardly anyone took note of it! The earth didn't move, the trees didn't dance for joy, and only a few people bowed down before the Christ to adore him. Yet there were numerous signs throughout the lifetime of Jesus for anyone who was paying attention.

One of these happened on a windy night in the middle of the Sea of Galilee. The previous day, Jesus had fed five thousand people with a few loaves and a couple of fish. After that, he sent his disciples out in their boat while he headed up the mountainside to pray. Matthew's Gospel tells us that something extraordinary happened between three and six o'clock the following morning. The disciples were in their boat, straining at the oars because of a strong headwind. Suddenly they saw a figure on the water and cried out in fear, thinking they were seeing a ghost. But it was only Jesus, who calmed them by saying, "Take cour-age! It is I."

To the Jewish people the sea represented chaos. It was a place where demonic powers ruled. Only Yahweh could control the sea, and here was Jesus walking on top of it! Then, Jesus said, "Take courage! It is I" which can literally be translated, "Take courage! I AM."

There was also the occasion of Jesus' arrest in the garden of Geth-semane. Judas came with a detachment of soldiers and some officials from the chief priests and Pharisees. Knowing exactly what was going to happen to him, Jesus took control of the situation by asking whom they were looking for. Has it ever struck you as odd that the gang of men who had come to arrest him, armed with torches and weapons, simply collapsed when Jesus identified himself, saying "It is I"? It may help to understand that the words Jesus spoke can literally be translated "I AM." His enemies fell to the ground, unable to stand in the presence of God.

Jesus, whose name means "Yahweh is Salvation," is the great I AM — the one who is always present with us whether or not we recognize him. Whatever difficulties you may face, whatever storms may threaten, pray for the grace to have eyes and ears wide open so that you may perceive the Lord saying, "Take courage! I AM."

Wednesday

PRAYING THE NAME

"Do not let your hearts be troubled. Trust in God; trust also in me. In my Father's house are many rooms; if it were not so, I would have told you. I am going there to prepare a place for you. And if I go and prepare a place for you, I will come back and take you to be with me that you also may be where I am. You know the way to the place where I am going."

Thomas said to him, "Lord, we don't know where you are going, so how can we know the way?"

Jesus answered, "I am the way and the truth and the life. No one comes to the Father except through me."

JOHN 14:1–6

Reflect On: John 14:1–6.

Praise God: For giving us a way back to him.

Offer Thanks: For the Spirit of God who leads us into all truth.

Confess: Any half truths or lies that you have allowed into your life.

Ask God: To help you to love and recognize the truth.

We sometimes speak of people who lack faith as being lost, which seems an apt description of those who feel aimlessly adrift in a meaningless world. But faith changes us. Belonging to Christ confers a sense of identity and purpose. We become grounded. We know who we are and where we are going. As Paul said, "In him we live and move and have our being" (Acts 17:28). Jesus alluded to this when he replied to Thomas's question about the way to the Father's house. Instead of saying, "I *know* the way," Jesus declared, "I *am* the way." He is not, then, a kind of Lewis and Clark, leading us on a path he has discovered through the wilderness. He himself *is* the path.

Jesus also declared, "I *am* the truth." He didn't say, "I know the truth," or "I teach the truth," though of course he did. The biblical idea of truth is of a reality that is solid, stable, and reliable, something strong enough to support you. Jesus is all of these things. But he is also the truth that challenges the lies we want to believe. It is no wonder that his public ministry lasted so short a time. It is hard for people, after all, to stand so much truth.

Our problems with truth began when our first parents believed the beguiling lie of the serpent: "You will be like God." When they embraced the lie and ate the fruit, Eve and Adam found how very unlike God they were. They became broken, alienated, unreliable, weighed down by sorrow.

Jesus tells us, instead of a beguiling lie, the stark truth—self-sufficiency will land us in hell. Ignoring God will defeat us. Going our own way will destroy us. "Apart from me you can do nothing," he said. "If you do not remain in me, you are like a branch that is thrown away and withers; such branches are picked up, thrown into the fire and burned" (John 15:5–6). Either we build our lives on the Truth personified, or we build our lives on something that will not hold us up.

Malcolm Gladwell, the author of *Blink*, tells the story of a fire department commander in Cleveland, Ohio, who recalled an experience he had as a lieutenant responding to what looked like a routine house fire:

> The fire was in the back of a one-story house in a residential neighborhood, in the kitchen. The lieutenant and his men broke down the front door, laid down their hose, and then, as firemen say, "charged the line," dousing the flames in the kitchen with water. Something should have happened at that point: the fire should have abated. But it didn't. So the men sprayed again. Still, it didn't seem to make much difference. The firemen retreated back through the archway into the living room, and there, suddenly, the lieutenant thought to himself, There's something wrong. He turned to his men. "Let's get out, *now!*" he said, and moments after they did, the floor on which they had been standing collapsed. The fire, it turned out, had been in the basement.

What a picture of what can happen to a life that is built on something other than Christ. Things may look normal for a while, but underneath a threat is growing. Sooner or later the whole structure of our life will collapse.

Join me today in asking Christ for the grace to reject the beguiling lies of our culture—that sexual gratification is all important, that life is about the pursuit of money and success, that the individual reigns supreme. Let us remember the words of St. Paul who urges us to set our hearts on things above, where Christ is, remembering that when Christ, who is our life, appears, then we too will appear with him in glory (Colossians 3:1–4).

Thursday

PRAYING THE NAME

"I am the true vine, and my Father is the gardener. He cuts off every branch in me that bears no fruit, while every branch that does bear fruit he prunes so that it will be even more fruitful. You are already clean because of the word I have spoken to you. Remain in me, and I will remain in you. No branch can bear fruit by itself; it must remain in the vine. Neither can you bear fruit unless you remain in me.

"I am the vine, you are the branches."

JOHN 15:1–5

Reflect On: John 15:1–16.

Praise God: For sending his Son to be the True Vine through whom the world would be saved.

Offer Thanks: That Christ has made you a branch of the True Vine.

Confess: Any disobedience that makes it difficult for you to abide in the Vine.

Ask God: To prune you in whatever way is necessary so that you can be as fruitful as possible.

◌

Unable to find a decent job after graduating from college, I did what many people do—I went to graduate school. But shortly before obtaining a master's degree, I attended a job symposium on campus regarding my chosen field. The news was dismal. New jobs were hard, almost impossible, to find. The experts were advising new grads to settle for low-paying, menial jobs if necessary until the employment picture brightened.

I felt my hopes for the future sinking fast. But then an old cliché flashed through my mind: "It's not *what* you know but *who* you know." Wait a minute, didn't I know the most powerful person in the universe? It couldn't be that hard for Jesus to help me find the job I needed. After all, I didn't need a million jobs—only one. A couple of months later I landed my first professional job, which proved to be the perfect entry into my career.

William Watley speaks about the importance of realizing that Jesus is the greatest of all connections:

> You are connected to somebody who is not only the Alpha and the Omega, but the Nu as well. *Alpha* and *omega* are the first and last letters of the Greek alphabet; *nu* is the middle letter. Thus, Jesus is not only somebody who will be with us in the beginning when we're born and at the end when death comes. He abides with us in all that is between ... in the middle. In the middle, when temptation comes to turn us around. In the middle, when Satan attacks to dismantle and destroy. In the middle, when friends become few. In the middle, when resources run short. In the middle, when the unexpected shakes the foundations of our lives. In the middle, when relationships are severed. Yes, in the middle. Therefore, we can continue to abide in Jesus. He is sufficient for whatever comes between our beginning and our ending.

The kind of abiding that Jesus speaks of in John's Gospel is a life-long abiding accomplished through faith and obedience. Furthermore, we abide not as a single branch, isolated from others, but in union with Christ and with other believers. Together we are branches of "the true vine."

It is no accident that Jesus uses the metaphor of a vine to describe himself and his disciples. In Palestine abundant vineyards were considered a sign of God's favor. Vines, in fact, were labor intensive forms of cultivation that grew best in peacetime, producing grapes that could be eaten fresh or made into raisins, grape juice, wine, and even a jelly-like substance called honey. No wonder the vine was a symbol of peace and prosperity. Numerous times in the Old Testament, God had referred to Israel as a vine. But Israel was a wild vine that had failed to produce the rich harvest God intended (Isaiah 5:4). By calling himself the "true vine," Jesus was saying that he was the true Israel. Jesus and those who belong to him will fulfill God's plan for the world.

For each of us, abiding in the true vine is a lifelong, sometimes painful process. Like branches on a vine, we have to be pruned so that we can be more fruitful in the future than we have been in the past. Apart from Christ we shrivel and die. But united with him we experience the God-blessed life, which, as Paul told the Galatians, produces "love, joy, peace, patience, kindness, goodness, faithfulness, gentleness and self-control" (Galatians 5:22–23). Indeed, we are called to bear fruit that will last.

Today, ask God for the grace to recognize your true purpose in life, which is not to *be blessed* but to *become a blessing,* bearing the sweetness of Christ to all who are hungry for him.

Friday

PROMISES ASSOCIATED WITH HIS NAME

Of all the promises of Jesus in the Bible none is greater than this: "I am the resurrection and the life. Anyone who believes in me will live, even though they die; and whoever lives by believing in me will never die" (John 11:25). If Jesus hadn't made this promise, every other promise would be only a short-term warranty set to expire on our death. His own resurrection forever validates his claims and promises.

Biblical scholar and theologian George Eldon Ladd once remarked about John's account of the resurrection that "it seems to be the evangelist's intention to suggest that Peter saw the grave clothes lying like a chrysalis out of which the risen body of the Lord had emerged." That's a picture we can claim for ourselves—that death for us will be like the butterfly's chrysalis—this life merely a shape we shed when we enter into the life that will never end.

By living and dying to save us, Jesus himself has become the Promise we live by. He is the Truth we stand on, the Bread that nourishes us, the Shepherd who leads us, the Vine that makes us fruitful. He is the Resurrection for which we hope and the Gateway to life eternal. He is all of these things and more—the Almighty, Everlasting God, the One who is the great I AM!

Promises in Scripture

"Lord," Martha said to Jesus, "if you had been here, my brother would not have died. But I know that even now God will give you whatever you ask."

Jesus said to her, "Your brother will rise again."

Martha answered, "I know he will rise again in the resurrection at the last day."

Jesus said to her, "I am the resurrection and the life. Anyone who believes in me will live, even though they die; and whoever lives by believing in me will never die. Do you believe this?"

JOHN 11:21–26

Continued Prayer and Praise

Remember that Jesus will never leave us. (Matthew 28:20)

Know that Jesus is God. (Matthew 16:15 – 16; Mark 14:61 – 62)

Realize that Jesus is the Beginning and the End. (Revelation 1:8, 17; 21:6)

SELECTED BIBLIOGRAPHY

Barker, Kenneth L., and John Kohlenberger III, eds. *Zondervan NIV Bible Commetary.* 2 vols. Grand Rapids: Zondervan, 1994.

Brown, Colin, ed. *New International Dictionary of New Testament Theology.* 4 vols. Grand Rapids: Zondervan, 1986.

Bruce, F. F. *The International Bible Commentary.* Grand Rapids: Zondervan, 1986.

Douglas, J. D., and Merrill C. Tenney, eds. *The New International Dictionary of the Bible.* Grand Rapids: Zondervan, 1987.

Freedman, David Noel, ed. *The Anchor Bible Dictionary.* 6 vols. New York: Doubleday, 1992.

Kittel, Gerhard, and Gerhard Friedrich, eds. *Theological Dictionary of the New Testament: Abridged in One Volume.* Translated and abridged by Geoffrey W. Bomiley. Grand Rapids: Eerdmans, 1985.

Lockyer, Herbert. *All the Divine Names and Titles in the Bible.* Grand Rapids: Zondervan, 1975.

Rhodes, Tricia McCary. *At the Name of Jesus.* Minneapolis: Bethany, 2003.

Richards, Lawrence O. *Every Name of God in the Bible.* Nashville: Nelson, 2001.

_____. *New International Encyclopedia of Bible Words.* Grand Rapids: Zondervan, 1999.

Shelly, Rubel. *The Names of Jesus.* West Monroe, LA: Howard, 1999.

Simpson, A. B. *The Names of Jesus.* Harrisburg, PA: Christian Publications, 1967.

Tenney, Merrill C., ed. *Zondervan Pictorial Encyclopedia of the Bible.* 5 vols. Grand Rapids: Zondervan, 1975, 1976.

Towns, Elmer L. *The Names of Jesus.* Colorado Springs, CO: Accent, 1987.

VanGemeren, Willem A. *New International Dictionary of Old Testament Theology and Exegesis.* 5 vols. Grand Rapids: Zondervan, 1997.

Watley, William D. *Exalting the Names of Jesus*. Valley Forge, PA: Judson, 2002.

Wiersbe, Warren W., ed. *Classic Sermons on the Names of God*. Grand Rapids: Kregel, 1993.

Wiersbe, Warren W. *The Wonderful Names of Jesus*. Lincoln, NE: Back to the Bible, 1980.

NOTES

Chapter 1: Immanuel

Page 24. Randall Frame, "Fixing Haiti," posted on the Power of Purpose Awards website, *www.templeton.org/powerofpurpose/winners/summaries.html*, accessed November 21, 2005.

Chapter 5: Physician

Page 74. Catherine Marshall, *Meeting God at Every Turn* (Grand Rapids: Chosen, 1980), 98–99.

Chapter 7: King of Kings

Page 97. *Epistle to Diognetus*, 7.

Page 101. King Farouk, quoted in *Life* (April 10, 1950).

Chapter 8: Prince of Peace

Page 115. David Fox (Reuters), "We Could Tell Something Strange Was Happening," *USA Today* (December 29, 2004).

Page 115. Dilip Ganguly (Associated Press), "Nine Women Claim One Tsunami Baby," *The Grand Rapids Press* (January 15, 2005), 1.

Chapter 9: Christ, Messiah

Page 127. Thomas Reese, quoted by David Bauder (Associated Press), "Networks Already Prep for Next Pope," *The Grand Rapids Press* (March 15, 2005), A7.

Page 127. Fraser Nelson, "Pope's Ordeal Gets His Message Across," *The Scotsman* (March 15, 2005). See *thescotsman.scotsman.com/opinion.cfm?id=229972005*, accessed March 16, 2005.

Page 128. George Weigel, "Lessons of a Pontiff's Twilight," *The Washington Post* (March 22, 2005), A17.

Chapter 10: Rabbi, Rabbouni, Teacher

Page 141. Augustine, as quoted in Jeffrey John, *The Meaning in the Miracles* (Grand Rapids: Eerdmans, 2001), 4.

Page 141. This interpretation is drawn from Jeffrey John, *The Meaning in the Miracles,* 4.

Page 143. William Barclay, *The Parables of Jesus* (Louisville: Westminster John Knox, 1970), 16.

Page 143. This interpretation is drawn from William Barclay, *The Parables of Jesus,* 52–59.

Chapter 12: Cornerstone, Capstone

Page 170. Attributed variously to John Keene, John Kirkham, and John Keith, 1787.

Chapter 13: Bright Morning Star

Page 177. The monk who set up the modern calendar miscalculated the date of Jesus' birth, making the likely date of his birth sometime between 8 and 4 BC.

Page 177. Cf. R. A. Rosenberg, "The 'Star of the Messiah' Reconsidered," *Biblica* 53 (1972): 105–9, as mentioned in Colin Brown, *New International Dictionary of New Testament Theology* (Grand Rapids: Zondervan, 1986), 3:737.

Page 181. William D. Watley, *Exalting the Names of Jesus* (Valley Forge, PA: Judson, 2002), 94.

Chapter 14: Lion of the Tribe of Judah

Page 190. For a more extensive discussion of the meaning of *orge*, consult Gerhard Kittel and Gerhard Friedrich, eds., trans. and abridged by Geoffrey W. Bomiley, *Theological Dictionary of the New Testament: Abridged in One Volume* (Grand Rapids: Eerdmans, 1985), 722–26.

Page 193. This interpretation of Jesus' last words is drawn from Tricia McCary Rhodes, *At the Name of Jesus* (Grand Rapids: Bethany, 2003) 104–7.

Page 196. William D. Watley, *Exalting the Names of Jesus* (Valley Forge, PA: Judson, 2002), 2–3.

Chapter 16: Friend

Page 221. Patricia Raybon, *My First White Friend* (New York: Penguin, 1996), 85, 96.

Chapter 17: Alpha and Omega

Page 229. A. B. Simpson, *The Names of Jesus* (Harrisburg, PA: Christian Publications, reprint 1967), 39.

Page 230. Warren Wiersbe, *The Wonderful Names of Jesus* (Lincoln, NB: Back to the Bible, 1980), 40–41.

Page 231. Herbert Lockyer, *All the Divine Names and Titles in the Bible* (Grand Rapids: Zondervan, 1975), 110.

Page 232. Gerhard Kittel and Gerhard Friedrich, eds., *Theological Dictionary of the New Testament: Abridged in One Volume*, trans. and abridged Geoffrey W. Bomiley (Grand Rapids: Eerdmans, 1985), 870.

Page 234. Jason Otis, "Life in the Big Easy," posted on *BigEasy.com* at *http://bigeasy.com/features/bigeasy.html*, accessed September 7, 2005.

Page 234. Ibid.

Chapter 18: Jesus the Savior

Page 242. Robert Farrar Capon, "The Lost Sheep and the Lost Coin," Program #4012, first aired December 29, 1996, posted on *http://www.30goodminutes.org/csec/sermon/capon_4012.htm*.

Page 245. The story of this hymn is told in greater detail by Kenneth Osbeck, *101 Hymn Stories* (Grand Rapids: Kregel, 1982). Posted at *http://www.webedelic.com/church/hailt.htm*, accessed September 14, 2005.

Page 246. Jim Cymbala, *Breakthrough Prayer* (Grand Rapids: Zondervan, 2003), 40–41.

Page 249. Carol Cymbala and Ann Spangler, *He's Been Faithful* (Grand Rapids: Zondervan, 2001), 15–16.

Page 249. Graham Kendrick, "Shine, Jesus, Shine," copyright ©1987 by Make Way Music (administered by Music Services in the Western Hemisphere). All rights reserved. Used by permission.

Chapter 19: Bridegroom, Husband

Page 260. Gary Thomas, *Sacred Marriage* (Grand Rapids: Zondervan, 2000), 32.

Chapter 20: Son of David

Page 275. A. B. Simpson, *The Names of Jesus* (Harrisburg, PA: Christian Publications, reprint 1967), 90.

Page 278. Jeffrey John, *The Meaning in the Miracles* (Grand Rapids: Eerdmans, 2001), 125.

Chapter 21: Priest, Prophet

Page 289. From an unpublished sermon by Reggie Smith, delivered at the Church of the Servant in Grand Rapids, Michigan, October 30, 2005.

Page 291. Michael Ramsey, *Be Still and Know* (London: Fount, 1987), 4, as quoted in Jeffrey John, *The Meaning in the Miracles* (Grand Rapids: Eerdmans, 2001), 152.

Page 292. Evelyn Underhill, "Life as Prayer," in *The Collected Papers of Evelyn Underhill*, ed. L. Menzies (London: Longmans, Green, 1946), as quoted in Jeffrey John, *The Meaning in the Miracles* (Grand Rapids: Eerdmans, 2001), 153.

Chapter 22: Son of God, Son of Man

Page 298. C. S. Lewis, "Reflections on the Psalms," in *The Inspirational Writings of C. S. Lewis* (New York: Inspirational, 1994), 199.

Chapter 23: Good Shepherd

Page 314. Jack Roeda, "Beloved," *Today, the Family Altar* (November-December, 2005), meditation of December 29, 2005.

Chapter 24: Servant, Servant of God, Man of Sorrows

Page 329. Jack Roeda, "Believing," *Today the Family Altar* (November-December 2005), meditation of December 28, 2005.

Page 330. Dorothy Ranaghan, *New Covenant Magazine* (July 1981).

Page 336. This story is posted at *http://home.comcast.net/~mothertersasite/stories.html*, accessed on December 2, 2005.

Chapter 25: The Redeemer

Page 341. Gerhard Kittel and Gerhard Friedrich, eds., *Theological Dictionary of the New Testament, Abridged in One Volume*, translated and abridged by Geoffrey W. Bromiley (Grand Rapids: Eerdmans, 1985), 545–46.

Page 343. This story is posted at *http://meltingpot.furtunecity.com/upper/271/Kolbe.htm*, accessed on December 15, 2005.

Page 344. Ibid.

Page 344. Ibid.

Page 347. Mary Reynolds was one of 2,300 former slaves from across the American South who were interviewed by journalists in a program undertaken by the Works Progress Administration. She and others provided firsthand accounts of what it was like to live as a slave. Her photo and the transcript of her interview is posted at *http://xroads.virginia.edu/~hyper/wpa/reynold1.html*, accessed on December 14, 2005.

Page 350. Paul Brand and Philip Yancey, *In His Image* (Grand Rapids: Zondervan, 1984), 53–54.

Chapter 26: I Am

Page 361. Malcom Gladwell, *Blink* (New York: Little, Brown, 2005), 122.

Page 364. William D. Watley, *Exalting the Names of Jesus* (Valley Forge, PA: Judson, 2002), 42–43.

Page 364. George Eldon Ladd, *I Believe in the Resurrection of Jesus* (Grand Rapids: Eerdmans, 1975), 94, quoted in Colin Brown, "The Resurrection in Contemporary Theology," *New International Dictionary of New Testament Theology* (Grand Rapids: Zondervan, 1986), 3:297.

Praying the Names of God
A Daily Guide

Ann Spangler,
Bestselling *Author of* Women of the Bible

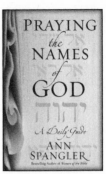

A twenty-six-week devotional study by the best-selling coauthor of *Women of the Bible*

Names in the ancient world did more than simply distinguish one person from another, they often conveyed the essential nature and character of a person. This is especially true when it comes to the names of God recorded in the Bible. *Praying the Names of God* explores the primary names and titles of God in the Old Testament to reveal the deeper meanings behind them.

El Shadday, Elohim, Adonay, Abba, El Elyon—God Almighty, Mighty Creator, Lord, Father, God Most High—these are just a few of the names and titles of God that yield rich insights into his nature and character. *Praying the Names of God* shows readers how to study and pray God's names by focusing each week on one of the primary names or titles of God.

- Monday—readers study a portion of Scripture that reveals the name.
- Tuesday—Thursday—readers pray specific Scripture passages related to the name.
- Friday—readers pray Scripture promises connected to the name.

By incorporating the divine names and titles into their prayers—and learning about the biblical context in which the name was revealed—readers will gain a more intimate understanding of who God is and how he can be relied on in every circumstance of their lives.

Praying the Names of God is a unique devotional, one that offers a rich program of daily prayer and study designed to lead people into fresh encounters with the living God.

Hardcover, Jacketed 0-310-25353-5

Pick up a copy today at your favorite bookstore!

Women of the Bible
A One-Year Devotional Study of Women in Scripture

Ann Spangler and
Jean E. Syswerda

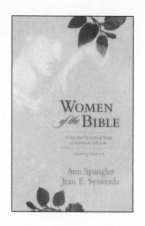

Women of the Bible focuses on fifty-two remarkable women in Scripture—women whose struggles to live with faith and courage are not unlike your own. And now this bestselling devotional study book has been updated and expanded to enhance its flexibility, usefulness, and relevance for both individuals and groups.

Small groups will especially welcome the way the Bible studies have been streamlined to fit the unique needs of the group setting. Other important changes include:

- A list of all the women of the Bible keyed to Scripture
- A timeline of the foremost women of the Bible
- A list of women in Jesus' family tree
- A list of women in Jesus' life and ministry

Vital and deeply human, the women in this book encourage you through their failures as well as their successes. You'll see how God acted in surprising and wonderful ways to draw them—and you—to himself. This year-long devotional offers a unique method to help you slow down and savor the story of God's unrelenting love for his people, offering a fresh perspective that will nourish and strengthen your personal communion with him.

Hardcover, Jacketed 0-310-27055-3

Pick up a copy today at your favorite bookstore!

Mothers of the Bible
A Devotional

*Ann Spangler and
Jean E. Syswerda*

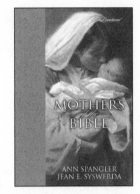

Children need the love, wisdom, and nurture that mothers are uniquely capable of
giving. *Mothers of the Bible* can help you fulfill your own calling
as a mother by offering insights from God's Word. Exploring the
lives of women in the Bible can help strengthen your faith and
your effectiveness as a mother. Like you, these mothers wanted
the best for their children. And like you, they sometimes faced
difficulties that challenged their faith. Looking to them can help
deepen your understanding of Scripture, enabling you to experience more of God's love so you can reflect that love to your
children.

Adapted from *Women of the Bible*, *Mothers of the Bible* fur-
nishes a unique twelve-week devotional experience. Each week
becomes a personal retreat focused on the life of a particular
biblical mother.

Designed for personal prayer and study or for use in small
groups, *Mothers of the Bible* will help you ground your relationship with your children on God's Word.

Hardcover, Printed 0-310-27239-4

Pick up a copy today at your favorite bookstore!

Women of the Bible

52 Stories for Prayer and Reflection

Ann Spangler

Though we are familiar with the Bible's most noteworthy men, many of us know little about women of the Bible and the important roles they played in the story of salvation.

The cast is long and colorful, including a parade of prostitutes, evil queens, peasants, and prophetesses. And though our culture differs vastly from theirs, we instinctively understand these women as they agonize over infertility, worry about their children, long for a little real affection, and struggle to find faith. Far from being one-dimensional characters, these are flesh-and-blood women whose mistakes and failings often mirror our own and whose collective wisdom yields rich insight into our struggle to live with faith and courage.

Taken from the bestseller *Women of the Bible*, each of the fifty-two stories in this book concludes with a brief reflection encouraging us to pray in light of the woman's story, thereby deepening our understanding of Scripture and our experience of prayer.

Hardcover, Printed 0-310-24493-5

Pick up a copy today at your favorite bookstore!

Women of the Bible

52 Bible Studies for Individuals and Groups

Jean E. Syswerda

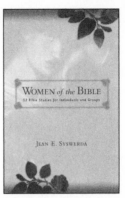

As you immerse yourself in their lives, you'll see more and more places where your life intersects with theirs.

Focus on fifty-two female heroes in Scripture, and you'll discover yourself in the process. *Women of the Bible: 52 Studies for Individuals and Groups* is designed especially for those who want to delve more deeply, either alone or in a group, into the lives of women like Ruth, Anna, Esther, Leah, Rachel, Mary, Elizabeth, and other women who encountered the living God.

This study edition of the bestseller *Women of the Bible* includes an introduction to each woman, major Scripture passages, study materials, and cultural backgrounds. There are fifty-two studies, one for each week of the year. Newly gathered study aids include helpful charts as well as a complete listing of all women of the Bible, with pertinent Scripture references. Space is included to record your thoughts and insights.

Each timeless biblical story mirrors the challenges and changes today's women face. Through understanding these women's lives, this easy-to-use study resource will help you discover the God behind their stories—and yours.

Softcover 0-310-24492-7

Pick up a copy today at your favorite bookstore!

Men of the Bible

A One-Year Devotional Study of Men in Scripture

Ann Spangler and Robert Wolgemuth

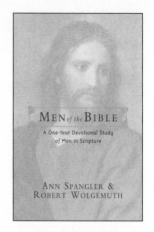

MEN *of the* BIBLE

A One-Year Devotional Study
of Men in Scripture

ANN SPANGLER &
ROBERT WOLGEMUTH

Men of the Bible takes a close-up look at fifty-two men in Scripture—complex flesh-and-blood characters whose strengths and weaknesses often seem strangely similar to our own. Heroes and villains, sinners and prophets, commoners and kings . . . their dramatic life stories provide us with fresh perspective on the unfolding story of redemption.

Though our culture differs vastly from theirs, the fundamental issues we face in relation to God and the world remain the same. We still reach for great dreams and selfish ambitions. We wrestle with fear and indecision, struggle with sexual temptation, and experience the ache of loneliness and the devastation of betrayal. And, like many of these men, we long to walk more closely with the God who calls us into an intimate relationship with himself and who enables us to fulfill his purpose for our lives.

Men of the Bible offers men and women today a unique devotional experience, as each week becomes a personal retreat focused on the life of a particular man.

Designed for personal prayer and study or for use in small groups, *Men of the Bible* will help you make Bible reading a daily habit. Whether you dip into portions or read every page, this book will help you grow in character, wisdom, and obedience as a person after God's own heart.

Hardcover, Jacketed 0-310-23944-3

Fathers of the Bible
A Devotional
Robert Wolgemuth

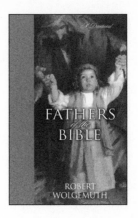

When we take a Bible in our hands, we are actually holding a user's manual for fathers. Story after story, it reveals our heavenly Father's love for his Son—and for us. It also shares the accounts of earthly fathers whose examples we'll want to either imitate or avoid.

The twelve chapters in *Fathers of the Bible* offer slices from the biblical stories of men who were fathers. From them, we can learn something about the tasks, privileges, challenges, and failures of fatherhood. We'll discover the faithfulness of Noah, the conniving of Jacob, the unbridled passion of David, and the quiet confidence of Joseph, Jesus' earthly father.

Each of these men were dads. Their geographic settings and life circumstances were vastly different from ours, but the struggles and challenges of fatherhood are remarkably similar.

Designed for personal prayer and study or for use in small groups, *Fathers of the Bible* will help you ground your relationship with your children on God's Word.

Hardcover 0-310-27238-6

If you would like to invite Ann to speak at your group,
contact her at annsdesk@annspangler.com.

We want to hear from you. Please send your comments about this book to us in care of zreview@zondervan.com. Thank you.

ZONDERVAN.com/
AUTHORTRACKER
follow your favorite authors

For more information on Ann Spangler, visit
www.annspangler.com.